...er Women on the Move

Southeast Asia

POLITICS, MEANING, AND MEMORY

David Chandler and Rita Smith Kipp

SERIES EDITORS

OTHER VOLUMES IN THE SERIES

HARD BARGAINING IN SUMATRA:
Western Travelers and Toba Bataks in the Marketplace of Souvenirs
Andrew Causey

PRINT AND POWER:
Confucianism, Communism, and Buddhism in the Making of Modern Vietnam
Shawn Frederick McHale

INVESTING IN MIRACLES:
El Shaddai and the Transformation of Popular Catholicism in the Philippines
Katherine L. Wiegele

TOMS AND DEES:
Transgender Identity and Female Same-Sex Relationships in Thailand
Megan J. Sinnott

IN THE NAME OF CIVIL SOCIETY:
From Free Election Movements to People Power in the Philippines
Eva-Lotta E. Hedman

THE TÂY SƠN UPRISING:
Society and Rebellion in Eighteenth-Century Vietnam
George Dutton

SPREADING THE DHAMMA:
Writing, Orality, and Textual Transmission in Buddhist Northern Thailand
Daniel M. Veidlinger

ART AS POLITICS:
Re-Crafting Identities, Tourism, and Power in Tana Toraja, Indonesia
Kathleen M. Adams

CAMBODGE:
The Cultivation of a Nation, 1860–1945
Penny Edwards

HOW TO BEHAVE:
Buddhism and Modernity in Colonial Cambodia, 1860–1931
Anne Ruth Hansen

CULT, CULTURE, AND AUTHORITY:
Princess Liễu Hạnh in Vietnamese History
Olga Dror

Khmer Women on the Move

EXPLORING WORK AND LIFE IN URBAN CAMBODIA

Annuska Derks

 UNIVERSITY OF HAWAI'I PRESS   *Honolulu*

© 2008 University of Hawai'i Press
All rights reserved
Printed in the United States of America
13 12 11 10 09 08   6 5 4 3 2 1

Library of Congress Cataloging-in-Publication Data
Derks, Annuska.
    Khmer women on the move : exploring work and life in
urban Cambodia / Annuska Derks.
        p. cm.—(Southeast Asia—politics, meaning, and memory)
    Includes bibliographical references and index.
    ISBN 978-0-8248-3128-8 (hardcover : alk. paper) —
ISBN 978-0-8248-3270-4 (pbk. : alk. paper)
        1. Young women—Cambodia—Social conditions.
    2. Urban women—Cambodia—Social conditions.
    3. Urban women—Employment—Cambodia. I. Title.
HQ1750.3.D47 2008
305.242'209173209596—dc22
                                        2007048704

University of Hawai'i Press books are printed on
acid-free paper and meet the guidelines for permanence
and durability of the Council on Library Resources

Interior pages based on design by Leslie Fitch Design

Printed by Edwards Brothers, Inc.

CONTENTS

ACKNOWLEDGMENTS

One of the first Khmer expressions I learned when I first went to Cambodia in 1995 was *'oh kun,* meaning thank you. The expression, my Khmer teacher taught me, comes from *'oh,* meaning "glad," and *kun,* meaning "goodness," "kindness," or "merit." It was, however, only during the field research for this study that I learnt about the deeper meanings of *kun.* The young Khmer women who are the focus of this study emphasized the importance of acknowledging the *kun* of those who contribute to one's life, education, work, or other pursuits. In order to complete this book, I relied on the *kun* of various people to whom I owe debts of gratitude. First and foremost are the young Khmer women who were the focus of this study and who shared their time, their stories, their joys and also their sad experiences with me. It is to them that I dedicate this study.

The field research for this study was supported by a grant from the Netherlands Foundation for the Advancement of Tropical Research (WOTRO) and the Prince Bernhard Cultural Foundation. In Cambodia, I was supported by a great number of people and organizations. I am greatly indebted to Lim Sidedine, a valuable colleague and friend, who never tired of exploring new places, new foods and new concepts with me, the latter also during long telephone conversations after I finished fieldwork in Cambodia. I thank Mak Sophea, Hun Thirith, Lath Poch, Som Somony, Heng Chhun Oeurn, Kim Sedara, Baureaksmey Kim, Lee Hong, Ek Salan, and the representatives of diverse international and nongovernmental organizations for their assistance and expertise. I would like to express special thanks to Hean Sokhom, director of the Center for Advanced Study in Phnom Penh, for providing me with the necessary institutional support and for sharing his knowledge about Khmer culture and Buddhism. I am also grateful for the friendship, warm hospitality and care with which San, Peou and other neighbors made me part of their—at times difficult—lives.

I profoundly thank Frans Hüsken and Huub de Jonge, my doctoral advisors at the Radboud University Nijmegen, the Netherlands, for their time, efforts, and valuable suggestions and insights at critical points in the research and writing process. I am very grateful to William Collins, who has been a great mentor since I first came to Cambodia and who sent me his stimulating and constructive criticism on earlier drafts of the manuscript. I greatly appreciated the academic exchanges at the Institute of Social Anthropology, University of Berne, Switzerland, where I worked during most of the writing process, and thank my colleagues and Professors Wolfgang Marschall and Heinzpeter Znoj for their encouragement and input.

This book benefited greatly from the invaluable suggestions from a number of scholars of Cambodia. Many thanks go to David Chandler for taking his time to thoroughly read and comment on the manuscript. His suggestions were very important for molding the manuscript into its present form. I am also very grateful for the supportive and constructive reviews of Judy Ledgerwood, Penny Edwards and Trudy Jacobson, which greatly helped me to strengthen the argument. The publication of this book would not have been possible without the support of Duncan McCargo, who introduced me to the University of Hawai'i Press in the first place, of Pamela Kelley, my editor, and of Keith Leber and Barbara Folsom, who helped bring the book to completion. Many thanks to them all.

Finally, I am greatly indebted to my parents, Wim and Alie Derks, who have consistently supported me, even though I know it is not always easy for them to have a daughter "on the move." I would further like to express my gratitude to my family and friends, all of whom, from various parts of the world, kept me aware of the fact that there are other things in life than writing a thesis. Special thanks go to Cristel Teusink who, with her great sense of humor, would always help me put my work in perspective, and to Judith Zweers, with whom I spent relaxing moments on the Tonle Sap Boulevard. And last, I would like to thank Florian Forster for his strong support, for his probing questions, and for occasionally taking me away from my computer and into the mountains, and Yorio, simply for existing.

NOTE ON THE TRANSLITERATION

There is no standard romanization of the Khmer language. I have followed, as far as possible, the spelling of common words and expressions as I found them in Khmer dictionaries (especially Headley 1977). In some cases, however, I slightly changed the symbols in order to make them easier for the reader, even though this deviates from the system that language experts use for transcription of the numerous vowels in Khmer. For an indication of the pronunciation:

a   = as in French "pas"
ae   = falling diphthong, as in *"khmae"* (khmer)
au   = as in "noun"
ay   = as in "Thai"
ea   = falling diphthong, as in *"neak"* (person)
eu   = as in French "peu"
ii   = as in "cheek"
o   = as in "long"
ou   = as in "loan"
u   = as in "June"
ˀ   = glottal stop

h after a consonant indicates aspiration
r at the end of a word is not pronounced
a double vowel indicates a longer sound

Introduction

Like many people, the main images I had of Cambodia before I first arrived in the country in 1995 were those of Angkor Wat and the Killing Fields. Not surprisingly, like most of the literature, news reports and films tend to focus on the splendor of Angkor, which symbolizes the glory of the country's past, and on the horrors of the Killing Fields, which evoke more generally the tragedy of Cambodia's modern history. History, it seems, is a central theme in the way the country is portrayed. This attention focused on Cambodia's past is also manifest in the labels of tradition, conservatism, timelessness and changelessness that are often employed in describing Cambodian society (Martin 1994; Ledgerwood et al. 1994; Chandler 1996a; Curtis 1998; Ayres 2000).

It does not, however, take long to find out that Cambodia is not as static or backward-looking as such labels or the dominant focus on the past may suggest; not only because of the centuries of history in which the country has continuously been (re)created and transformed, but also because of the variety of influences and processes that have affected the country in more recent times. The transition from a closed socialist system to an open-market system and toward peace and reconstruction has contributed to a new framework for the country's future, and to new opportunities, expectations and needs for its inhabitants.

Hence, on a closer look we find a country full of contradictions in which past and present constantly interact. While the majority of the population are subsistence farmers, growing rice and using technology similar to those depicted on the Angkorian bas-reliefs, the ancient temple itself has become a site of (post)modern achievement due to its function as a major tourist attraction as well as a backdrop for Hollywood productions.[1] Contradictions can also be found in the lives of Cambodians themselves, which are, for the majority, dominated by poverty and the rhythms of rural life, while a small, mostly urban, elite enjoys the "benefits of democratic happiness-cum-consumerism" (Thion 1993). And while many Cambodians aspire to take part in an officially proclaimed "new era" of prosperity and development, dominant discourses still revolve around the timeless concern about the perceived loss of Khmer tradition, land and national identity.

In such a context there are ample challenges for an anthropological study of what Fischer (1999) has called "emergent forms of life." By exploring such forms, this book aims to give a dynamic picture of Cambodia and the way Cambodians deal with new aspirations, opportunities and constraints. It analyzes the interrelations of individual experiences, symbolic constructions and structural inequalities that shape the country as it adapts to the global pressures of the twenty-first century. The focus is on young Cambodian migrant women, who are directly involved in, affected by and also shape current processes of change as they leave their villages to work in the city.

SOPHEA'S STORY

"I think that I have two hands and two legs so I can earn money to support myself without having to steal from others. My siblings know about my character and remain silent. They know that I will not become a prostitute like other women. I told my siblings that they need not worry about me, that I know how to take care of myself and that I am well aware of the good and bad roads to follow."

Through her remarks, the young woman whom I call Sophea points out how her move to the city was guided by the need for cash income, moral dilemmas and, above all, self-determination. It is the last for which I remember her most fondly. I met Sophea for the first time in a restaurant where she was working as a beer promotion girl. In her charming and open way, she told me that her brand of beer was still unknown among most customers, and that she therefore had a hard time selling it. Her arguments convinced me and my companions to support her by ordering her brand of beer. As we continued to talk about her work and life in Phnom Penh, it turned out that we were living very close to each other, and we arranged to meet again later that week.

On several occasions afterwards I learned about Sophea's story. Her parents died during the Pol Pot era while she was still very young. The eldest of her seven siblings took care of her. When she was about sixteen years old, she ran away from home because she no longer wanted to live in the household of her oldest brother, who blamed her for being lazy and denied her a much-wanted bicycle and wristwatch like those a neighbor possessed. She decided to try her luck somewhere else and left for Phnom Penh with three friends from her village. Two of these friends have since returned to marry and live in the village, but Sophea has stayed in Phnom Penh. She found work first as a domestic servant, later as a market trader, as a factory worker in several factories and, finally, as a beer promotion girl.

When she came to Phnom Penh, she stayed with the family she worked for, then moved to live with the family of her cousin, who helped her settle as a market trader. When she started working in the ironing section of a factory, she rented a room with a friend from her village who worked in the same factory. Sophea later found a job in another factory, where she could work with a sewing machine. In this factory she befriended Sophoarn, a young woman from her work unit, who joined them in living in a small, wooden room located on a compound close to where I lived. Of the three women, only Sophoarn continued to work in a factory. Sophea and her other friend quit after they got fed up with night shifts, forced overtime and arrogant behavior of the Chinese supervisors. Sophea tried to find another factory job, but was unsuccessful and remained without work for a few months. She was in urgent need of money: "I spent the money that I'd earned before [. . .] and didn't want to go back to my native village. I didn't know what to do, so I decided to sell beer."

When I met Sophea, she had been working as a beer promotion girl for two months. She worked on the basis of commission and had diffi- culties earning enough to cover her living expenses. Sophea is well aware that her job, often seen as an indirect form of sex work, is not good for her reputation as a woman. At work she has to wear a short, tight blue dress, which she tries to cover with a long black skirt when she takes a *motodup* (motorbike-taxi) to go to work. Her work also requires an adaptation in behavior and speech. She has had to learn how to soothe unknown men, sit, talk and drink with them in a familiar, intimate way. Further, Sophoarn, her friend and roommate, criticizes her for incorrect behavior outside work, for going out with men, wearing too tight tops and skirts with a long split. Sophoarn and others consider such style and behavior as "too modern" and not proper for Khmer women.

Sophea knows that urban types of work, styles and behavior set her apart from other women in her village: "When I compare myself now with women of my age in my native village who have one or two children, I am very different: I have my own money to buy rice." She attaches high value to the autonomy she has in the city, which is possible through the money she earns herself. Sophea likes to buy new clothes, go out for fun *(dae leeng),* and sing karaoke—activities she could not indulge in or afford back in her home village. No wonder that Sophea vehemently refuses her siblings' repeated calls to come back to her village and get married. For Sophea, twenty-four years old when I befriended her, it is clear: she wants to stay in Phnom Penh a bit longer and "have some more fun." She finds life in the village too boring *(opsuk)* and, as she admits, she always longs to go back to Phnom Penh after a short visit with her family. As a result her siblings joke that Phnom Penh is her native village: "They love me very much, but I am obstinate and I want to outdo them, even if it is only a little."

Sophea is one of tens of thousands of young women who have left their villages to find work in Phnom Penh. Her story is one of many, neither exemplary nor unique in its facets of mobility and determination. Her career so far illustrates part of the spectrum of jobs available to young women without much education. At the same time it shows a young woman's mobility, switching between jobs, places and styles. Sophea is accommodating her work, housing, friends and behavior to the possibilities and constraints that make up the lives of young Cambodian women like her. Her behavior does not fulfill the conceptions of traditional proper behavior for women, as shown in the reactions of her family and roommate. Though such notions are both assumed and referred to as a given, they are, like Khmer tradition in general, constantly being created (Ledgerwood 1996a: 412).

Women like Sophea who make their way from the village to the city to find work, and with it an income to support themselves as well as their village-based families, are very much part of a process in which meanings of "proper" female behavior, tradition and being Khmer are renegotiated. This renegotiation takes place in the face of the social upheaval and destruction associated with Cambodia's recent past, and also in the face of its present road toward reconstruction and the related concerns with development, globalization and modernization (see also Edwards and Roces 2000). It is within this context that this study will explore, in detail, stories of young rural women's work and life in Phnom Penh, the teeming capital of Cambodia.

MY STORY

Before I started this study I had worked for three years for a local research organization in Cambodia. During this time I worked on research projects focusing on such topics as ethnic minorities, conflict resolution and democratization. I was frequently assigned to work with female Cambodian researchers on gender issues. A great deal of my work involved research on the trafficking of women and children, an issue that drew increasing attention from local and international organizations, policymakers and the media. It was, and is, commonly associated with young women and girls who are brutally forced, kidnapped, or deceived into a globalized sex industry. What I discovered in my research, however, was a much more differentiated and complex picture. Not only were the target groups, the recruitment practices and the services or activities in which "trafficked" persons ended up much more varied than the general picture of young women forced into "sexual slavery," but also those women who ended up in the sex industry did not necessarily see themselves as victims of organized "global sex traffic" (Derks 1997, 1998a, 2004; see also Law 2000: 11). I encountered young women in search of a better life for their family and themselves, wanting some adventure and using some of the opportunities open to them, leading them into diverse new, positive and negative, experiences.

This discovery inspired me to focus on different forms of female mobility. Instead of looking at the forced forms of it, and instead of focusing on sex work, I wanted to take a broader look at the migration and opportunities available to young women coming from the countryside to Phnom Penh. These young, often poorly educated, women are most likely to end up working in the sales, service and industrial sectors, performing jobs that contrast sharply to those performed in their home villages. I decided for comparative reasons that it would be interesting to focus on specific categories of unskilled or low-skilled, low-paid employment within these three sectors.

Within the sales sector, I look particularly at female migrants working as street traders. Trading is an activity in which women traditionally prevail and contribute cash to the household economy. There is a large variety in trades and traders, but young, rural women—who are the focus of my research—dominate in small-scale street trading that often involves food items.

Work in the industrial sector, contrary to trading, is a relatively new economic activity for women. It is related to Cambodia's integration into the global capitalist economy. This concerns in particular the garment industry, which has been pinpointed as one of the main catalysts to development. I therefore focus on migrant women working in this particular industry.

Within the service sector I concentrate on those "service providers" that I was already familiar with, namely sex workers. Prostitution, as such, is not a new phenomenon in Cambodia, although the scale upon which it has been practiced within the past decade is unprecedented. Sex work takes place in nightclubs, brothels, and parks, as well as more indirectly by some women working in the entertainment or service sector, such as beer promotion work in restaurants. I will examine these different forms, but I focus mainly on brothel-based sex workers. Since sex work most strongly defies cultural notions of proper behavior and sexuality of women, it is an interesting case for comparison with small-scale trading activities and factory labor.

By studying three different categories of work, the question I seek to answer is how to understand the differences and similarities in rural-urban migration and urban employment of young Cambodian women. I will do so by exploring the interrelationships among structural conditions, social and cultural constructions, and individual experiences. I concentrate on the processes and practices of migration and employment with an initial set of research questions. What are the individual and familial motivations for migration and urban employment, and how do these relate to structural conditions? How are migration and urban employment related to contacts with family and village of origin? What are the conditions of women's work and life in the city? And how do these motivations, contacts and conditions differ between women in factory work, sex work and street trade?

Although the three categories of work have specific entry routines, working, earning, and related living conditions, as well as specific interventions and regulations, Sophea's story shows that the borders between these categories of work are porous and easily crossed. Soon after starting my fieldwork I realized that mobility is not only related to geographic movement of women from the countryside to the city, but also relates to women's ever-changing work and living situations, and to the flexible patterns of behavior these young rural women display as they try to make sense of ambiguities and contradictions in their pursuit of fulfilling personal desires, family obligations, or cultural ideals.

This finding motivated me to look in detail at women's experiences and the ways in which women view themselves in the city and in relation to their rural background. With a second set of research questions I focus on these urban experiences and their consequences. What does urban work and life mean to young rural women? To what extent do they aspire to and achieve participation in urban life? How do women perceive their rural backgrounds in relation to their desired "modern" urban experiences? How are contradictory moralities and ideals regarding financial obligations, responsibilities, female behavior and individual desires reworked through social relationships, networks and employment in the city? And do these urban experiences influence decision-making processes that affect their own lives as well as those of their families?

Over the past two decades many studies have analyzed the migration and employment of women in Southeast Asia (e.g., Enloe 1983; Ong 1987; Murray 1991; Wolf 1992; Chant and McIlwaine 1995; Mills 1999; Law 2000; Elmhirst 2002). In this sense, the focus of this study is not unique, and neither, at first glance, are the experiences of Cambodian migrant women, which parallel those of other women in Southeast Asia and other parts of the world. Yet, by paying attention to local conditions, meanings and consequences, and by taking a comparative look at migrant women in different categories of work—which also required high mobility and flexibility for myself as a researcher—I hope to provide insight into the ways that young Cambodian women with similar rural, economically poor, rice-farming and poorly educated backgrounds involve themselves in urban employment and thereby contribute to a multiplicity and dynamism in social practices and the production of cultural meanings. In Cambodia, which has recently opened up to the global economy, the ideas of social reconstruction and the ways in which people handle new possibilities, changes and insecurities have so far hardly been analyzed. Women definitely play an important role in these processes, not simply, as we shall see, as pawns in the country's pursuit of national development or as simple cultural images of "tradition" and "modernity," but also as agents in their own right.

SUBJECTS AND SYMBOLS
Studies focusing on women in developing countries tend to highlight how they are used to symbolize the state of "tradition" in their societies or how women are subjected to structures of dominance. The former perspective points to women as the symbolic bearers of culture, honor,

or national identity, and as such carrying the "burden of representation" (Yuval-Davis 1997: 45–46). The last perspective relates more specifically to female migrants and laborers, who are often portrayed as exploited subjects, forced to leave their village and work under unequal, capitalist conditions and patriarchal control systems in order to provide their families with much-needed cash earnings (e.g., Enloe 1983; Heyzer 1988; Sassen 1998). While such portrayals of women as symbols of tradition or subjects of capitalism can be criticized for suggesting passivity and homogeneity among women who differ in class, ethnicity, and age as well as in the ways they respond to and act upon changing opportunities and constraints, they continue to appear quite regularly in analyses of female labor migration.

Approaches to female labor migration variously emphasize the role of economic rationality, structural conditions, household strategies and agency. An approach that focuses on economic rationality explains population movements merely as a function of individual decisions based on "pull" factors, such as employment opportunities, better wages, working conditions and other advantages in usually urban industrialized areas, and on "push" factors that are related to the deteriorating conditions in the usually rural areas of origin, such as declining productivity, increased landlessness, or demographic growth. This approach has been rightly criticized for failing to take into account the structural determinants, or the underlying inequalities, that are fundamental to understanding processes of migration. To consider migration, Fernández-Kelly argues, "as the result of aggregate individual decisions does not adequately explain why migration begins, increases, and diminishes at certain historical stages nor does it account for the direction of migratory flows" (1983: 206).

An approach that focuses on structural conditions and links labor migration and participation to specific economic, political and ideological conditions, can therefore be seen as an important corrective to the more functionalist individual, rational actor approach to labor migration (Fernández-Kelly 1983: 221). Feminist authors have in this way examined the gender-linked characteristics of migration. Sassen (1998) analyzes the systematic relationships between globalization and the feminization of waged labor. She argues that the fundamental processes leading to an increase in migratory movements of so-called Third World women, within their country as well as abroad, are related to economic restructuring at the global level. These include, most obviously, the shift of factories and offices to developing countries that promotes a demand for cheap female labor. The connection between female migration, labor participation and unequal developments within the world market, resulting in an international division of labor, is also explored by other authors. Mies (1986), for example, argues that women in developing countries form a cheap, easily controllable, flexible workforce, serving international male-dominated capital by producing commodities for the world market, and by fulfilling subsistence and reproductive services in the informal sector or the sex business.

In an effort to link this overly deterministic focus of the structural approach to the individualistic focus of the rational actor approach, some researchers have resorted to a household strategies approach (cf. Wolf 1992: 13). Female labor migration has, in their view, to be considered above all as part of a household survival strategy, because women who migrate are doing so in order to earn an income that can contribute to the household economy. The diverse tasks associated with household maintenance are, as Chant and Radcliffe (1992: 22) argue, as important as labor opportunities in explaining female labor migration. Gendered divisions of productive and reproductive tasks, and decision-making structures within the household are, according to these authors, crucial in analyzing who moves, whether other household members move with them, and who stays behind. Such divisions should therefore be considered in combination with the structural elements that lead to a gender-segregated labor market (Chant 1992; Chant and Radcliffe 1992).

Although the household strategy approach attempts to mediate between macro-structural and micro-individual levels of analysis, it fails to take, as Wolf (1992: 17) argues, sufficiently into account that household reproduction cannot be considered as a given, and that households are in fact sites of conflict, loci of contestation and negotiation between contradictory positions and expectations among household members of different genders and ages. These contestations and negotiations are partly related to women's own aspirations regarding consumption, beauty, fashion and commodified leisure. State-based pursuits of development, as well as the capitalist images spread by television and other media, play an important role in young women's material aspirations. These pursuits and images also influence the employment strategies of young migrant women, such as those described by Murray (1991), who abandoned informal economic activities such as street trading and adopted a more profitable economic activity, namely prostitution.

This all points toward a complex interplay among the different levels—individual, household, state, and global—in processes of female labor migration. On the one hand, we can, like Mills (2003: 42), speak of a "profoundly gendered global economy." Gender inequalities serve to define women around the globe as supplementary or devalued workers in the new sites of industrialization, the informal sector, and domestic service as well as the sex industry. On the other hand, there is "considerable diversity in discursive forms and material practices that gender hierarchies take within the global labor force" (Mills 2003: 43). This diversity relates, besides ethnicity, class, or age, to women's diverse positions as unmarried daughters as against wives or mothers, and to the dynamics and experiences of women in migration and labor participation. Women's experiences are differently affected by employment-related disciplinary strategies (and resistance to these), by the ways in which women are positioned as consumers rather than producers, as well as by the multiple gender roles and meanings. This complexity results, as Ong has written, in a "gap between our analytical constructs and workers' actual experiences" (1991: 279).

Increasingly, studies therefore try to come to terms with the complex dualism between the unequal structures of power and wealth within the global economy, and the daily lives and views of young women in the global labor force. The concept of female agency, the "socioculturally mediated capacity to act" (Ahearn 2001: 112), plays an important role here. Law, for example, speaks in her study about sex work in Southeast Asia of a "negotiated tension" (2000: 121) between free will and the constraints that make certain kinds of employment, such as in the sex industry, an opportunity for women. She adds that sex workers themselves, contrary to the views of many observers, do not view their position and encounters with men in strictly oppressive terms, and points therefore to the possibilities for resistance—albeit in a complex, unanticipated, or culturally relevant way.

Contestation and struggle have become critical themes in studies of women's experiences of migration and employment. Women may be confronted with diverse forms of exploitation or domination within the family, at work or in society, and yet by "manipulating, contesting and rejecting these claims, working women reassess and remake their identities and communities in ways important for social life" (Ong 1991: 296). This is clearly visible in courtship and marriage practices, in which young working women increasingly gain autonomy, as well as in their engagement in "new patterns of consumption linked to desired and often globally oriented standards of 'modernity'" (Mills 2003: 49). These are, however, at the same time the arenas of life that most interfere with ideas about women's symbolic role in national development and modernization, as well as in embodying the maintenance or loss of traditional values. It is in this context that portrayals of female migrants as capitalist subjects contrast most strongly with portrayals of women as symbols of tradition.

Young women working away from the direct control of their parents in the sex industry, factory labor, or trading are easily depicted as "loose women" who are behaving in improper, immoral, or nontraditional ways. Such concerns affect not only women and their parents but also society at large. While women's lives are affected by external forces such as the global economy, changes in their behavior may be interpreted as a threat to "tradition" and "national identity." It is for this reason that Ong and Peletz (1995: 2) suggest placing gender both in relation to specific historical and political economic forces and in the framework of symbolic meaning.

The argument that gender and sexuality are in fact symbolic constructs with various meanings in different social and cultural contexts—and thus not natural categories—has long been discussed among feminist anthropologists.[2] Studies about gender in Southeast Asia tend to emphasize these symbolic meanings of gender. Local constructions of gender relationships, Atkinson and Errington (1990: viii) argue, demand understanding in their own terms. As a result, gender should be viewed as a cultural system of meaning that pertains to the differences and similarities between women and men as they are lived and interpreted in particular contexts (ibid.: 8). Whereas attention for the impact of exogenous factors on these gender meanings is, in early works, minimal, they become central in later works on gender in Southeast Asia (Steedly 1999: 438). Ong and Peletz (1995: 2) argue that "indigenous notions bearing on masculinity and femininity, on gender equality and complementarity, and on various criteria of prestige and stigma are being reworked in the dynamic postcolonial contexts of peasant outmigration, nation building, cultural nationalism, and international business." Gender should therefore be considered as fluid and contingent, characterized by contestation, ambivalence and change.

Few studies and analyses focus on the complex interplay between symbolic meanings of gender, and the processes and developments that have shaped post-conflict Cambodia.[3] Contestation, ambiguity and change are especially relevant themes in relation to years of warfare, the Khmer Rouge terror regime, and isolation under the guidance of their "traditional enemies," the Vietnamese. This heritage has led to the pervasive idea of the destruction or even loss of Khmer culture, and "[i]n the face of a threatened loss of their culture, Khmer emphasize certain cultural symbols as the embodiment of 'Khmerness'" (Ledgerwood et al. 1994: 9). The cultural symbol of the Khmer woman has thus taken on a special meaning. Ledgerwood writes: "They—the Khmer—are focusing on women. The sense of their importance goes beyond the fact that more women than men survived the horrors of their recent history, or the fact that women are somehow "culture bearers" par excellence. There is something of central importance to this focus that is linked to the proper behavior of women" (1990: 2).

Ledgerwood goes on to explain that to be Khmer means to live in accordance with a certain hierarchical order of society, one that places a strong emphasis on gender roles. "To move outside these roles is to enter the realm of chaos where, having lost what it is to be female in Khmer terms, one loses also what it is to be Khmer" (ibid.: 3). Symbolic images of the woman, and of proper female behavior, thus not only function to preserve culture but the Khmer social order and people in general. This does not, however, mean that these images are fixed or internally coherent. Gender relationships—in Cambodia, Southeast Asia, or indeed anywhere—cannot be considered as fixed systems, if only because they are typically comprised of contradictory ideologies that are constantly undergoing change (Ong and Peletz 1995: 4).

Such ambiguous gender imagery is especially important in times of rapid social change, as it can be used to put forward new issues and categories that become restated as "tradition" (Ledgerwood 1996a: 412). Studies on Khmer gender typically refer to the *Chbap Srey,* or "Code of Women's Behavior" that advises women how to behave properly and is often referred to as a kind of blueprint for the traditional, submissive position of women in Cambodia. Yet, a detailed reading of such and other texts shows that the "proper," or virtuous, woman in the Khmer context is a multivalent symbol, through which she is simultaneously many different and contradictory things and can thus be made to fit new situations (Ledgerwood 1990: 317). A proper woman must be "soft and sweet" as well as a "hard-headed businesswoman," and while daughters are supposed to be protected, they are also expected to go to the city in order to earn money to help support the family (Ledgerwood 1994: 123; 1992: 5). Such multiple ambiguous notions of femaleness allow ideals to be discussed as being retained, even though the action has significantly changed (Ledgerwood 1996a: 139–140). In this sense, the contradictory and changing meanings of ideals with regard to women are of major importance to our understandings of young women who temporarily leave their families and villages in search of work in the city.

CAMBODIA AND THE EXPERIENCE OF MODERNITY

Whereas Ledgerwood focuses in her work mostly on how the changing symbolic meanings of "proper" Khmer women are restated as tradition, at the same time, especially in the media and advertisements, women are portrayed as symbols of progress and modernity.[4] These images of modernity certainly exert appeal as they reach villages through occasional TV sets and the stories of those who have experienced a stay in Phnom Penh. They contribute to the perceived attractions of city life and jobs, particularly for young people, and are important for generating a flow of migrants to the city. Working and living in Phnom Penh gives these young people the opportunity to become, if only temporarily and to a limited extent, part of a "modern" urban world. This "modern" experience plays an important role in young rural women's perceptions of their work, life, and position in the city. Yet, in their desire to be modern women *(srey samay)*, they struggle to find a proper balance between what they consider to be "old" or "traditional" in village life and what they see as "too modern" in the city. This struggle occurs between parents and daughters, managers and workers, men and women, or among women themselves, and interrelates with the constraints and opportunities that are set within the specific Cambodian context.

In the 1950s and 1960s, journalists, tourists and diplomats who visited Cambodia described it as "an idyllic, antique land unsullied by the brutalities of the modern world" (Shawcross 1986: 36). Such descriptions referred to Phnom Penh, a quiet riverside city with a provincial charm and, unlike cities such as Bangkok and Saigon, seemingly untouched by the pressures of trade and war. They referred even more so to the countryside, where the majority of the "friendly," "smiling" population lived in villages built around Buddhist temples and surrounded by green rice fields. Although this idyll was already by then an illusion, it was brutally destroyed by the years of war, terror and geopolitical forces that dominated the country's history from the late 1960s up to the 1990s.

This violent past is now thought to be a result of a confrontation between the traditional and the modern. Only during the French protectorate (1863–1953) did Cambodia become part of a modernist, colonialist project while, as Ayres (2000: 2) states, continuing to uphold its system rooted in "time-honored notions of power, hierarchy and leadership." He speaks of a "Cambodian veneration of tradition" that made modernity only a limited success (ibid.). Hence the Pol Pot regime is often seen as synonymous with what is regarded as the "tragedy of modern Cambodia." While similarly focusing on this interplay between the traditional and the modern in Cambodian political history, Marston (2002) argues that Cambodia never met the criteria for modernity as defined within the modernization theory relating to industrial development, mass media, liberal democracy and social diversification. Yet, modernity also refers to individual identity in relation to the modern world, a modern world that is increasingly complex, globalized, ideologically diversified and self-reflexive (Marston 2002: 39–40).[5] Seen from this perspective, modernity has touched Cambodia to the extent that global processes created its recent past, not only the Pol Pot regime, but also the economic, political and social developments that have influenced Cambodia up to the present day. Even more important for Marston is the conception of modernity—that is, the configuration of what, in different ways and in different places and times, is conceived of as modern—and how this is played out in what is conceived of as "traditional," leading every society to spin its "modernities" out of the fleece of the "traditional" (2002: 59).[6]

How, then, do past and present developments shape the "face" or "character" of modernity in present-day Cambodia? As we have seen, Cambodia's recent past, marked by war and destruction, is crucial to understanding the present meanings of modernity, which constitute, above all, a break with this past and the onset of better times. Developments in Cambodia since the early 1990s have brought hopes of what Prime Minister Hun Sen has called a "new era of growth and prosperity" (Ministry of Commerce 2000). This new era involves a necessary "process of modernization and national economic development" and integration into a capitalist global economy (Minister of Commerce Cham Prasidh, in Ministry of Commerce 2000). Such ideas and hopes of prosperity, development and modernity, proclaimed at the highest political levels, have reached people at all strata of Cambodian society.

Young women and their mobility play a decisive role in this pursuit for prosperity, development and modernity. First, their labor contributes significantly to national economic development, especially in the factories that produce for a global market. Second, their earnings contribute to fulfilling, if only to a limited extent, the needs and aspirations of their rural families who, through new commodities, agricultural inputs, as well as the education of younger siblings, hope to enhance their own position and comfort. Third, women are pursuing their own aspirations regarding modern consumption and display as these are promoted in images of modernity in advertising and the mass media as well as in stories of peers who live and work in the city. These three roles are not easy to reconcile, especially when taking into account the symbolic and limited positions of women in a rapidly changing society like Cambodia according to which women are simultaneously symbols of tradition and yet subject to, and thus constrained by, structures of dominance. Edwards and Roces (2000: 10–11) speak therefore, more generally, of a "modern" Asian woman who "exudes contradiction and ambivalence as she straddles between tradition and modernity, victimization and agency, between being a subject and an object."

Are these oppositions reflected in lived experiences? This central question runs throughout this study. By paying attention to Khmer women's own stories, as well as to their responses, actions, consumptions and creativity, I hope to gain insights into their subjective experiences and the ways in which these are based on practices that can be considered neither wholly acts of free will nor completely socially determined products.

PLAYING GAMES

Studying Khmer women who move to the city to work involves reaching an understanding of the conditions that contribute to the demand for female labor, the constraints and opportunities that are set in a Cambodian historical context, and the ways in which these relate to cultural and social constructions of gender that are characterized by contestation, ambivalence and change. Furthermore, a study of Khmer women on the move will need to explore the role of the experience of modernity, existing at large but variously practiced and conceived (Berman 1988; Appadurai 1996). And maybe most important, this study calls for an understanding of the ways in which women themselves are agents in these processes. How can one understand the links between subjective experiences and actions, constructions of gender and the broader historical context, and structures in which these are situated?

Probably the most influential framework in which such questions are dealt with is so-called practice theory, as it tries to overcome dualistic conceptualizations such as those of structure/individual and objective/subjective. Within the practice framework, the emphasis is on the idea that human action is constrained by the given social and cultural order—usually condensed to the term "structure"—but also on the idea that human action creates structure—that is, it reproduces or transforms it, or both (Ortner 1996: 2). The actions, or practices, of individual actors are produced by what Bourdieu (1977: 72) calls the habitus,[7] the "strategy-generating principle enabling agents to cope with unforeseen and ever-changing situations." Bourdieu pays significant attention to the reproductive tendencies and unintentionality of practices. Ortner (1996), however, insists that it is important to pay due attention to agency as both a product and a producer of society and history.[8]

As noted earlier, agency refers to a capacity to act within specific contexts. These capacities are neither passive reactions to sociocultural prerequisites nor simply acts of free will or resistance (Rapport and Overing 2000; Ahearn 2001). Instead, agency concerns the mediation "between conscious intention and embodied habituses, between conscious motives and unexpected outcomes, between historically marked individuals and events on the one hand, and the cumulative reproductions and transformations that are the result of every day practices on the other" (Ortner 2001: 77). In an effort to develop a model of practice embodying agency, Ortner refers to an image of what she calls "serious games." The idea of the "game" is to capture simultaneously the actors, rules and goals that make up social life, the different webs of relationships and interactions between "multiple, shiftingly, interrelated subject positions" as well as agency, because the actors "play with skill, intention, wit, knowledge, intelligence" (Ortner 1996: 12). Through the adjective "serious," Ortner means to bring in "the idea that power and inequality pervade the games in multiple ways, and that while there may be playfulness and pleasure in the process, the stakes of these games are often very high" (ibid.).

As far as the migration of young rural women to Phnom Penh is concerned, it may be useful to keep in mind the dimensions involved in what Ortner called "serious games." Doing so allows us to go beyond ideas of economic rationality, determining structures, and household strategies, and emphasizes the embeddedness of women's practices and the complex ways in which they go about life in a particular time and place. The seriousness of the games refers to the global economic, but also to the national and regional historical context that influences the constraints and possibilities these women face in their lives. The actors, rules and goals that are culturally organized and constructed contribute to specific understandings and meanings of practices and experiences related to employment, duties and desires, and arrangements for the future. Through the webs of social relationships and interactions, these understandings, practices and experiences are sustained, contested and changed. This is possible due to the agency of these women, which suggests that they are knowledgeable about, and skilled in, using the rules and goals of the game and also aware of the intentions of the different subject positions that make up their lives as they move to the city.

RESEARCH AND RESONANCE

Doing research in a city involves a different setting from the village in which anthropologists tend to conduct field research. In cities, places and people are more diverse, scattered and unknown. Since the focus of my research was on young rural women working in different sectors, I had to find a way to gain access to these diverse, scattered and mostly unknown women. Although the help of Cambodian friends and former contacts with organizations facilitated access to places and people, I still had to create my own network of women working in the sex industry, factories and street trading. I decided to find a place to live in the northern part of Phnom Penh, Tuol Sangkeo, located close to a market and situated within easy reach of one of the most famous brothel streets in Phnom Penh and close to a conglomeration of garment factories. Among my neighbors living in small rooms in the same compound were factory workers, families from the countryside, as well as the landlady and her family, who possessed a TV set in front of which we all assembled several times a week to watch and comment on popular Thai soap operas.

My living situation allowed me to talk to my neighbors on a daily basis, so I could cross-check information and the meanings of concepts during our evening talks, and provided at the same time enough privacy to receive people, most notably sex workers, who are not necessarily welcome in all houses. This relative independence to maintain relationships with different kinds of people in my own house would have been almost impossible if I had lived with a family. I also bought a small, secondhand motorbike—the kind mostly used by students—in order to be able to move around independently and visit places not considered proper for young women.

On many occasions Lim Sidedine accompanied me and assisted me with the Khmer language when needed. I had worked with Lim Sidedine for several years, especially in research projects on trafficking of women and children. She proved to be an open-minded person with very good interview skills. We have worked well together for many years and became close friends, discussing not only the situations and stories of the women we met, but also our own stories and insecurities. The fact that she is a university teacher in her forties did not hinder her communication with younger women. On the contrary, it made it easier for her to communicate about all kinds of subjects, including sexuality, and to enter sex establishments without feelings of shame and fear, something that would have been more difficult for younger research assistants.

My fieldwork took place from September 2000 through May 2001, and was followed up in 2002 and 2003. During these times I tried to address the context within which the daily life of the women I wanted to study is set. Through life histories, interviews and focus-group discussions I gained insights into the ways these women present themselves, and how they see their urban experiences and their individual accommodations to different situations, sometimes contradictory expectations, and sociocultural imperatives. Several in-depth interviews were recorded, transcribed and translated. More often, however, we took notes during or after interviews, discussions and informal talks, so that women would feel more at ease in telling us personal stories.

However, as Wikan states, anthropologists cannot only rely on people's own narratives. A "person must also respond to events, create and consume resources, and influence the events and course of social interaction" (Wikan 1995: 265). Thus, besides women's own presentations, their actions are important for understanding their positions and the way they deal with the constraints and possibilities in their positions. In this sense, participant observation can give important clues with regard to, for example, how sex workers interact with their brothel managers, their clients, or among themselves; the consumption practices of factory workers in their free time; or the ways in which street traders create and use urban spaces for themselves. I visited brothels at different times of the day, spent time with factory workers on Sunday afternoons (I also visited some factories, but gaining access to them was difficult), and spent time with street traders as they prepared curry or sold pickled mango, noodles, or fruitshakes on Phnom Penh's streets.

It was not always easy to move among the women working in different occupations and living in different parts of the city. Initially, I focused on factory workers and sex workers, presuming that it would be easy to get in contact with street traders, easily visible and accessible as they are, later on. This was not as simple as I had thought, because of the high mobility of street traders during work time, and also because of their frequent visits to their home villages. As a result, I spent more time with sex workers and factory workers than with street traders. Since my field research took place in the city, I know the rural perspective only from hearsay through my informants. I did, however, accompany a few women when they visited their families and home villages. In this way I saw how these women interacted with their families and other villagers, showing off their acquired urban styles and experiences.

In order to gain insight into the cultural and symbolic constructions of gender, I explored diverse Khmer texts, such as the *chbap* (didactic codes), folktales, religious stories and popular songs that describe, advise and indicate the importance attached to proper behavior for Khmer in general, and for Khmer women in particular. These sources do not give us a blueprint of how "it should be" or "used to be," but are helpful in understanding how gender ideals, concepts and patterns are part of the everyday discourse and how they relate to the lives and views of young rural women in Phnom Penh today. Views from religious specialists, family members, neighbors, village chiefs and other authorities in state institutions or civil organizations extended such understandings, and the different perspectives of these people proved helpful in shaping the contexts and positions in which women find themselves (see also Barth 1994; 2002).

These contexts and positions are framed by material and structural constraints, such as those reflected in statistics on female labor, education, marital conditions, migration on a national level, and by historical conditions. To document these, I relied on records and documents from government departments, international and national organizations involved in the collection of economic and social data, on archival sources, and on the valuable insights and accounts in anthropological and historical literature on Cambodia.

The difficulty and the beauty of ethnographic research is that it is never finished and always in motion. During my stay in Cambodia, I saw how the upgrading of a brothel street changed the image it had had when I arrived. The brothels located in a squatter area that I used to visit regularly had disappeared when I returned a year later. People moved on, so I occasionally got new neighbors, noticed that a sex worker had changed brothels, found that an ambulant street trader had turned to selling alternative products at a local market, or lost contact with a factory worker who had gone back to her village. Thus the lives of these women—like my own—carry on, and my presence may have been after all nothing more than a pleasurable, enriching, temporary experience.

For many young rural women seeking to become part of modern urban life, I was a symbol of the "modern woman." While I wanted to learn about their life and work, these young women showed a fascination with my world. When visiting me, some of them were more interested in the photos and magazines that friends or family had sent me than in answering my questions about their own life and work in Phnom Penh. Furthermore, by borrowing my trinkets to show off in the factory, framing the pictures I gave them, bringing me along to go *dae leeng*, or to the village, I guess that our willingness to engage in each other's worlds not only brought me, but also these young rural women, new kinds of cherished experiences. It is such resonance that Wikan (1992) describes as evoking sameness, but without denying difference.

There are, indeed, obvious differences, which are difficult to bridge and which made me uneasy about my position as, depending on the person concerned, older sister *(bong srey),* younger sister *(p'oun srey),* friend, neighbor, or foreign student. I encountered women in extremely difficult positions, from fractured families, working hard to make ends meet, or living with AIDS, without—except for some small contributions—being able to help. I do hope that this book will give these women a voice, and that, by exploring the forces that shape their position, it will be helpful to all who seek a more comprehensive understanding of the interplay between individual experiences and structures of inequity.

Rice People in the City   2

Même en ville le Cambodgien reste un campagnard.
—Jean Delvert, *Le paysan cambodgien*

A "mixture of Asian exotica" and the "gateway to an exotic land"—
this is how Cambodia's capital city, Phnom Penh, is portrayed
on the Web site of its municipality. Phnom Penh is now, we can read
on the same Web site, "within the midst of rapid change" similar to
that taking place in other Asian cities. Although such associations may
recall images of high-rise office buildings, flyovers, traffic jams, shopping malls, bright lights and signs promoting the products of an endless
diversity of small-to-big businesses within Southeast Asian cities such
as Bangkok, Ho Chi Minh City, Kuala Lumpur and Jakarta, these do
not really fit with the relatively provincial outlook of Phnom Penh. The
charm and colors for which Phnom Penh was famous in the 1960s, with
its tree-lined streets and small parks, the yellow royal palace, the red
national museum and the faded colors of the French colonial houses,
still shape the city's outlook. The orange robes of the monks living and
studying in the many pagodas of the city, the colorful boulevard along
the Tonle Sap River—a favorite place for young and old to go for a
stroll or ride a motorbike—and the newly painted stupas and replanted
flower clock of Wat Phnom, the hill designated as the birthplace of
Phnom Penh[1] that solemnly towers over the city's bustle, all add to the
charm and colors of the city.

It would, however, be wrong to describe Phnom Penh only in terms
of its past glory and refreshed coloring. The heritage of war and revolution cannot be ignored, if only because of the poor condition of many
streets, the visible presence of handicapped mine victims who, as beg-
gars, try to collect money for a meal, or the institutionalized memo-

rial to the brutality of the Khmer Rouge in the form of the Tuol Sleng museum, once a school but turned into a torture center from which virtually no proclaimed enemy emerged alive.

In the face of this historical legacy, Phnom Penh has, in the past decade, experienced a diversity of developments and influences that shape street life and business activities, as well as architecture. Motorbikes, cyclos, white land cruisers from aid organizations, and other cars now fill streets that were nearly deserted until the early 1990s. Markets scattered throughout the city function as the main centers for sales and services varying from food to imported clothes and medicine, from jewelry and spare parts to hairdressing. On the outskirts of the city factories produce cigarettes, shoes, and above all garments. These factories and a few high buildings, especially hotels, business buildings, shops and market halls are shaping a new face of Phnom Penh. In the unpaved back streets it is nowadays not uncommon to see a pink Thai-style villa rise up next to a wooden Khmer house on stilts. Along the main streets Western and "modern" Asian style products and lifestyles are promoted on huge advertisement boards, which display young women in office dress using mobile phones, Western men drinking French cognac, or "exotic" snowboarding heroes who are meant to promote a certain brand of cigarettes to people who have never seen snow.

Improvements in security, electricity and wealth during the past decade have contributed to a bustling street life in Phnom Penh. Throughout the day one can hear traders praising their *numpan* (bread), scavengers calling for *etchay* (old glass), or sounds of the *tok-tok*, clacking wooden sticks, indicating the arrival of the noodle-soup cart. On the sidewalks food stalls offer street food and drinks till late at night, while new restaurants, bars, nightclubs and other establishments offer food, alcohol and sex. This dynamism has, however, not benefited everyone. With the developments that have taken place since the socialist economic system was abandoned in the early 1990s, class differences have become more evident. And thus, on Phnom Penh's streets, luxury cars move alongside the old, skinny cyclo driver from the countryside. While the rich build huge villas for themselves, many rural migrants find housing in flimsy squatters' hovels located near the river and other unused spaces. Class differences are also visible in other aspects of urban life, such as the newly established computer and internet shops that provide the wealthy urban dweller with global access—features of a modern world far away from that of the city's poor inhabitants.

FROM ANCIENT ANGKOR TO PRESENT-DAY PHNOM PENH

The role of the capital city has varied considerably over time in Cambodia. Once a political-religious center with great regional influence, it changed not only in position but also in function as it moved from Angkor to the area of Phnom Penh in the fifteenth and sixteenth centuries. Its strategic location at the crossing of the Mekong and Tonle Sap made Phnom Penh an ideal site for an international port town in which trading played a major role. Although not always the city where the court resided, Phnom Penh remained the main urban center of the country.[2] In the nineteenth century it became a colonial city, and by the mid-twentieth century, a postcolonial capital with modernizing aspirations. These aspirations were destroyed in 1975 by the revolutionary forces, who referred to Phnom Penh as a "great prostitute on the Mekong" (Chandler 1991: 247). In the 1980s, Phnom Penh slowly resumed its role as the political and economic center of the country. The political and economic opening-up of the country in the 1990s strengthened this role and led to major transformations within the city. Notwithstanding these recent developments, Phnom Penh keeps a relatively marginal position within the global economy—especially when compared to the capital cities of some other Southeast Asian countries—which is why it has also been labeled a "fourth world" city (Shatkin 1998).

The historical developments are reflected in the changing size of Phnom Penh (see Table 1). Reid (1993: 73) estimates that Phnom Penh contained, in the seventeenth century, up to fifty thousand people. After Cambodia lost its main sea access to Vietnam, international trade declined, and so did Phnom Penh's population. At the beginning of the French protectorate, Phnom Penh had about one-fifth of the population it had had two centuries earlier and consisted of "little more than a string of huts" (Igout 1993: 4). Under influence of King Norodom—who had moved the royal seat from Udong back to Phnom Penh—and the French administration, this "string of huts" gradually changed into a colonial city with the construction of the Royal Palace, Chinese shop-houses, administrative offices, and later hotels, schools, and other edifices that contributed to the "emergence of a modern city" (Igout 1993: 7).

During the French protectorate, which lasted until 1953,[3] the urbanization and modernization of Phnom Penh had progressed considerably. This was not only visible in its population, which by the 1950s was about seven times the size it had been at the beginning of the twentieth century, but also in city planning and architecture. The city was divided

TABLE I   Population of Phnom Penh (in thousands)

Year	Phnom Penh
1860s	~10
1897	~50
1939	108
1942	111–120
1950	354–363
1958	355–450
1962	394–400
1970	900–1,000
1975	1,500–2,000
April 1975	evacuation
1975–1979	~50
1979–1980	90–100
1985	427
1989–1990	500–615
1998	1,000
2004	1,043

Sources: Igout (1993); Blancot and Petermüller (1997);
National Institute of Statistics (2000b; 2004); Delvert (1961)

into ethnic quarters, each with economic specializations. Around Wat Phnom, a French colonial quarter developed. In the center of the city, around the central market, was the lively Chinese quarter, where a new market (Psar Thmey) had been erected as a *"chef d'oeuvre* of modern architecture" (Igout 1993: 12). A predominantly Cambodian quarter surrounded the area of the Royal Palace and the National Museum. A smaller Vietnamese quarter was located to the west of Phnom Penh and in the suburb of Russey Keo.

After independence the Khmer part of the population quickly grew to outnumber other groups (Goulain 1967: 17–19). From the early 1950s until 1970, when Sihanouk[4] was toppled in Lon Nol's coup d'état, the population of Cambodia's capital city almost tripled. This population growth was related, above all, to the migration of peasants leaving behind their insecure situation in the countryside and profiting from improvements in transport and new educational possibilities. Many of these rural migrants maintained a rural outlook after their arrival in the city. With their small vegetable gardens and their pigs and chickens roaming around, the Cambodian quarters of Phnom Penh looked, according to Delvert (1961: 31), more like villages than part of a "modern" capital city.

Sihanouk was determined to make Phnom Penh into a city that fitted with its status as the state capital of an independent Cambodia. He centralized all administrative, political, economic and cultural operations that were under French rule tied to Saigon (Igout 1993: 16). With the new function of the city, its appearance also changed through a series of public works, often developed by young French-educated Khmer architects influenced by ideas of the "Modern Movement"[5] (Lemarchands 1997: 44). The combination of these "modern" projects and the colonial-style houses, the pagodas, green parks and boulevards, contributed to Phnom Penh's image as the most charming city of Southeast Asia (Osborne 1994: 123). Little of this charm could, however, be found in the shantytowns that grew on the outskirts of the city (ibid.: 130). The overwhelming majority of rural newcomers lived in wooden shacks without clean water, sewage, or electricity and tried to make a living through harsh and low-paying laboring jobs. Those who completed their education pursued positions in civil service or, in the case of the Sino-Khmer, strove to become successful in business (Osborne 1994: 124–126).

The late 1960s was a time of rising tensions. Located between capitalist Thailand and partly communist Vietnam, Cambodia maneuvered in an international field between the leading players of the Cold War in an attempt to remain neutral, which became increasingly difficult. Within the country, political opposition to Sihanouk rose, as did his attempts to suppress it. Meanwhile, Cambodia's economy was faltering (Chandler 1996a: 202). Increasing numbers of poor peasants lost their land due to the worsening socioeconomic situation, and had to earn incomes as agricultural laborers or as migrant workers in the city (Hou Youn 1982; Chandler 1996a). This mounting pressure on the peasantry may not, as Vickery (1984: 16–17) states, have been the only reason for the revolution to come, but was certainly responsible for serious rural-urban antagonisms. The relationship between the city and rural villages was characterized by a situation in which, as Hou Youn stated, "[t]he tree grows in the rural areas, but the fruit goes to the towns" (quoted in Kiernan 1982: 13).

The mounting crisis eventually led to the overthrow of Sihanouk by US-allied Lon Nol in 1970, and led the country to a civil war that lasted until the 1990s. In an effort to eliminate the Vietnamese communist trail through Cambodia, the United States intensified their air campaigns, destroying many villages, harvests and lives. These ongoing air campaigns, together with the widespread corruption of Lon Nol's officials, made it easier for the Khmer communists to gain support and recruits among the rural population (Chandler 1991: 230). In that sense, the war was also "a war between town and country," as the towns fought to preserve privileges while the rural areas suffered (Vickery 1984: 26). Not surprisingly, growing numbers of rural people tried to escape this suffering by fleeing to Phnom Penh. As a result, Phnom Penh's population rapidly grew and consisted by April 1975 of up to two million people. Also in the city, the situation soon became desperate as the few existing social services broke down, causing a pitiful state of medical care, hundreds of thousands of school-age children to stop their education, the malnutrition of thousands of the new city dwellers, and the hasty erection of improvised shelters (Chandler 1991: 230). Within only a few years, the spontaneous urbanization had swept away the previous urbanization plans for a "modern" Phnom Penh (Igout 1993: 18).

Urbanization plans became even more obsolete after the Khmer communists, the Khmer Rouge, entered Phnom Penh on April 17, 1975. Almost immediately the Khmer Rouge started to evacuate the city.[6] According to the leaders of the newly installed regime, Democratic Kampuchea (DK), Khmer culture was based on rice cultivation. The urban way of life of the educated elite, along with money, markets, education, Western medicine and private property, were considered elements of foreignness that needed to be abolished. The urban residents, who were called "new people," were put to work within the rice fields alongside the peasants, called "old people" or "base people."[7] Within the three years and nine months of Khmer Rouge rule, perhaps as many as 1.7 million people died as a consequence of overwork, disease, malnutrition, or execution after being accused of being counterrevolutionary enemies.[8]

The regime ended with the Vietnamese invasion of Cambodia in January 1979. While the Chinese-backed Khmer Rouge leaders fled to the jungle and started a guerrilla war, the Soviet-supported Vietnamese swiftly established the People's Republic of Kampuchea (PRK). Almost immediately after the Vietnamese invasion, the population started moving, crisscrossing the country looking for lost relatives and returning to their homes. In addition, thousands fled to the Thai border in order to escape what they felt was an occupation by the Vietnamese and a submission to another form of communism (Martin 1994). In the early 1980s over thirty thousand Cambodians were staying in eight camps located in Thailand along the Thai-Cambodian border (Chandler 1996a; Mysliwiec 1988).

The new PRK government inherited a country whose infrastructure had been badly damaged. Besides a lack of professionals, many of whom had been killed or had fled, the country had no currency, no markets, no postal system, no financial institutions, no public transport and virtually no industry. Moreover, electricity, clean water, sanitation and education were hardly available. In the countryside, many villages were abandoned or destroyed, and the capital and provincial cities had become ghost towns (Mysliwiec 1988: 10–11). The repopulation of Phnom Penh proceeded slowly, also because access to Phnom Penh was initially limited to those who had positions in ministries or factories, or permits to work as waiters, construction workers, or small-scale merchants. They were often not former Phnom Penhois, but villagers who squatted in empty villas and buildings (Vickery 1984; Gottesman 2003).

During the 1980s the city slowly recovered from the years of abandonment and destruction, as streets and buildings were restored, public markets reestablished, and small numbers of tourists came to visit the Royal Palace, National Museum, and Tuol Sleng Genocide museum. Over time, the movement of urban residents and their rural families also became less restricted, allowing the city's population to grow from about ninety thousand in 1979 to more than half a million in 1989 (Ty Yao 1997).

After Soviet financial support for Vietnam ended in 1989, the Vietnamese withdrew their troops from Cambodia, bringing an end to the PRK. Its successor, the State of Cambodia (SOC), adopted more liberal policies regarding private property, the market economy, and freedom of religion, and reinstated some national symbols. In 1991 warring parties signed the Paris Peace Agreements, giving way to the establishment of the United Nations Transitional Authority in Cambodia (UNTAC). UNTAC, at the time one of the largest UN operations ever, had the main responsibility for overseeing the ceasefire between the warring parties and organizing the electoral process. The operation, involving twenty-two thousand military and civilian peacekeepers and costing two billion US dollars, boosted the local economy through the demand for imported goods, the employment of Cambodians, the construction and rental of buildings, and the purchase of local services in restaurants, transport and prostitution. This massive inflow of dollars was mostly directed at Phnom Penh and some smaller urban centers, whereas the rural areas continued to be marked by poverty (FitzGerald 1994).

After the elections in 1993, the Royal Government of Cambodia formally adopted market-oriented reforms and created conditions for the establishment of a labor-intensive and export-oriented industry. As a result, the garment industry began to develop, which, along with the arrival of international aid and lending institutions, and of increasing numbers of tourists, stimulated Cambodia's reintegration into the global economy. Most of these developments were concentrated in Phnom Penh. The burgeoning opportunities in the urban areas, combined with the continuing poor conditions in the rural ones has led to rapid rural-urban migration, and with it, a reemergence of old social inequalities between a privileged elite enjoying newfound wealth in their fenced villas and the ongoing struggle for survival in the squats of the urban poor. These developments have, according to Shatkin (1998: 383), "changed Phnom Penh's meaning for its inhabitants, creating opportunities for some while immiserating others."

In the meantime, the city municipality is determined to make Phnom Penh once again into the "Pearl of Southeast Asia."[9] With the support of international donors and investors, roads, sewage and drainage, electricity, as well as important public buildings such as schools, hospitals and markets are being repaired and constructed. Phnom Penh's important tourist spots have been renovated, painted, or provided with new flowers. As part of a city beautification plan, house owners along the major streets are being urged to repaint their houses in a fresh yellow color. Slums in the city are being destroyed and their habitants resettled on land outside the municipality. A contract with a new garbage collection firm assures that the city, at least along the main streets, remains clean, while newly installed—but not necessarily respected—traffic lights try to impose order on Phnom Penh's growing and chaotic traffic. It is, however, not order but disorder that fixes the image of some observers. This concerns not only Phnom Penh's traffic, but most notably problems that relate to squatting, urban poverty, the criminal economy and the sex business—all of which have flourished in the wake of unequal development, foreign influences and weak state structures (Blancot 1997; Shatkin 1998; Beyrer 1998). These inequalities, influ-

FIG. 1. A street in Phnom Penh

ences and instabilities, as well as the charm, exotic outlook and modern aspirations, make up the many faces of present-day Phnom Penh.

RICE PEOPLE AND CITY PEOPLE

"The Cambodian is a peasant," Delvert (1961: 31) concluded in his study *Le paysan cambodgien,* after pointing out that the Cambodian left all, or almost all, other occupations to foreigners. It may seem that not much has changed in this regard. Cambodia is still a predominantly agricultural society, with about 85 percent of the people living in rural areas, and more than three-quarters of the population working in the agricultural sector. The majority of the rural population is peasant, cultivating rice mainly for subsistence. These peasants refer to themselves as *neak srae,* "rice people," [10] or *neak chamkar,* "people from the garden farmlands." While *neak srae* live in villages throughout the countryside, the *neak chamkar* usually live along the riverbanks (mainly the Mekong, Bassac, and Tonle Sap) and focus, instead of on rice, more on the cultivation of vegetables, fruit, maize, beans, tobacco, cotton and other products for the market (Delvert 1961; Ebihara 1968).

Given this predominantly rural outlook of Cambodian society, scholars tend to contrast the life of the majority of the Cambodians living in the countryside with the life of people in the city, the *neak krong.*

Martin (1994: 7) stresses that a "distinction must be made between the peasantry [. . .] and prosperous townspeople, well-off financially, intellectually, politically, or working in the public sector." This distinction between peasantry and townspeople concerns not only social and economic status but, as Ovesen et al. (1996: 39) argue, also a way of life, which "in many ways felt incompatible, or at least at variance with, so-called traditional Khmer cultural ideas and values." In this sense, "rural" has become, as Rigg (1997: 157) writes in relation to Southeast Asia more generally, "a metaphor for much more than open spaces and green trees: it also implies a way of life, a set of values, and a shared commitment to a certain livelihood." Rural livelihoods are, however, not static arrangements. The same is true for the meanings of the "rural ways of life" and "rural values" that are related to changing perceptions of rural life and people, and their relation with their urban counterparts. The contrasts between the countryside and the city are neither new nor restricted to Cambodia. Yet the Khmer Rouge drove this dichotomy to extremes. The Cambodian case therefore vividly shows how positive and negative images of rice people and city people have shifted over time and in relation to "political-economic determinants that have a logic of their own" (see also Gupta and Ferguson 1992: 11).

The images of changelessness, traditionalism and conservatism of Cambodian society in general, and of the Cambodian peasantry in particular, are persistent and were prevalent, if not created, during French colonial times. To the French, the "lazy" Cambodian, who lives "day by day, poor and contented" (Porée and Maspero 1938: 186), compared unfavorably to the active and flexible Vietnamese. The French found in the disinclination of Cambodian peasants to increase their rice production a confirmation of this stereotype.[11] Sihanouk, the leader of independent Cambodia, similarly ignored the hard work of wet-rice cultivators, but cherished a more positive picture of "happy peasants" who could "just pick the fruit off the trees" (Becker 1998: 7). In Sihanouk's newly independent Cambodia, Khmer peasants came to be portrayed as poor but "pure" figures, and the Cambodian countryside was "sanitized" into lush green landscapes as depicted in paintings, films and theaters. These were mainly produced by an urban elite interested in constructing a "modern Khmer culture" (Ly and Muan 2001: vii) and using "ruralist themes" in order to express an "authentic" view of "Khmerness."

As Cambodia's urban population expanded, however, perceptions of rural-urban distinctions became more negative (Vickery 1984: 25). For many wealthy and westernized city dwellers, peasants represented not only the idealized "pure" Khmer, but also the poor and backward people who, because of the agricultural slack season, did not work enough (Vickery 1984: 26). On the other hand, for villagers who had either visited or heard about Phnom Penh, the city symbolized, besides "noise, confusion, crowding, unsavory characters, immorality, danger and expenses," also "excitement, sophistication, [. . .] glamour, [. . .] wealth and escape from peasant life" (Ebihara 1968: 569). In the late 1960s and early 1970s, an increasing number of peasants actually sought to escape there, as Phnom Penh remained relatively unaffected by the war that had created so much destruction and insecurity in the countryside, thus becoming a "safe haven" for hundreds of thousands of refugees.

The Khmer Rouge also saw a clear rural-urban dichotomy, but they reversed its terms (McIntyre 1996: 758). For the Khmer Rouge the capital city was a bastion of foreign influence, corruption, oppression and capitalism (Hinton 2002: 63). As formulated in the thesis of Khieu Samphan, who later became the head of state of the Khmer Rouge regime, the rural-urban dichotomy existed above all in the oppressive relationship between productive countryside and the unproductive city (McIntyre 1996: 742). To remedy this situation, the Khmer Rouge turned to radical measures by evacuating Phnom Penh and other towns and forcing their inhabitants to become agricultural workers. Although these radical policies were abandoned as the Vietnamese-backed socialist regime overthrew the Khmer Rouge in 1979, preventing the reemergence of class differences and rural-urban inequalities remained important themes within the ideology of the PRK.

Notwithstanding these socialist efforts and ideals, the gradual repopulation and reconstruction of Phnom Penh in the 1980s and, especially, the accelerating developments since the 1990s contributed to its recovery as the biggest city in the country—almost four times larger than the second-largest city—and to a widening of what is commonly called a "rural-urban gap." A survey conducted on Cambodia's socioeconomic situation in 1993–1994 showed that, after a period of only fifteen years since its total evacuation, the average household monthly income in Phnom Penh was twice that of the other urban areas and four times that of the rural areas[12] (National Institute of Statistics 1995; Zimmerman 1997: 63). The widening division between rural and urban living situations is related not only to income but also to the availability of running water, sanitary facilities, electricity, and educational and medical services. This rural-urban gap has, as will be discussed in more detail later in this book, made Phnom Penh in the eyes of many—especially young, rural residents—into the country's leading example of the road toward development, wealth and modernity.

RURAL-URBAN LINKAGES

One could easily conclude that city people and rice people are imagined, as in the time before the war, to represent "two completely distinct subcultures" (Bit 1991: 55). Yet, are these rural and urban worlds as distinct as these descriptions suggest? Cambodians, rural as well as urban, will likely point to some obvious distinctions between rural and urban worlds, most notably those related to landscape, economic activities and lifestyle. The picture of the rural world is dominated by rice fields and villages, and an associated "traditional" way of life, whereas the large and diverse population that fills the city landscape of brick buildings, traffic and commercial signs engages more in trade, services, industry and to a lesser extent administration, thereby giving it a more "cosmopolitan" and "modern" feel. Statistics, however, only partly support this commonly believed picture. Agriculture takes place not only in rural areas, where 78 percent of the labor force work in this sector, but also in urban areas it is the largest single occupation, involving 34 percent of the urban labor force (National Institute of Statistics 2005b: 22).[13] The distinction drawn between "rural" and "urban" is also in other terms open to question. This is the case not only in Cambodia but in Southeast Asia more generally, where Rigg (1998: 499) finds a "blurring of these two worlds." Rigg sees this blurring as multidimensional, existing in physical terms due to the expansion of metropolitan areas, in economic terms due to the growing interdependency of agriculture and industry, and in human terms due to the "increased movement of people over a vital landscape of rural-urban interaction and the diversity of livelihoods." Such blurring of rural and urban boundaries, though in varying degrees, can also be observed in Cambodia.

The physical extension of Phnom Penh is visible along the roads that lead out from the city in diverse directions, along which squatters have been resettled and where factories have mushroomed in the midst of a landscape of rice fields and sugar palms. Industrialization, however, is still largely concentrated in urban areas. Also, the economic linkages between agriculture and industry are less evident in the Cambodian context than elsewhere in Southeast Asia. Although a few agro-industrial projects have been set up, agriculture is still predominantly small-scale and, except for the growing use of fertilizers and pesticides, low-input. Mechanization and intensification have been introduced only selectively (Chan and Kim 2003: 2).

Most important, especially for this study, are therefore the linkages between the rural and the urban in human terms. These have changed in important ways over time. Whereas the rural hinterlands for long periods provided tax and labor for urban dwellers, this relationship was turned upside down when the Khmer Rouge forced urban residents to work alongside the peasants in the rice fields. This revolutionary experiment has been particularly relevant in the urban developments that followed the fall of Democratic Kampuchea, when people once again left the countryside to live in the city. Most of these people had not lived in a city before the war. A large part of the urban elite of former days was either killed or had left Cambodia seeking refuge elsewhere.[14]

As Table 2 shows, Phnom Penh's migration rates are clearly among the highest in the country.[15] About three-quarters of Phnom Penh's population consist of migrants, more than one-fifth of whom moved there during the past five years.[16] Notable, however, is also Cambodia's overall migration rate of around one-third of the population, most of which is rural-to-rural. This gives a clear image of a population on the move. These migrations are not only connected to population shifts during and after the Pol Pot regime; observations concerning the mobility of Cambodians also exist before these years of war and social upheaval (Ledgerwood 1990). Delvert (1961: 199) even describes the Cambodian character as "nomadic." He found that Cambodians, individuals but also complete hamlets, move easily (1) for economic reasons, to be closer to a prosperous center; (2) for family reasons, most notably the husband leaving to live with his wife's family; or (3) for religious reasons, be it to enter a monastery or to leave a place that is cursed. Kalab (1968: 525) also speaks of "the great mobility of the Cambodian peasant." In the village she studied, 20 percent of the village's inhabitants had left in the five years prior to her research, and she estimated that at least 24 percent of those living in the village were migrants. It is, however, questionable to what extent such mobility rates can be generalized to Cambodian villages in general. Ebihara writes that the inhabitants of Svay, the village she studied, "spend most of their lives and satisfy many of their social and material needs within its confines, and their outlook on the surrounding world is basically provincial and insular" (1968:

TABLE 2   Population (%) by Migration Status, Sex and Residence

	Both sexes				Males				Females			
	Migrants		Recent migrants		Migrants		Recent migrants		Migrants		Recent migrants	
	1998	2004	1998	2004	1998	2004	1998	2004	1998	2004	1998	2004
Cambodia	31.5	35.1	34.0	23.7	32.5	35.2	36.6	25.9	30.5	35.1	31.3	21.6
Rural	26.4	31.4	31.7	22.0	27.5	31.8	34.6	24.5	25.3	31.0	28.8	19.5
Urban	58.9	56.2	39.3	29.2	58.7	54.2	41.5	30.7	59.1	58.2	37.1	28.0
Phnom Penh	73.4	67.4	30.5	21.7	72.0	65.4	30.7	21.9	74.7	69.2	30.3	21.6

Source: National Institute of Statistics (2000b: Tables 2.4, 2.12, 2.14, C3; 2005a: 42, 45)

553). This does not mean that Svay was an autonomous, isolated village. On the contrary, Ebihara describes the linkages between villagers and other communities, the district town, and also Phnom Penh, where people went to visit relatives, exchange or buy goods, attend ceremonies, or search for temporary employment.

Cambodian peasants are not dependent on agriculture alone for their income, and Kalab argues that "people shift between agriculture and other employment as easily as they move from place to place" (1968: 527). Though in present-day Cambodia agriculture is still the principal source of income, most rural Cambodians earn a living from multiple sources (Chan and Kim 2003; Ministry of Planning 1999). These include foraging, fishing, small-scale business activities and wage labor. Wage labor and non-farm jobs, however, have become increasingly important for rural households, as they are confronted with growing food insecurity linked to population growth, low yields and inadequate facilities (e.g., credit, irrigation, infrastructure, or market linkages) for increasing production or marketing their produce (Chan and Kim 2003: 3–4). Cambodian villagers, like their counterparts in other Southeast Asian countries, facing "an absence of sufficient opportunities within agriculture," are thus "looking further afield, both spatially—beyond the village—and in sectoral terms—beyond agriculture" (Rigg 1997: 169). This means that Cambodia has, since its opening up, slowly come into line with many other developing countries, where changes in global patterns and modes of production have brought about a gradual shift away from agriculture toward industry and services (Mehra and Gammage 1999: 533).

RURAL-URBAN MIGRATION

As outlined above, the distinctive worlds commonly perceived within the dichotomy "rural–agriculture/traditional" and "urban–industry/ modern" are fluid and ambiguous. We have seen that agriculture continues to be an important occupation for a third of the people living in the city and that Phnom Penh's population consists predominantly of migrants. One may thus wonder whether the city is urbanizing or ruralizing (see also Li [1996: 45] about Hanoi).

Rural-urban migration contributes to an important interchange between rural and urban areas, as many of these rural migrants maintain ties to and identify with their rural homes. A focus on social networks brings to light the encompassing rural and urban relationships of migrants that stretch across boundaries of what used to be seen as separate social systems (Hannerz 1980: 172). The notion of social networks, or the connections between locality and wider contexts, has challenged the conceptual relationship between the social and the spatial, and the corresponding use of "urban" and "rural" as surrogates for social change that characterized migration studies in the past (Rogers and Vertovec 1995: 18). Analyses of the importance of kinship and other social networks in migration processes, and the enduring impact of such relationships on migrants and their community of origin, have long dismissed the proposition that family and community structures break down due to the migration flows brought about by changing market and labor regimes (Choldin 1973; Mitchell 1974; Fawcett 1989).

Within the Cambodian context, family and village relationships play an important role in the motivation for migration and choice of occupation as well as in the migration patterns. Census data indicate that the majority of the migrants in urban areas moved because their family moved (National Institute of Statistics 2005a: 32). This is even more the case among female migrants. Conversely, more male than female migrants cited work-related reasons—either transfer of work or search for employment—for their migration. However, these statistics may somewhat underestimate the role played by work in migration. When a family moved because of the employment of one family member, other family members may in fact have also moved in the hope of finding employment (ibid.: 30).

The social ties—also called *ksae*[17]—that facilitate rural-urban migration are not only based on family relations. The sheer number of people moving from their rural base in search of employment has created increasing possibilities for mediation within the migration process. Such a mediator, or broker, is also referred to as *meekcol*. Literally, *meekcol* means "leader of the wind," which symbolizes the impermanence and situationality of his or her capacity.[18] This mediator can be a fellow villager or someone from outside the area who recruits laborers for employers elsewhere. In the diverse studies on trafficking and migration, I have come across many stories about *meekcol* who turned out to be cheaters, running off with the recruitment fee or leading young women into abusive situations.

For the young rural women of this study, I found that the mediators were especially peers who bring experiences, new clothes and remittances back from Phnom Penh. Peers play an influential role in motivating fellow female villagers to come to the city for work and facilitating this move. These acquaintance networks constitute, as Portes (1995: 12) formulates in more general terms, the more immediate settings that influence the goals of individuals and the means but also the constraints in their paths. The experiences, knowledge and contacts of earlier migrant women help to calm the fears of parents regarding the risks of migration, most notably those relating to sexual experiences and exploitative working conditions, by making it possible to find a secure shelter in the big, unknown city and a "proper" job for newcomers. The more women from one area that migrate, the lower the perceived risks for individuals, as networks for potential migrants become denser, and reliable information about the opportunities and dangers associated with the city and the job situation become more readily available (Massey 1990; Curran and Sugay 1997). Although such networks are effective in linking newly arrived women to jobs, employment opportunities remain mostly limited to those low-wage, low-skilled ones in the informal sector, services, or manufacturing in which experienced migrant women found work.

Despite such constraints, rural women in the city comprise an important link between "rice people" and city people. They form an important bridge between what is perceived as the "traditional" peasant world and the "modern" urban world. Although it might be tempting to hold onto the rural and urban dichotomy in order to emphasize the contrast in lifestyles or economic activities that are still observable in Cambodia, these are clearly two interconnected worlds.

Women, Ideals, and Migration

3

Discussions about gender in Cambodian society have confusingly pointed to male dominance, the relative equality and complementarity of men and women, and the "high status" and "considerable authority" of women (C. Zimmerman 1994; Ebihara 1968; Martin 1994; Népote 1992). Although these statements appear incompatible, they can all be true and reflect above all the complexity of gender constructs within Cambodian—or in fact any—society.[1] Therefore, as Ledgerwood (1990: 19) points out, we should get away from a fixed view on *the* status of men and women, gender and sexuality, because they are symbolic constructs assigned various meanings in different contexts.[2]

Gender is "highly contingent and fluid, taking shape as it does in contexts created in different and overlapping webs of power" (Ong and Peletz 1995: 9). Authors writing on gender in Southeast Asia have pointed out the need to pay attention to the historical context, global capitalist expansion, and development, as well as to the local complexities arising from contradiction and ambivalence and the historical specificity of gender constructions. Such an approach will help us understand how various gender constructions and historical developments inform the varying subject positions that exist between and among men and women, as well as the ways in which they creatively use, contest and change these subject positions, thus influencing broader processes of change. By focusing on the contradictory and ambiguous interpretations of gender conceptions, ideals and positions, I set the stage for a later exploration of the processes of female mobility and employment, and the diverse ways in which these influence young rural women as they make sense of their lives in the city.

KHMER CONCEPTS OF GENDER

An often-repeated cliché suggests that women in Southeast Asia enjoy "high status" (Van Esterik 1996: 1). Historians and anthropologists speak of the "comparable status of the sexes in Southeast Asia" (Wolters 1982: 5), of a "pan-Southeast-Asian pattern of female autonomy" extending from sexual and marital to economic matters (Reid 1988), and cite the "relatively high status of women" as a "pan-regional cultural trait" (Steedly 1999: 439; see also Van Esterik 1996; Atkinson and Errington 1990; Ong and Peletz 1995; Karim 1995). Explanations for this regional cultural trait often refer to the ubiquity of the cognatic kinship system, the associated inheritance rights for both men and women, and women's active participation in economic activities.

The "relatively high status" of Cambodian women is often compared to the more disadvantaged situation of Indian or Chinese women. Some see this as a social relic of a lost civilization where women held political power, and an indication that Cambodia and Khmer culture at some point in the past constituted a matriarchy (Ovesen et al. 1996: 42). The Cambodian National Council for Women, for example, argues that foreign cultures and influences destroyed the powerful position of women, for which they find evidence in the common use of the prefix *mee* (mother) for leadership positions (CEDAW 2006). The argument that foreign influences have put an end to, or concealed, the true matrilineal and matriarchal organization of Cambodian society can also be found in other sources. Népote (1992) argues that the matrilineal organization of Cambodian society has long been ignored in ethnographic literature because of a biased view in European and classical Indian writings. He maintains that the life of every Cambodian, of every social group in the whole nation, is created in the frame of temporal cycles dominated by female personages (Népote 1992: 168).

This argument is criticized by authors such as Parkin (1990) and Ledgerwood (1995: 247), who rightfully note that the presumption of Cambodian society as matrilineal is often conflated with the notion that, in some distant past, Cambodian society was matriarchal, a view that is derived from the evolutionist frame of thinking. They refer to the work of Ebihara and Martel, as well as to similar research done in other countries in Southeast Asia, which "suggests that women's actions have social value, that women are accorded respect in certain contexts, and that they have status in society based upon a range of characteristics, of which their sex is but one" (Ledgerwood 1995: 257).

The cognatic or bilateral kinship system here plays an important role, as it allows an emphasis on either the female or the male family lineage in different situations and gives woman's relatives a central role in her life and in decision-making processes that affect her and her family. The importance of the woman's relatives is also reflected in the preference for uxorilocal residence, where a newly married couple chooses to live (often temporarily) with the parents of the woman. This preference is also seen as a remnant of former times when it was common for the new son-in-law to move in with the family of his wife and perform labor services attesting to his suitability for marriage (Ovesen et al. 1996: 39; Tarr 1996: 24–25). The system of bride service has, over time, been replaced with bridewealth. Both tend to enhance the position of female children in the family because they are not seen as a burden, as is the case in some dowry systems. The position of female children is also valued in social terms. Ebihara (1974: 325–326) suggests that the preference for uxorilocal residence relates to the strong bonds between mothers and daughters, which begin in childhood and continue in adolescence as mothers and daughters share common tasks and concerns, and which result in girls being reluctant to leave their mothers, who can give them help, advice and support after their marriage.

Besides the kinship system, other features also point toward relatively equal positions of men and women. Ebihara (1968: 113–114) writes about this: "[T]he relative positions of male and female, husband and wife are virtually equal. The husband is technically the supreme authority who is owed deference, respect and obedience by his family. But the peasant wife is by no means a totally docile and submissive creature. Her role in the maintenance of the family is critical and her activities are varied." Ebihara goes on to describe the responsibilities of the woman, which are related to the domestic domain and the household economy. The latter has been linked to the economic autonomy of Cambodian women. Both women and men can inherit property (and keep it after divorce), both are engaged in a broad range of activities with no strict gender division of labor, and women have a strong, if not decisive, say in the family economy and finances (Ledgerwood 1995: 256–257; Parkin 1990: 213–214). Women's economic autonomy is also visible in their obvious dominance in trade. This often surprised foreign observers who found themselves dealing with women in a domain that in Chinese and European cultures is dominated by men (Reid 1988: 164).[3]

All these features have led to the view that women in Cambodia are "virtually equal" to men (Ebihara 1968: 113) or even have a "privi-leged place" (Martin 1994: 25). Yet, as Ledgerwood (1990: 21) suc-cinctly points out, whereas women in Cambodia and other Southeast Asian societies are often described as possessing "high status," power is usually described as being a "male game" in which women play no role.[4] It is to this that I will now turn.

GENDER AND THE SOCIAL ORDER

This issue of power is commonly related to the concepts of order and hierarchy that are consistently used to describe Southeast Asian societies. Within Khmer society, hierarchy is, according to Chandler (1996b: 77–78), part of the orderliness sought to overcome the threat-ening and dangerous—because unknown—"wild," or *prey* (forest). As he suggests, "to many Cambodians, things, ideas and people—societies, in fact—were thought to be safer and more authentic when they were ranked and in balance, arranged into the same hierarchical patterns (however ineffectual or unhappy) which they had occupied before" (Chandler 1996b: 78).

The interrelated concepts of merit, karma and dharma are important within the legitimization of this explicit hierarchical order (Ledgerwood 1990: 14). The human social order is a segment of the cosmic hierarchy in which, according to Buddhist beliefs, "all living beings stand in a hierarchy of variable ability to make actions effective and of varying degrees of freedom from suffering." Within the cosmic hierarchy, dei-ties and angels stand on top, human beings form the middle level, and animals occupy the lowest echelons (Hanks 1962: 1247–1248). The hierarchy, and similarly a person's position within the social order, is based on the balance of merit and demerit in previous lives. Success, wealth and influence are based on one's store of merit in previous lives, manifest in good karma.[5] A way to accumulate merit is to fulfill one's role (within the hierarchy) to the best of one's ability, which is the start-ing point of dharma (Ledgerwood 1990: 13–20; see also Thion 1993; Népote 1992; Ovesen et al. 1996). The concept of dharma[6] refers to cosmic, spiritual, temporal and moral aspects of life, but on the level of daily life its meaning is, above all, related to the preservation of the social order and harmony between all members of a community. This order and harmony is primarily achieved through laws or moral codes *(chbap)* that guide the behavior of each individual within society (Pou 1988: 4–5).

In this regard, Buddhist notions about gender and merit are also important. Within Khmer Buddhism women occupy, according to Ebihara (1968: 397), a "lower religious status than men" because "their sex presumably reflects a limited amount of merit in the previous incarnation." Whereas there is disagreement regarding the validity of this view of the "religiously inferior status" of women, it is generally agreed that there are major distinctions in male and female definitions within Buddhist gender imagery (Keyes 1984; cf. Kirsch 1985). Ledgerwood (1990: 34) notes, in simple terms, that "Khmer Buddhist sex roles are that men become monks and women feed monks." A man gains merit when he becomes ordained as a monk for a period of time, which was, in former times, the only way to learn reading and writing and to become familiar with Buddhist prayers and other religious texts that were respectable sources of knowledge. Since women are not allowed to enter the *sangha,* Buddhist monkhood, or other religious positions, they do not have the same opportunities to gain merit as men do.[7] Women gain merit by donating food, wealth, and their sons to the pagoda; in other words, they are primarily donors (Ledgerwood 1990: 36–37).

Gendered distinctions between "Buddhist sex roles," according to Kirsch (1985), are reflected in the sexual division of labor found in Theravada Buddhist countries (he focuses on Thailand). The specialization of women in entrepreneurial activities and their embeddedness in relationships with others (children, men, family, etc.) refer to their rootedness in worldly attachments (Kirsch 1985: 303). Men, in contrast, are thought to be more ready to give up such attachments and specialize in religious and political-bureaucratic activities that have a form of positive Buddhist valence, which economic-entrepreneurial activities do not.

Whether due to their position as nurturing mothers and donors, or to their rootedness in worldly attachments, authors find that women's relation to and possibilities to gain merit are distinct from those of men. Yet, while Buddhist notions of maleness and femaleness may influence the social status of men and women, social status is not fixed, and not related to sex alone. Everyone is responsible for his or her own karmic status, which can change over the lifetimes of a person. Gender is one of several components that define a person's position within the social order. When the focus is solely on differences between men and women, differences between women and between men, as well as similarities between some women and some men, may be concealed.

As in other contexts, relative positions between Cambodians are influenced, besides gender, by age, occupation or specialization, official position, wealth, and individual character and personality (Ebihara 1968: 187–198). Among these different components, age is generally considered to be a prime marker, and relative age has a strong influence on behavior. This is most obvious in language use. Different terms are used to distinguish the hierarchical order of people. Thus, depending on who one addresses, a variety of words may be used for the verb "to eat," from the pejorative *sii* for animals, the more colloquial *ñam* for children or peers, the more rural *hoop* or the more polite *pisaa,* to the royal *soay* for addressing the king.

This is just one example illustrating the various arrangements among gender, age and the social order, and the way they interfere with other structures of social asymmetry that are constructed in local, culturally specific ways (Ortner 1996: 116; see also Rosaldo 1980). Constructions of symbolic and ideological images of male and female are not consistent, but rather multiple, conflicting and ambiguous, as will be further exemplified in the case of Khmer gender ideals.

KHMER GENDER IDEALS

In her analysis of Khmer conceptions of gender, Ledgerwood stresses that the status or potency of women has always been linked to "proper behavior." Women demonstrate their high status through proper behavior, and this is also true for men. Several rules and codes of conduct prescribe what proper behavior is in a Cambodian context, while ancestral spirits guard over their observance. Nonetheless, it remains open to exploration just what "proper behavior" means and how so-called traditional rules and codes of conduct inform the lives of Cambodians, especially women, in present-day Cambodia.

Authors writing about Khmer gender relationships usually point to the texts, tales and sayings that portray the perfectly virtuous or proper woman—the woman full of qualities, also called the *srey krup leakkhana.* Ledgerwood (1990: 64) states that "women are taught to be virtuous, provided with images of what it means to be virtuous, in part through performances of Khmer literary works." The best-known source portraying the ideal behavior of women is the *Chbap Srey,* the Code of Women's Behavior. Other examples include the *Reamker* (Cambodian version of the Ramayana), folk stories that exemplify the virtues of the perfectly proper woman, texts and rules published in the Khmer-language journal *Kampuchea Suriya* (e.g., "31 rules for the *srey krup leakkhana*"), as well as several other publications and books that aim to instruct about women's conduct (see Aing 2004).

The *Chbap Srey* is part of a whole series of *chbap:* moral codes or normative poems (Chandler 1996b: 45). These *chbap*, written according to a rhythm or melodic line, were composed between the fourteenth and nineteenth centuries and passed down from generation to generation as moral advice for different categories of people (Thierry 1985; Pou 1988; Ayres 2000).[8] The *Chbap Srey* specifies women's place in and responsibility for maintaining order and peace within the family and broader society. One version of the *Chbap Srey* was composed by King Ang Duong in the mid-nineteenth century and modeled on a lecture by the Buddha (Thierry 1985). A more recent version, written by a former monk, Min Mai, became the version taught and memorized in schools (Pou 1988; Ledgerwood 1990: 86). This version of the poem, with a length of 227 verses, is written from the point of view of a mother advising her daughter how to behave as a proper woman. The importance of proper, virtuous behavior for women is reflected in the mother's statement that "one receives good, one obtains honor, one acquires well-being and peace, thanks to a daughter of a good family" (Pou 1988: 413). The advice goes on at length about how to speak—not too much or too loud; walk—not in such a way that one can hear the skirt rustle or that it makes the house tremble; sit—with legs crossed, neatly; and work—devotedly and without a moment of distraction.

An important part of the *Chbap Srey* is devoted to how a woman should serve and respect her husband and how she should keep peace in the house. The woman is responsible for containing the three fires, or "potential areas of anger and trouble" (Ledgerwood 1990: 99), which are related to the parents, the husband and others. The woman should not bring fire from outside into the house, not take fire from inside the house outside, and she should take care not to spread or overheat such fires. A perfect woman is a caring mother, a protective sister, a devoted friend and a patient servant. She devotes herself to her husband, her parents and her children. She should not be arrogant and look down on her husband, even when he is weak, poor, uneducated, ugly, lazy, drunk, or when he comes from a lower-ranking family. Instead, she should be patient, guiding, and serve him. She should not try to be bigger *(thom cieng)* than or look down on *(meul niey)* her husband, as that would lead others to look down on him as well. Due to her virtue, her silence, her softness and her devotion, the perfectly virtuous woman, or *srey krup leakkhana* brings fortune, peace and honor to her husband and to the whole family (Pou 1988: 407–456).

When unmarried, the *srey krup leakkhana* is ideally a shy, ignorant, vulnerable, industrious young woman. She is devoted to her parents, follows their advice and helps her mother at work. Proper speech, proper behavior and proper appearance are of utmost importance. This is exemplified by the eight verses of the *Chbap Srey*, which Rha, working as a sex worker in a karaoke bar, had memorized and recited during an interview (see also Pou 1988: 410–413; Institut Bouddique 1995: 20–21):

> Oh my dear daughter, my darling, it is very difficult, my child,
>   to apply the *Chbab Srey*.
> First difficulty: a woman who does not speak right, and is
>   incapable of using soft words that will please the family.
> Another difficulty: a woman who does not think carefully,
>   and at the sight of relatives close or far, doesn't invite them
>   to eat betelnut.
> Whether she is provided with wealth or not, if she speaks
>   sweet words, she will be loved by others.
> Don't be rude, shameless, or greedy, don't fall short of
>   devoting yourself to all members of your family.
> One obtains wealth, one acquires happiness, one acquires
>   well-being and peace, thanks to a daughter.
> When you talk, or converse, think of your reputation as a
>   woman; don't make frivolous remarks.
> Don't babble affectedly like little girls. And at the sight of young
>   men, be cautious in making the impression of liking them.

With these precepts a young woman is taught to be aware of her behavior at every moment, with regard to her parents and especially to men. The *Chbab Srey* states that a woman who "glimpses at men, teases with them and makes fun of them, is detestable, without dignity, and has no fear of compromising herself with conduct against the rules" (Pou 1988: 413). Other texts (e.g., Kampuchea Suriya 1966) tell women not to be provocative by walking with swinging hips, speaking loud, waving their arms, seeking eye contact, or letting their hair hang loose.

Because men are portrayed as being naturally attracted to women, women are warned not to seek attention from them. Her sexuality is of utmost importance to the reputation of a woman as well as to that of her family, and her virginity needs to be protected. A virgin *srey krup leakkhana* should therefore ideally stay at home and preferably never leave the house without the company of a trusted relative. Men, on the other hand, are warned against the charms of young women, as "an unmarried girl is like good food, which provokes hunger, excites appetite, something only few men can resist" (in *Chbap Subhasit*, Pou 1988, 339). This also shows the potential "danger" women pose to the reputation of men. Just as the *srey krup leakkhana* can lead her husband and family to success, the opposite means that a woman who is *'at leakkhana*, who is not behaving properly, can destroy the reputation and wealth of a man and her family.

The importance of virginity for young women and the danger of female sexuality for men are reflected in the spiritual world. In Khmer folk belief there exists an array of supernatural beings that watch over and protect the human world. Among them are the ancestral spirits, which can be male or female, or both, such as the *meebaa,* literally "mother and father." The *meebaa* oversee the order and stability in the family by watching over the behavior of young unmarried women, especially their virginity, as well as cases of adultery and quarrels within the family. When morals are violated they are capable of causing illness to someone in the family (Ebihara 1968: Ang 1986; Ledgerwood 1990; Pou and Ang 1992).

Other kinds of spirits are only female. Some of these female spirits are idealized figures,[9] while others are associated with evil and can be especially dangerous for men. The latter kind are called *bray,* which are the spirits of women who died while they still were virgins or of women who died during childbirth. The *bray* belong to the "most wild domain of nature" and are therefore far from everything that is associated with culture, the tamed and civilized. A *bray* derives her magical power from the essential impurity of her death (Pou and Ang 1992). A *bray* is insatiable, always hungry for sex and food, extremely mean, fearsome and impulsive.[10] The *bray kramom,* or "virgin *bray,*" tries to seduce young men. She appears as a beautiful young woman, but reveals her true nature as men respond to her advances, when her appearance changes into that of a frightening woman with a long tongue, large round eyes and straggly long hair. The young men who see her will try to flee before she can penetrate their bodies. A *bray kramom* can be extremely violent, not only toward young men, but also toward young unmarried women, as they may also possess and thereby destroy other virgin women (Ang 1986: 128–129; Ledgerwood 1990: 50–54).

In Khmer folk belief, spirits have also been incorporated within Khmer Buddhism. There are *bray* who reside in the pedestal of the main Buddha within the central hall of a pagoda and function as a protector of the Buddha (Ang 1992). This symbol of the woman as protector or nurturer of Buddha is also observable in the *Chbap Srey*, as a woman who follows all the rules will eventually be reborn as the mother of a Buddha.

From this it follows that, within the spiritual world, as well as in the ideals of behavior, a woman "can, through her virtue and proper behavior, create the perfect environment for success; or she can be tempting, greedy, and the cause of decline" (Ledgerwood 1990: 64). Ledgerwood clearly points to the contradictions between the character-ization of women as shy, serving and dependent, and their "strength" or "potency," which lies especially in their sexuality:

> The virgin, the woman capable of reproduction yet not yet married and thus controlled, is the most dangerous—both in her human form and as a spirit. As a person, she holds the reputation of the entire family in her hands, and yet she is young and ignorant and incapable of protecting that critical interest. As a spirit, she will be insatiable, coming to woo and destroy young men. [. . .] Women, throughout their reproductive years, can be dangerous; their reproductive fluids can be draining, poisoning.[11] There is always the possibility that they will cheat outside marriage. Women without male supervision, most particularly widows and orphans, present ever-present sources of temptation and danger. (Ledgerwood 1990: 287)

This suggests, on the one hand, the importance of virtuousness, which some have related to a subservient and inferior status of women (e.g., C. Zimmerman 1994) and, on the other hand, the kind of potency women possess because they can assert great influence over men and affect the status of her husband as well as her family.

However, the question is not only how we may understand gendered meanings of power and subservience in Cambodian society but also how present-day women perceive and deal with such positions. How useful are texts like the *Chbap Srey* that were written centuries ago? Do these texts hold any relevance for present gender ideals or should they be seen as merely an idealized picture of norms and values of a minority elite in a previous time? As Chandler (1996b: 46) argues, these written documents are principally useful for understanding the social order in precolonial Cambodian society because, unlike chronicles and inscriptions, they are concerned with the activity of an entire society and not only the ceremonial behavior of an elite. Further, he argues that such texts may well hold relevance for the present time as well, and that with the perceived loss of order in recent history "it is possible that many Cambodians [. . .] will return to the *chbap* from time to time in response to nostalgia, to curiosity about an earlier time, or to more compelling personal needs" (Chandler 1996b: 60). The *Chbap Srey* and other texts may therefore gain renewed relevance in the effort to restate a social order that is thought to be either lost due to years of war and destruction or at stake in the face of foreign influences. In such a context, as several authors point out, gender ideals become emphasized and used as cultural symbols that embody "Khmerness" (Ledgerwood et al. 1994).

The ease with which Rha quoted several verses of the *Chbap Srey* gives the impression that this text is widely known among young women in present-day Cambodia. Part of the *Chbab Srey*,[12] and the *Chbap Proh* (Code for Men's Behavior), are printed in the textbooks for seventh-grade students. The majority of the women I met, however, had not even completed grade four and had therefore not read or even heard of the *Chbap Srey*. Still, as a representative of a women's organization argued, "women are brought up to behave as described in the *Chbap Srey*." If not in the form of a poem, the advice young women receive from their mothers and grandmothers as they grow up seems indeed to be very similar to the advice put down in the *Chbap Srey*.[13] Peou, a fruit-shake seller, remembered that her grandmother told her that "even when we eat, we should not make a noise with plate and spoon; a girl cannot go out a lot, she must know how to sew, do the dishes, clean the house, but not go to the neighbor's house and talk about other people—that is no good." Whenever Peou made a noise while washing the dishes or walking in their thatched house, her mother used to warn her not to be like a *srey 'at leakkhana,* or a woman without qualities. Similarly, Srey, a factory worker, noted, "good girls stay at home. And if we have work to do, we do it seriously. We don't quarrel with our brothers and sisters. We obey our parents. When our mother tells us to do something, we have to do it without complaining." Srey emphasized that good behavior involves "respecting old people, helping parents with their work, not playing around with men and, when we go to the pagoda, thinking about the proper prayer."

Such advice is not taken uncritically. Rha thought that it was not sensible to live according to the rules of the *Chbap Srey*, because she did not see why she should be patient with a husband who acted wrongly. Moreover, the conditions of sex work, in which she is involved, demand ways of talking, behaving and dressing that are not easily reconcilable with those demanded of a *srey krup leakkhana*. Yet, what is important is not just whether one is a *srey krup leakkhana*, but whether one behaves properly within a given situation. The question is therefore, not whether women like Rha are knowledgeable or ignorant of, subservient or resistant to the values regarding gender ideals, but how they can, and do, inventively adapt their "qualities" to the various situations that comprise their daily lives.

BALANCING LIVES

The concerns with order and ideals in Khmer society suggest a search for balance between high- and low-ranking, young and old, men and women. In that sense, the above-discussed rules, codes and ideals are relevant. They can be creatively used by actors in diverse positions as well as to enforce relations of asymmetry. Much recent women-centered literature on Cambodia emphasizes these relations of asymmetry and often focuses on how issues such as domestic violence, rape and trafficking influence the lives of many Cambodian women (e.g., C. Zimmerman 1994; Surtees 2003; Derks et al. 2006).

This focus on relations of asymmetry, however, is difficult to reconcile with the "happy balance" that Ebihara (1974) described in regard to the position and lives of Khmer women before the years of civil war.[14] She characterized the lives of village women as rather harmonious, as they, at least informally, exerted influence in the household as well as in the community, possessed considerable "authority, independence and freedom," while men and women performed complementary activities in the division of labor. Overall, Ebihara gives an impression of happy women, living balanced lives, in that the positions of men and women are "relatively equal," that work, play and sadness are balanced, as are the duties of men and women (Ledgerwood 1990: 170).

Ebihara describes this balance in the various phases of the life cycle of village women. Petted baby girls develop into young girls, who start feeling embarrassed to be naked. They are gradually involved in household chores and school—then still a relatively new development—to prepare them playfully for life as grownups. As a girl begins to menstruate, and her body develops bosoms and hips, she becomes a *kramom,* or a female eligible for marriage (Ebihara 1974: 311). From then on, she is expected to become more seriously involved in domestic and agricultural tasks, to show more responsible behavior toward her parents, to observe moral values, especially regarding the protection of virginity, and to maintain a reputation as a virtuous young woman. After marriage, a woman bears the primary responsibility for domestic tasks and the care of children, is a necessary coworker in rice fields, and becomes an active participant in Buddhist and other ceremonies. As mothers become grandmothers *(yeey),* these religious activities become more important. With the gray hair cropped short, symbolizing "renunciation of worldly concern with physical beauty" (Ebihara 1974: 332), and with the main burden of subsistence passed on to the younger generation, elderly women, like men, can turn their thoughts to spiritual concerns, thereby earning religious merit in the final years of life (Ebihara 1974: 335–336; Guthrie 2004).

The duty of a woman is, according to Ebihara (1974: 338) above all related to her main role as "wife-cum-mother." This suggests that marriage marks an important change in a woman's life. In former times a special ritual prepared a girl for this change. The so-called entrance into the shade *(coul mlup)* marked a girl's transition from childhood to a female eligible for marriage, preparing her for the tasks associated with a good wife and mother. Since this ritual had already been abandoned in most parts of the country during the time of Ebihara's research, it is not easy to find women who can recount their experiences "in the shade."[15] I met one elderly woman inhabiting a pagoda close to where I lived who remembered her "entrance into the shade" after she had her first menstruation. For half a year she had to stay at home and was not allowed to see any men, not even her father and brother. She had to perform tasks inside the house, make mats of sugar-palm leaves and could only leave the house at nighttime, when she was sure that no men were around. She was not allowed to eat meat or fish, instead only "sesame seeds and peanuts." She described her "coming out of the shade" as a festive event ending with her marriage. As the elderly woman stated,

"I entered the shade when I was *krup kaa* [literally "complete for marriage"; sexually mature] and when I got out, they came to *dondeng* [ask for my hand in marriage]."

For other women, the duration of seclusion could vary from several months up to a year. After such a long time in the shade, a girl would come out "pale, with a truly wonderful skin" (Porée and Maspero 1938: 208). This "coming out of the shade" used to be celebrated with food offerings to monks and spirits, and rituals similar to those performed at weddings, signifying that the girl was ready to marry (Ebihara 1974; Porée and Maspero 1938). Even though girls nowadays are not prepared for adult life through such a special ritual, their maturation does involve changes in responsibilities and concerns regarding sexuality. This is also evident in the case of young migrant women in Phnom Penh. Their usually temporary employment in the city allows them to literally "enter the shade," most obviously when working in a factory, and to leave it when it is time to get married.

At the same time, however, women's employment in the city takes them away from the control of their relatives, thus giving rise to suspicions regarding their sexual behavior. Young women are, in that sense, much more subject to rules and guidance than are young men. A representative of a woman's organization referred to *kanloh*, or the tether that goes through the nose of cows and other animals (Headley 1977: 19), which, as is commonly said, can be taken out for a male, but is necessary to guide and keep a female under control. Loss of control over unmarried daughters could mean loss of virginity, a cause of "great shame" for the girl as well as her family (Ebihara 1974: 314). It may not only decrease a young woman's own chances of marriage but also the chances of her sisters. This was also the reason why the sister of a sex worker tried to keep the "shameful" behavior of her younger sister secret. She was afraid that this behavior would affect how others would evaluate the whole family, and "if they know that our lineage is bad, they will also criticize my children and no one will ask my daughters to marry."

This points to the connection between marriage and female sexuality. Surtees (2003: 101) speaks of a "strictly structured social field of sexuality." Violations of this social field, that is, sexual relations between unmarried partners, are to be mediated through certain sanctions, most notably forced marriage or financial reparation in the form of fines. For example, such sanctions are applied in cases in which a woman is sexually violated, which means that rape can result in the couple being forced to marry.[16] However, they can also be manipulated by young women and men—for example, by casting the man a young woman wants to marry as her rapist, or by claiming to be raped when being caught in the very act. This shows that social sanctions that appear to be restraining and disadvantaging women can also be used to "make demands of sexual partners and receive recompense" (Surtees 2003: 101).[17]

Such demands and recompense are relevant for young women and men, and their families. Ideally, marriage arrangements involve the families of both the young woman and the man, where reputation and economic position play an important role.[18] The betrothal procedures do not take place directly between the families on both sides, but through a go-between who, on behalf of the young man's parents, contacts the parents of the young woman, as well as the spirits, to ensure their acceptance of the new relationship (Porée and Maspero 1938; Ebihara 1968; Ovesen et al. 1996). These betrothal procedures include negotiations concerning the bridewealth, which is variously called *cumnuun* (gift), *tlay tik doh* (price of the mother's milk), *tlay pteah* (price of a house), or *khanslaa* (payment during the wedding ritual with sword and betel). Marriage arrangements, however, do not take place without the consent of the spouse-to-be. A daughter has a say in rejecting or accepting a marriage proposal, and many proposals in fact commence with an attraction between the two young people (Ebihara 1968; Martel 1975).[19]

Marriage is an often discussed topic in relation to perceptions of tradition and societal developments in Cambodia. Elderly people complain that nowadays wedding parties last only one day, or even half a day, instead of three days as in former times, and express their concern regarding the "shortening," or loss, of "Khmer tradition" *(propeinii khmae)*. Religious teachers I met argued that, these days, "the cake is bigger than the scale" *(num thum cieng niel)*, purposely inverting the old saying according to which the cake cannot be larger than the scale, which means that children should obey their parents in matters concerning marital choice and arrangements.

Recent reports and newspapers, however, tend to argue that the persistence of "age-old customs" leads to "horribly mismatched marriages" such as forced marriages, underage marriages, polygamy, and the regular breakdown of marriages (e.g., Yun Samean 2002; CEDAW

2006). This view on marriage customs is not necessarily supported by previous ethnographic research, which tends to emphasize consent and choice (Ebihara 1968; Martel 1975), or by recent census data that indicate a mean age of marriage of almost twenty-three for women and twenty-four for men (National Institute of Statistics 1996; 1999). (The legal age for marriage is eighteen for women and twenty for men.) Forced marriages and polygamy were already prohibited under previous marriage laws, and a newly adopted marriage law has even made adultery a criminal offense. While it is thus questionable to what extent marriage customs actually lead to forced or underage marriages, there is more substantiation for the regular breakdown of marriages. Statistics indicate that more women than men experience marriages that have been cut short due to the death of a husband, divorce, or separation. This may be related to the sex imbalance, especially in the middle and older age groups where women exceed males in number, and to the fact that higher proportions of women than men have not remarried after losing their husbands or being separated (National Institute of Statistics 1999: 15).

Widowed and divorced women are commonly referred to as *srey meemay*.[20] Although some researchers find that these women without husbands are considered "fully adult and full-fledged members of the community" (Ebihara 1974: 328), others speak of a particular stigma attached to *srey meemay*. This stigma concerns particularly a divorced woman, as she may be considered to have fallen short, according to those who take the *Chbap Srey* as a reference, in serving her husband under all conditions, even when his behavior is unlike that of a good husband (see, e.g., C. Zimmerman 1994). Besides being an imperfect woman, a *meemay* may also be considered incomplete, or a socially disabled person, which is seen as a result of individual karma (see, e.g., Ovesen et al. 1996). Yet, regardless of the rules of the *Chbap Srey* or ideas of social incompleteness, women running a household without men are not exceptional in present-day Cambodia. More than one in every four households is headed by a woman (National Institute of Statistics 2004). Among this group, the older *meemay* are more likely to remain single, whereas young *meemay*, who are often seen as potentially sexually mature and as such a threat to married women, may be more concerned with remarriage.[21] Still, some of the young *meemay* I met openly questioned whether the idea of remarriage is desirable. As *meemay*, these women, especially when they have no children to take care of, enjoy a degree of independence, freedom and mobility that is very unlike what they experienced when they were an unmarried daughter or when they were married.[22]

While it is thus difficult to generalize about women's positions as daughters, wives, mothers, or widows, restrictions in behavior related to symbolic and cultural constructions of femininity, as well as influences of social and historical developments, do affect women's lives in ways that may place them at a disadvantage in relation to other women as well as men. Women's lives are therefore not (or no longer) as happily balanced as Ebihara suggested in the 1960s. Yet, too strong a focus on imbalances and disadvantages, such as is found in more recent discussions about gender in Cambodia, will obscure women's own subjective understandings of their situations and women's creative use of "traditions and customs" to their own advantage.

WOMEN AND THE BURDEN OF THE PAST

Recent history has affected Cambodians in many ways. Among policymakers at the national level, as well as in the assessments of development organizations, there is a tendency to assign women a greater burden from civil strife and recent developments. As we can read on the Web site of the Ministry of Women's Affairs,[23] the effects of war have placed "extraordinary strains on the status of women in the country."

This, among others factors, is visible in the demographic imbalances that lead to a surplus of women in the age groups of twenty years and older, which, some argue, has lowered their status and value. Ledgerwood (1996b), for example, saw a devaluation reflected in a decline in bridewealth payments, while others have linked the surplus of women on the marriage market to the rise in prostitution (e.g., Ministry of Planning 1998). Such alleged linkages, however, are not that evident. The demographic imbalance is most extreme in the higher age groups (forty years and older), whereas the younger age groups of marriageable age and from which prostitutes are recruited show more equal demographic balances. A clearer connection can be drawn between demographic imbalances and the high rate of female-headed households. The female heads are predominantly aged forty and above and are thought to meet with more difficulties in their daily survival than married women (see also Ebihara and Ledgerwood 2002: 278–280).

Not only the composition of households, but also the social relationships within families have changed over the past three decades. The importance of the bilateral kinship system and women's position within this system has, it is commonly believed, changed due to the disruption of family life and social norms. At the same time traditional social norms are blamed for hindering "modern-day pursuits" such as education and wage labor, areas in which women are clearly disadvantaged compared to men (Ministry of Planning 1998: 44). Parents are more inclined to allow their sons to pursue education, perhaps because of the view that the economic returns of an educated daughter will not be beneficial. Furthermore, attending schools usually involves traveling, which parents are reluctant to let their daughters do, as it would run counter to the Khmer ideals according to which a young woman needs to be protected and cannot travel too far from home unaccompanied by relatives. A well-known and highly respected monk remarked on this:

> In our society, we have to take care that our daughters are good daughters. A good daughter, from the Khmer point of view, does not venture far from home. As the Khmer saying goes "Do not keep a good dessert for tomorrow; do not allow a woman to go far." [. . .] Our society values the virginity of women. It is not like Europe or America, where they don't care about daughters who go away. But Khmer value virgins, and if parents do not allow their daughters to go to study far from home, we cannot blame them, because they know their daughters will lose their future if they lose their virginity.[24]

Such attitudes are now often criticized for reinforcing a disadvantaged position of Cambodian women.

The ambiguous position of women in relation to "tradition" and "social norms" that are either abandoned or form a hindrance to their advancement can also be observed in the economic and political developments that have taken place in Cambodia over the past decade. On the one hand, there are women who, due to traditional norms of female behavior, are hindered in participating in those spheres of life that would allow them to be part of the new developments taking place in Cambodia, while these new developments are, on the other hand, seen as causing women's situation to deteriorate even further. The National Policy for Women (Asian Development Bank 1996: 15) states that "[o]verall, the social status of Cambodian women is in a state of flux with traditional and hierarchical tendencies controlling social mores, attitudes and behaviors while at the same time the necessities of economic growth and national reconstruction are demanding a more prominent and influential role for women." Yet, where women are influenced by the new economic and political developments, it is perceived to be mainly in a negative way. In a report of the Ministry of Women's Affairs, Chhoy Kim Sar et al. (1997: 44) state that "[i]n the atmosphere of liberalization, many women are in debt, lose their land, become maid-servants of the rich or are forced to leave their villages to come and live miserably in the suburban slums."

These tendencies, which are mostly assumed rather than carefully documented, show that earlier and more recent developments have had contradictory influences on women's lives, and especially on the discourses about women's lives. There are now numerous programs and projects set up by international and national organizations that focus on these negative influences and making efforts to improve the situation of women. At the national level, the Ministry of Women's Affairs is mandated to promote a new image of Cambodian women, "moving from a disadvantaged group to the nation's invaluable assets and its economic potential" (Ministry of Women's and Veterans' Affairs 1999: 1). It is, according to former Minister of Women's Affairs Mu Sochua (quoted in Green 2002), the role of the ministry to be an "advocate and catalyst for women to transform and take hold of their lives." Yet, even without such a formalized catalyst, I observed that this is exactly what women in Cambodia are trying to do in their own way.

WOMEN AND MIGRATION

Visions of a new image for women and the transformation of women's lives are not necessarily a new phenomenon or the outcome of war and capitalist developments. Already in 1974, Ebihara foresaw alternatives or additional possibilities for the younger generation of women who aspired to live outside the village and outside agriculture, and whose education could open up new horizons. The purported alternatives and possibilities for the younger generation were soon obstructed by the years of civil strife that followed, but they are more possible than ever for the present generation of young women. For most rural young women it is not so much education, but rather migration to the city that makes life outside the village and agriculture (at least temporarily) an option.[25] Some women I met even told of abandoned and quiet villages because of the increasing number of young women leaving them to work in Phnom Penh's factories.

The nature of urban migration on the part of young women may give the impression that they are leaving villages en masse, but this is certainly not the case in many villages. Male and female migration flows toward urban areas do not differ much. There are, however, notable differences relating to age and motivation: there were higher female migration rates in the age group from fifteen to nineteen years, whereas males had comparatively high migration rates in older age groups; and work-related motives more often played a role in the case of male migration, whereas females more often named family-related motivations for their migration (National Institute of Statistics 2005a: 32, 37). Such observations support the common view according to which labor migration is especially connected with men, whereas female migration is considered to be mainly associational, linked to the migration of close family members.

Yet, as elsewhere in Southeast Asia, the changing circumstances in Cambodia and the growing demand for female labor have increased employment-related motivations in female migration. Such an increase in autonomous female labor migration has the potential to reshape gender relations, whereby such increased migration and labor participation is often—and not always rightfully so—put on a par with increased independence and decision-making power (Hugo 1993). Ledgerwood (1996b: 42) argues that "Khmer cultural constructions of gender [. . .] have caused women to pay a price for their mobility and economic activity." She points to the pervasive idea that women are less capable today of fulfilling the idealized standards set by classical Khmer literature when they leave the guidance and supervision of the family and village. Even though migration to the city has now become a viable option for young women from the countryside, the reputation of a young woman leaving her village for work in Phnom Penh may be quickly called into question by villagers speculating about her virtue and the nature of her work. A young woman who leaves the village is considered to be vulnerable to the dangerous influences associated with being outside the social order of the village and against which she is supposed to be protected. A woman who leaves such a protected environment is, as Peou noted, like a flower outside the gate: as long as the flower is inside the gate, the owner will take care of and protect it, but a flower outside is unprotected, and therefore susceptible to the harassment, scorn, and games of others, most notably in relation to sexuality.[26]

Yet while, on the one hand, autonomous female labor migration is not in accordance with the gender ideals held in Khmer culture in that it necessarily means leaving the protected environment of home, family and village, it is, on the other hand, a means through which young women can fulfill other important ideals. For example, migration offers an opportunity to contribute to the household economy and thus help accumulate family wealth. Female migration is therefore often explained as a response to poverty in rural households (e.g., Chant 1992). Moreover, female migration, according to some authors, is informed by a cultural mandate. Connecting Theravada Buddhist notions of karma and merit with the filial obligations of daughters, Muecke (1992), for example, argues that it is through the growing employment possibilities for women outside the village and their earnings from working in the city that Thai daughters fulfill their cultural obligations toward their family and the pagoda.

Still, it is essential to consider the importance of agency on the part of these young women. Their motivations for migrating to Phnom Penh are, I found, varied and not solely prompted by the economic necessities of their family or by cultural mandates. For example, although enabling financial contributions to the family economy and the pagoda did play a role for Piseth, a sex worker, her motivations for migrating were also related to her desires for material gain, a "modern" lifestyle, or adventure. She told me that other women "who had gold and money and nice clothes to wear" influenced her. She remembered that these women also "provided food and money to their parents and old people during seasonal ceremonies. And therefore, I was eager to leave the village and earn money." Nary, a factory worker, similarly heard from a cousin that she should go to Phnom Penh in order to earn money in order to have some jewelry to wear and experience life in the city. Then, she recalled, "I went to challenge my mother. I didn't think of myself as being too young. I just wanted to go. I told my mum that when my cousin went to Phnom Penh, I would go along with her." These comments all point to the importance of visible, material manifestations of women's involvement in urban employment. By showing off jewelry, or by providing support for old people and ceremonies, young women symbolically mark their position in culturally appropriate ways.

Besides the attraction of earning money, the city also offers advantages for women faced with difficulties in the village. The motivation to move to Phnom Penh was, for divorced women like Sokha, working as a sex worker, or Son, working as a street trader, also influenced by their desire to escape an abusive husband or the gossip of villagers. Although young women working in Phnom Penh usually see their urban experience as temporary and expect that marriage will take many of them back to the village and the rice field, divorce gives others the freedom to find their own way in the city.

We thus need to take into account that young women's motivations for migration are often predominantly guided by their own desires, needs, expectations and sorrows, and that family members are not necessarily involved in, and may even oppose, their decision to migrate to the city. Further, while economic necessity always plays a role in the desire to migrate, young female migrants do not necessarily remit earnings to their families, but may instead use them to fulfill their own aspirations regarding consumption.

Women's rural-urban migration thus illuminates, as Mills observed in Thailand, "both how social relations of domination and exploitation are reproduced as well as how they are negotiated, contested, and reworked in individual experience" (Mills 1999: 5). Such negotiation, contestation and reworking are above all possible when faced by multiple and ambiguous gender constructs that are assigned different meanings in different contexts. While gender constructs and ideals do inform women's lives in constraining ways, they can also be creatively used by women as they shift between various positions in their interactions with their rural home, urban work, and with their peers, including the opposite sex.

In what follows I shall explore the migration experiences of young rural women working in Phnom Penh and how these are related to the conditions of their employment, to constraints and possibilities arising from social relations, cultural images, and economic inequalities, as well as reveal the ways in which young women creatively "balance" their duties and desires as they move among spaces, employment, styles, and interrelated subject positions.

Factory Work $\qquad$ 4

Tuol Sangkeo, Phnom Penh, on a Tuesday morning around half past six: thousands of young female workers fill the streets leading to a range of factories to disappear again through the small, guarded factory gates. Some wear identifiable clothes, such as the gray Sam Han T-shirt, the purple polo shirt of the factory around the corner, the blue head-scarves of Rho Sing jeans factory, or the blue-striped blouses worn in a shoe factory down the road. Others are dressed in wide trousers and blouses, fashionable in the countryside, or in a more urban style, with jeans, long skirts with high-heeled shoes and tight shirts. Lipstick and sunbonnets in screaming colors complete the typical style of the factory workers on their way to work. Food stalls along the road serve those who did not have breakfast at home with rice porridge *(bobo),* noodle soup *(kuy-tiew),* or a sweet dessert. Some buy fruit, fried bananas, or cakes to take along to the factory, while others have a quick look at the small stalls where clothes, hair bands and make-up items are sold. Shortly before seven, when work begins, the streets are quiet again.

This scene can be observed in various parts of Phnom Penh, especially in the outskirts, where garment and shoe factories behind high walls are providing work for thousands of people, most of them women. The demand for their labor in these factories has brought new jobs and a chance to experience city life. Cambodian women now engage in the processes of migration and industrial production, just as other women did in nineteenth-century western Europe, the United States, and more recently, for example, in Mexico, Thailand, and other developing countries. These processes are thus not new. In Cambodia, however, they started much later and in a different historical, cultural and social context than in other developing countries. It may be argued that only by the end of the second millennium had Cambodian women entered the so-called new international division of labor, thereby taking their place in the "global assembly line." Though such abstractions can be useful for analyzing structural consequences of global industry, they are inadequate in understanding how deeply this experience cuts into the lives of these women and how strongly it influences societal outlook. For Cambodian garment factory workers, as for factory workers in other developing countries, abstractions are therefore "meaningful only from the vantage point of their own experiences and beliefs," which are shaped by their particular historical and cultural contexts (Mills 1999: 9).

CAMBODIAN GARMENTS AND THE GLOBAL MARKET

Factory work is relatively new in Cambodia. The first efforts toward industrialization took place during the postcolonial regime, especially in the 1960s. The industrial sector, however, had a minor position within the national economy and this position was reduced even more due to the major blows it suffered during the years of civil war and revolution. As a result, industrial production was restricted and exclusively directed at the local market, producing goods for everyday use, and later also the industrial goods that are essential to increase agricultural output. It was only after the reforms of the early 1990s that the industrial sector started to play a prominent role in Cambodia's economy.

Formal adoption of comprehensive market-oriented reforms took place after the UN-sponsored elections in 1993. The reforms aimed at reducing the size of the public sector through the privatization of state enterprises, the opening up of the country to international trade by the rationalization of the trade and tariff regime and the reduction of subsidies and protection, and the promotion of domestic and especially foreign investment through adoption of the Liberal Foreign Investment Law (World Bank 1999). These reforms created conditions for the establishment of a labor-intensive and export-oriented industry, most notably due to incentives such as tax holidays of up to eight years, full import duty exemption, no export tax, free repatriation of profits, land leases up to seventy years, and no nationalization or price controls. Such incentives were intended to attract domestic as well as foreign investors who, confronted with rising wages in the industrial sector in other countries in the region and with limitations on imports from manufacturing countries like China and India, could profit from Cambodia's low labor costs and "young and willing workforce with tradition-encouraged discipline, ready to learn and apply state of the art technology" (Ministry of Commerce 2000: 119).

Investment incentives and cheap labor are seen as important factors in attracting foreign investment and stimulating growth in Cambodia's industrial sector. However, the image of Cambodia as a war-torn country with a weak infrastructure, security problems, corruption and an unstable government has strongly influenced investment patterns. Investors concentrate predominantly on the garment industry, which relies on a large inexpensive workforce and requires less capital investment than some other industries, thus risking only minimal loss in times of trouble. The political crisis in July 1997 illustrated to several investors the risks and, also, the monetary losses potentially associated with investing in Cambodia. The fighting between two political factions, and the subsequent looting, caused considerable damage and loss to several factories, especially those situated on the road to the airport where most of the fighting took place. The front of the June Textiles factory, for example, was severely damaged by rockets and the factory itself looted, including the loss of machines. According to the general manager of the factory, the total damage amounted to five million US dollars. Replacement machines had to be purchased abroad and imported, and new workers had to be recruited, as many went back home or found jobs in other factories.

Despite these political insecurities, the garment industry has become the largest and fastest-growing one in the country, expanding from 7 factories in 1994 to 238 factories registered at the Garment Manufacturers Association in Cambodia (GMAC) at the beginning of 2005 (cf. Sok Hach et al. 2001; Sok Hach 2005). The majority of these factories are owned by investors from Hong Kong, Taiwan, China, Korea, Macau and Singapore who are subcontractors to clothing companies, including Nike, Gap and Hennes & Mauritz, and produce garments predominantly destined for the US and European markets. Concomitant with the growth in the number of factories, the value of garment exports has increased considerably, from 27 million dollars in 1995, to 985 million in 2000, and reaching 2.175 billion in 2005, accounting for about 80 percent of the total Cambodian export (Ministry of Commerce 2000; Sok Hach et al. 2001: 50; Better Factories Cambodia 2006).

The expansion of the garment industry has accelerated Cambodia's integration into the global economy, which the Royal Government of Cambodia considers to be "not only a necessity for its sustained growth but as part of the irresistible worldwide process of globalization" (Ministry of Commerce 2000: vii). Cambodia's garment industry has initially benefited from the worldwide quota system, imposing restrictions on textile and clothing exports from certain highly competitive, low-cost countries, and from the granting of General System of Preferences (GSP) and Most Favored Nation (MFN) status by its major trading partners, which gave Cambodian exports preferential access to their markets. As of 2005, the quota system for textiles expired, as members of the World Trade Organization have committed themselves under the Agreement on Textiles and Clothing to remove the quotas and open all manufacturing countries to competition in the global market. While many predicted that this would result in a collapse of the Cambodian garment industry due to the fierce competition from countries like China and Vietnam, this did not happen. In fact, export and employment even increased during the first year after the end of the quota system (Better Factories Cambodia 2006). This is in part because as a relatively small producer Cambodia tries to set itself apart as a "niche" market where workers are treated well.

The economic importance of the garment industry in Cambodia goes beyond what is shown by investment and export statistics. The new factory sites have stimulated a range of other, informal, economic activities. A range of food stalls, fruit stalls, karaoke bars, beauty salons, clothes and other vendors can be found close to most of the factory sites. The presence of thousands of factory workers has also stimulated the demand for housing. Residents within the area have profited from this great demand by offering rooms for rent. Often these rooms consist of thin wooden shacks in a housing compound, but also complete houses and barrack-like, small brick or wooden houses have been built especially to rent out to the women who came from the countryside to work in the garment factories.

INTO THE FACTORIES

When my father was still alive, I asked him to let me go [and work in Phnom Penh]. He replied "There is no need to. We can farm a little rice and what we have is enough. No need to become miserable in a place far away."

This is how Srey, an eighteen-year-old woman from Battambang, described her decision to go and find work in Phnom Penh. At that time, her father was opposed to the idea of her working in the city and preferred to live on what they had. When I first met Srey, she had just arrived in Phnom Penh to look for a job in a garment factory three months after her father had died.

Srey told me that, until a few years ago, she did not have to bother much about making a living. Her parents had enough rice land to support her and her four siblings. Rice farming was what she was brought up with, and it provided the basis of subsistence for her family. She attended a village school for two years, but had to leave due to attacks by Khmer Rouge soldiers who were still in the nearby jungle. Things started to change when her family fell into a spiral of indebtedness. First, her older brother got sick and money had to be borrowed to pay for his cure. After he had recovered, her mother contracted malaria and more money had to be borrowed to pay for treatment. She recovered, although Srey's younger brother also caught malaria and died. The rice harvest did not yield enough to repay their debts. The situation became even more difficult when her father became seriously ill. He was brought to Phnom Penh for treatment, but he did not survive and Srey's mother was left with a debt of three *damlung*[1] (around 1,020 US dollars). The moneylender kept coming to their house pressing for repayment of the loans. Interest rates are very high in Cambodia. For Srey's family they amounted to 50 percent per year. As the previous year's rice yield had been very low due to a lack of rain, Srey's mother had to sell part of their land to repay the debt. Confronting the hardship of her mother, Srey decided that she had to go to find work in Phnom Penh, but was not sure how to proceed. "I could not do it just like that. I was afraid people would talk bad about me, that they would say that I am not a good girl because I stay far away from home. People in my village would think that I was going to be a prostitute to earn money in order to repay the debt of my mother."

Srey's story sums up some of the difficulties that rural households in Cambodia have to deal with. Although physical security has improved considerably since the demise of the Khmer Rouge in the late 1990s, a range of economic and social insecurities still plague the lives of rural Cambodians. Small-scale agriculture provides the greater part of their livelihoods, but the crops they grow are extremely vulnerable to floods, drought and insect infestation. Loss of (wo)manpower, high indebtedness, a deficient social infrastructure, and a lack of economic alternatives, furthermore, contribute to rural poverty in Cambodia.[2]

Garment factories created new possibilities for these households, especially for young women, in their struggle to make a living. In the

case of Srey, the motivations for going to Phnom Penh to find a job in
a garment factory were directly related to the debts and difficulty of
repaying these after the death of her father. While her oldest brother
took up employment in the construction industry in the provincial town
in order to return home when it was time for plowing, Srey planned to
go to Phnom Penh to work in a garment factory. However, it was not
only the financial crisis back home that motivated Srey to seek work in
the city. She had also seen village women who worked in one of Phnom
Penh's factories returning with money, nice clothes, gold jewelry, and
a "whiter" skin, and was attracted by their appearances and stories.
Factory work had, for her as for many other rural women, the attractive image of working and living with other young women, being able
to "enter the shade" by working indoors, thus changing one's skin to
lighter shades, and receiving a monthly salary paid in US dollars as
opposed to the Khmer currency (riel) or gold, the more common cur-
rencies in the rural areas.

For young rural women like Srey, these attractions of city life and
working in a factory become more real when they meet other young
women from their village who are already working in Phnom Penh and
who form the possible *ksae* ("rope" or "string") through which they
can go as well. Srey saw her chance to go and find work through neighbors and peers from nearby villages, who came home for a few days in
September to celebrate Bon Pcum Ben, the Buddhist celebration for the
dead. They came with news about upcoming selections for new workers
in their garment factories during the days immediately after the Buddhist holiday. Srey was excited and talked to her mother about it. Her
mother, after learning about the money other village women brought
home and the social protection and support that existed among factory
workers from the same district, decided to set aside her worries. She
borrowed five *hun*[3] from neighbors and packed a bag with rice and
prahok,[4] thus supporting her daughter's wish to go to Phnom Penh.
Not all factory workers I met came to Phnom Penh in similar agreement with their parents. Some claimed that they did not want to go but
were pushed to do so by their parents, while others left without parental
approval.

Srey left her village after Pcum Ben with four other young women
from the neighborhood. They all stayed on the upper floor of a house
in Tuol Sangkeo, which some twenty women from the same district
(*srok*) in Battambang had rented together, sharing beds, food, joys and

sorrows. The house in which Srey and her friends stayed was close to many factories in the area and provided, for these newcomers, a secure place and social environment in the large unknown city. Although far from their villages, they were with known and trusted people. The presence of one of the women's aunt, a divorced woman in her thirties, was especially comforting, since she was more experienced and took it upon herself to guide and advise the young women about city and working life.

Such networks of people from the same village or area of origin is common among young women migrating to the city in search of a job in a factory. Young rural women seldom come to Phnom Penh on their own; they usually stay with relatives or friends already living in the city. Besides providing shelter, a trusted social environment and a first introduction to city life, these social networks are critical for finding a job in a garment factory.

FINDING A JOB

Although the demand for factory workers is high, supply seems to outstrip it. Factories therefore do not need to put much effort into labor recruitment and can select from a constant stream of young people eager to work. Nonetheless, for young women finding a job is not always easy, and either some luck is required to be recruited from among the masses that appear at announced selections, or alternatively, connections and money are needed to assist in finding a job.

Many newly arrived women start by taking sewing classes in order to acquire the skills that are necessary for passing the test at a selection procedure. Several shops that provide sewing classes with machines discarded by factories have popped up near the factories. Here one can see groups of women, fresh from the countryside, waiting their turn to try sewing a straight line or a perfect circle. It may take several hours, at two thousand riel[5] per hour, before a beginner is sufficiently skilled in handling a sewing machine and can sew a given pattern.

Possessing sewing skills, however, is not the only key to getting a factory job. When factories recruit new workers they tell them to spread the word among relatives and friends. When large numbers of new workers are sought, factories hang a sign outside the factory with information about their call for workers and the date and time of selection. Such an occasion attracts tens to hundreds of women, who stand for hours at the gate of the factory, waiting for someone to come out and start the selection procedure. A supervisor of a particular section in a factory will come out and choose potential workers randomly from the mass, choices more often based on appearance, height and healthy looks than on any demonstrated skills. It is interesting to hear how the women themselves judge the selection procedure. Srey repeatedly told me that Chinese managers select only beautiful, white-skinned women. This explained to her why she had not yet been chosen: "I am not a beautiful girl and therefore they did not point at me, but at my friend. I think I don't have a chance to work in that factory."

Factory managers claim, however, that the criteria for selection are not random or based on beauty. Instead, they are often related to the particular manufacturing procedures for which new workers are sought. For some procedures, such as knitting, height and literacy are important in order to be able to handle the machine and read the knitting patterns, whereas working in quality control does not require any specific skills or stature. Some factories conduct a second selection procedure, or test, after the initial one, when they take a closer look at the capacities of a woman, such as the ability to sew a straight line or handle a machine. When a woman passes this test, she will be further trained in a specific procedure.

However, there are also more direct ways of getting a job through the mediation of a *ksae*. Such a *ksae* may be a Cambodian supervisor in a garment factory, or someone connected to a supervisor, who can arrange access to a job. A *ksae* usually demands one or several months' salary for her (or his) service. In some factories, security guards may also accept money to let potential new workers enter the factory and make contact with a supervisor who might employ a new worker in her section. "Buying a job" *(tiñ kaa ni'e tweu)* in this way is a common practice in Cambodia, in which foreign supervisors and managers are usually not involved. A sign, spotted at one factory gate, stating that the factory selects people on merit and that paying an intermediator to gain entry is not allowed does nothing to stop this practice. While for newcomers, payment is a more reliable way of finding a job quickly, there is the risk of losing the money if the *ksae* does not live up to the promised arrangement, or when the worker gets fired during her probation period.

In practice, getting a job may take weeks or months and requires perseverance and funds. After almost one month in Phnom Penh, Srey and her friends still had not found jobs. Whenever selections were taking place at a garment factory in the neighborhood, they waited in front of the gate from early morning in the hope of being chosen. Srey was selected to do a test twice, but failed, which she blamed on the fact that she did not have enough money to attend more sewing classes. She had hoped, in vain, that their "local" *ksae,* a woman from the same district who had helped others get jobs before, would contact them and help them. A neighbor woman had offered to help Srey and her friends get a job in return for forty-five dollars, but the aunt told them not to get involved with this unknown and untrustworthy-looking woman. Srey considered bribing the guard at the Sam Han factory to get in contact with a supervisor. Yet she knew that she could not produce the money to pay for their services. Srey feared that if she had a problem during the first three months leading to her dismissal, she would have worked without income. Thus, she decided to wait to be selected and pass a test without having to pay for it.

In the meantime, after about a month in Phnom Penh, she slowly ran out of money. The amount she had brought from home was not sufficient for the expenses of food, photos for an identification card, and transport. Through visiting relatives of one of the women in the house, she sent her mother a message asking for extra rice, *prahok,* salt and dried fish, which she hoped relatives of other women would transport when they came to visit Phnom Penh. She did not dare to ask for more money, since she knew her mother would have to borrow it at high interest rates from a moneylender in the village. Srey also thought that if she had to pay someone to get a job, she could ask to borrow some money from her roommates. Yet she knew already what the consequences would be if she did not find a job soon: "If I cannot find a job within the next two or three days," she told me, "I'll have to go back. I do not have any rice and money left. [. . .] I am afraid that they will say that I just came here without a job and spent all my money without having an income. That's why I feel ashamed to go back home while I am running out of money."

For Srey, there were only two possibilities: work in a factory or in a rice field. She thought that other job options in Phnom Penh were beyond her reach, since she lacked education, money and contacts. Though Srey and her unemployed friends made jokes about selling each other to the Son San hotel, a karaoke club-cum-brothel, on the main street nearby, sex work was beyond her imagination. It was not something a "good girl" would do. It would be better to go back home,

FIG. 2. Factory worker

where she could always go into the forest to cut trees, plants or rattan, or catch fish and crabs, which were widely available around her village. This she did, when her mother came to Phnom Penh to collect her for the hundredth day ceremony for her deceased father. Sad as she was about it, during her first stay in Phnom Penh Srey had not succeeded in fulfilling her desire to find a factory job.

Srey was not the only one who returned home disappointed, with no money left. Three of her friends followed her one week later. Before Srey and her friends, there had been other young women who failed to find a factory job, or at least one that paid enough to survive in Phnom Penh.

For these women, the perceived profitability of factory work became a net loss, leading to higher debts, which had to be paid for by their families through the sale of rice, a pig, or even a piece of land.

Yet, the determination to find a job in a factory is not necessarily stilled after an initial failure. One of the four friends who came with Srey to Phnom Penh did not want to return home without being able to bring back some money for her family. She went to stay with an uncle and aunt who lived in a squatter area in the city, and waited for the next selections of workers. The women who stayed in Phnom Penh kept those who had returned to the village informed about forthcoming selections. I saw Srey's friends come back to Phnom Penh several times after a call from their friends regarding new chances for work in a factory, and return home when it did not work out.

About half a year after she had left Phnom Penh Srey unexpectedly came to visit me at my house. Together with a group of new young women and men from her district, she had arrived after Khmer New Year, when returning factory workers had told them about announced selections at some of the major factories. Srey was very excited when she told me she had passed a test at the Sam Han factory, where she was assigned to sew the hems around the neck and arms of shirts with machines she had never seen before. That she had to work the night shift, and did not know how much she would earn, could not temper her delight that she had finally found a job in a factory.

WORKING IN A FACTORY

The factories in which women like Srey work are mostly located in and around Phnom Penh, but some have begun to extend production to nearby provinces and the port town of Sihanoukville. Typically, the factories are one-story buildings, although some have several floors, with separate halls filled with machines for knitting, cutting, sewing, ironing and other steps of the production process. Other parts of the factory buildings are reserved for storage, administration and, depending on the size and products of the factory, washing and coloring of clothes. The size of factories varies, as they may employ from a few hundred to as many as several thousand workers.

At the beginning of 2006, the garment factories together employed over 290,000 people (Better Factories Cambodia 2006). Young women constitute between 85 and 90 percent of the workforce in these factories. Single women still form the highest proportion of the employed females in manufacturing, which reflects an apparent preference of employers for employing young and single women, often with little or no education (National Institute of Statistics 2000a: 25; 2005b: 20). The stereotypes about Asian female characteristics regarding nimble fingers, the capacity to endure long hours of tedious work, and docility also exist in the Cambodian context. As an official from the Ministry of Industry put it, women do the work on the floor because they know how to sew and can learn quickly. They can also sit for a long time, and have a willingness to work. They are, as he put it, "smooth workers." In the same vein, a general manager of a garment factory claimed that Cambodian men are harder to control and more violent, and therefore women are preferred as employees.

Feminine labor recruitment is, however, neither set in stone nor universal (Rigg 1997: 216). More and more young men are standing outside the factory gates when the selection of new workers is announced. Even the general manager who claimed that Cambodian men are harder to control saw advantages in employing men for some parts of the production process that had been performed predominantly by women. He complained that female workers often could not meet the production schedule and that, compared to other countries in Asia, most notably China, Cambodian factory workers were less skilled and less productive.[6] Cambodian women, he thought, were not as strong and faint easily, especially during menstruation, but also due to stress caused by homesickness. His factory was therefore planning to extend production into the countryside, where he hoped to attract more men, as the proximity to home would make it easier to combine their agricultural tasks with work in the factory.

BENEFITS AND BURDENS

In her song "The Weeping of the Garment Factory Worker" Hem Sivorn, a popular Khmer singer, portrays the hardship of a young woman who came to Phnom Penh to work in a garment factory. She sings:

The moon moves and sets, rain is slow. Clouds cover the moon, while the sun is almost rising. My heart hurts, because I broke my promise. When I left home, you reminded me that when the rainy season comes I'd come back home again with the money earned.

I arrived in the city as an ignorant girl. I became a garment factory worker in order to earn money to support myself. A salary of forty dollars a month, hardly enough for food, rent, yet not enough to return home. I have only my body left, no money to bring along.

The rainy season started already. I miss you, I am not happy. But what can I do? I have no free time, have to work day and night. The boss doesn't allow me to stop. Oh, my dear, who will help you to transplant rice?

I regret, I should not have come here. I was cheated, because I was ignorant. I wanted to earn money to help you. Instead, I earn less than when growing rice during one season. But now I am obliged to continue, the evil boss oppresses me so much.

Although this song suggests that growing rice is more profitable and more respectable, this is certainly not the dominant view of factory work among the women I met. For newcomers, the idea of working in a factory seems preferable to working under the sun in the fields. Although Srey had yet to experience it for herself, her roommates warned her "to wait and see what it means to sew from seven in the morning to ten in the evening without time for resting. If we do farming, there is nobody who orders or scolds us. On the contrary, we have fun and rest as we wish." Nary, who came with Srey to Phnom Penh, noted: "I did not believe it. I thought that it could not be difficult when one only has to sew and stay inside. How could this be harder than life back in the village?"

This contrast between the forms of hardship and oppression in agricultural and factory work is an issue that preoccupies not only factory workers themselves but also authors who analyze the relationships between industrialization and exploitation (Ong 1987; Wolf 1992; Rigg 1997; Mills 1999). Factory work entails new forms of labor organization for workers who were previously embedded in rural life. Peasant women, Ong (1987) states in her study about Malayan factory workers, undergo two major changes when they become integrated into factory work. The first is a shift from a flexible work schedule to the hierarchical structure of industrial production. The second is the transition from autonomy in the work process to the usually oppressive compulsion of labor discipline (Ong 1987: 151). Although hierarchical structures and labor discipline are also part of the organization of peasant production (Wolf 1992), their forms differ for rural women who "enter the world of laboring by the clock" (Ong 1987: 10).

Indeed, factory work requires for most workers, especially those from the countryside, adaptation to new forms of labor discipline. Back home it is not the clock but the season that guides daily routine. In the factory, strict working hours are maintained, during which chatting is not allowed and permission to go to the toilet has to be granted. New forms of labor discipline therefore involve, not only fragmented working patterns under the supervision of an unrelated and often foreign hierarchical authority, but also a strict division of time between working time and free time.

For Sophanna, who is from the same village as Srey, a typical working day starts at six in the morning. She gets up, washes herself, gets dressed and makes sure to leave the house before half past six, so that she has time to eat a bowl of rice porridge and some sweet dessert before clocking in at the factory. She takes her place at the work floor and chats with her colleagues until the bell rings at seven as a sign that it is time to start working. Sophanna works in a group of thirty-five workers at the control section *(khaan pinut)*. Their task is to carefully look for spots, wrongly sewn parts, or little holes in the finished shirts. Sophanna gets 350 pieces to control per day, but hardly ever manages to finish all these by four o'clock. In fact, only a few women, who are very serious about their work and do not let themselves be distracted by their colleagues, manage to finish their quota on time. Most of the workers end up working overtime until six.

The workers in Sophanna's factory have a one-hour lunch break at noon. Sophanna takes her lunch together with some of her colleagues at one of the food stalls outside the factory. Since supervisors tend to be rather strict about talking during work time, lunch is the time to gossip, tell about the latest outings, or lament about the lack of money for a much wanted pair of trousers she saw the day before. After work time, Sophanna sometimes passes by the stalls with clothes, hairpins and make-up to see whether something new has arrived. More often, however, she goes home to prepare dinner with her sister who is working in another factory in the neighborhood. They spend the evening together with the neighbors or with other women who rent rooms in the house. Sometimes they watch television, mostly Thai or Khmer soap operas, with the family of the landlord until it is time to go to sleep between nine and ten.

Factory workers have an official work week of forty-eight hours. Most factories have working hours from 7:00 a.m. until 4:00 p.m. with an hour lunch break, six days a week. Working until 6:00 p.m. is, as in the case of Sophanna, more the rule than the exception, and working until 9:00 or 10:00 p.m. is common, leaving women little time for relaxing during the week or even on their only free day, since they may be called to work on Sunday as well. Some factories have divided workers into shifts, from 6:00 a.m. to 2:00 p.m. and from 2:00 to 10:00 p.m., and when there is pressure to complete large orders a night shift is added. The pressure on workers is not constant but very much related to the seasons in Europe and the United States. Thus, the advent of Christmas means overtime for the factory workers.

Working overtime is voluntary according to labor legislation. A general manager of a garment factory employing several thousand workers did not see this as a great issue, since workers know from the start of their employment that they are at times expected to work overtime, and that it would therefore not be correct to refuse when the factory needs them. Factory workers, on their part, expressed fears that their salary would be cut or that they would be fired if they refused. This could even lead to a situation, described by a few, in which workers are called to work several days in a row from seven in the morning until after midnight in order to finish an order on time. Although this is an example of excessive overtime, which goes against legal and health regulations, a certain amount of overtime is also desired, as it gives the workers the opportunity to earn something extra. As the aunt in the house of Srey said, "We have to do it, because we need the money."

The legal minimum wage of factory workers working a forty-eight-hour week is forty-five dollars per month, which includes a raise of five dollars negotiated after massive strikes and demonstrations in May and June 2000. This minimum wage is about twice what regular civil servants and teachers earn. With overtime, the monthly wage of factory workers can rise to sixty or even over one hundred dollars. In 2005, the average wage was seventy-two dollars per month (Better Factories Cambodia 2006). Overtime hours have, according to the labor law, to be paid at a rate of 50 percent higher than normal hours. If overtime hours are worked at night (between 10:00 p.m. and 5:00 a.m.) or during the day off, the hourly rate should be doubled. Actual payment of these overtime rates is, however, not yet the practice in all factories. Some factories provide food instead of the required overtime rate; others pay just the regular hour or piece rate.

Depending on the kind of work, wages are calculated either by the month or by working hours, *sii khae* (lit. "eat a month"), or based on piece rate, *sii bon* (lit. "eat a bill"), also called *sii lou* (lit. "eat a dozen") when pieces are counted in units of a dozen. For the more experienced workers, piece-rate wages are financially more attractive, as they can earn more than the legal minimum even when working the normal work week. This also leads to competition among workers. There are always a few workers in one line who work faster than the others and thus earn more money. This may lead to feelings of jealousy and gossip among the others in the group, but also to admiration. As Sophanna noted about a worker in her factory: "Within our group of controllers, there are four or five women [out of thirty-five] who are the fastest. One of them is a relative of my mother. She can work the fastest of all. She earns more than one hundred dollars per month. One month, when I worked a lot, I earned 170, but she earned even more than that, up to 210 [dollars]."

For new workers, monthly earnings often remain below the legal minimum. Many factories use a progressive salary scale, whereby workers in their first month, for example, are paid thirty-five, the second month forty, and from then on forty-five dollars per month, which may be increased again after a year of work. In this way, factories try to avoid losing money when they train workers, as newcomers are usually unable to reach the required production rate, while at the same time making it more attractive for workers to remain at the same factory, avoiding a high turnover.

A few factories provide food for their workers, which is in fact paid for by the worker through deductions from her monthly salary. A meal usually consists of rice with two side dishes, soup *(samlo)* and a fried dish *(chaa)*. Workers in factories that provide food consistently complained, however, about the quality of the food, which is prepared in huge quantities to cater sometimes for thousands of workers. Most prefer to get money rather than food, and eat either at home or in one of the food stalls around the factory sites. These stalls operate from early morning until late in the evening in order to serve those working overtime or the night shift.

Although working overtime has the benefit of earning something extra, it also means that workers have to leave after dark, when young women would ideally already be at home. Young women consider walking back home late at night to be undesirable and dangerous, and these fears are confirmed by repeated stories about gangs of young men robbing and raping women in the area where I lived. In response to these concerns, the larger factories arranged minibuses to transport workers living far from the factory to their homes. Those who lived close by sought extra protection by walking back in groups or having someone pick them up from work.

Problems related to overtime are not limited to failures to pay the required rate and returning home after dark. Long working hours and a heavy workload affect the health of the workers. In one factory I visited, workers noted that almost on a daily basis at least one worker fainted, which they blamed on the long working hours and hot environment (and not on their physical weakness, as the general manager claimed). They also noted that supervisors did not take workers' complaints about headaches or other physical ailments seriously, which meant that a worker was only allowed to stop working when she fainted. This may, of course, mean that women sometimes resort to fainting in order to get breaks.

The factory environment also affects the circumstances of work spiritually. Stories about ghosts *(khmauc)* that inhabit the factories and come out at night, or when only a few people are around, are common. Although I have never heard of these spirits possessing workers (cf. Ong 1987), they do give rise to occasional alarm and distraction. Srey told about a *khmauc* who inhabited the toilet of the factory where she worked. She had not seen it for herself, because after she had heard about it she did not dare to enter the toilet. The women joked that it was the *khmauc* of the boss *(thawkae)* who did not want the workers to go to the toilet while they were at work.[7] Such perceptions indicate that both the working and the spiritual environment in the factory are related directly to the forms of supervision under which workers find themselves.

FACTORY HIERARCHIES

Given the highly fragmented production process, workers are divided up among the different stages involved in the production of a pair of trousers, a sweater, or a T-shirt. The number of procedures— from cutting or knitting, through mending, linking, washing, ironing, buttoning, labeling, and quality control to packing—are twenty-one for a sweater and many more for blouses. The major part of the production process, and therefore the majority of the factory space and workers, is related to sewing. In large open areas, sometimes equipped with air conditioners or fans, sewing machines are set up either in straight lines, two in a row, or facing each other. Individual workers are assigned to one place and are responsible for one small part of a piece of clothing, such as the collar, pockets, sleeves, or buttons, with the tables for quality control at the end of the production line, or separate in other halls. These parts of the production process are predominantly performed by women, and the sewing segments provide the most esteemed and desirable jobs. Certain parts of the production process, such as ironing and storage, are considered more suitable for men, as these activities require more physical strength.

The spatial arrangements form part of the factory discipline and allow supervisors to keep control over the stages of production and the workers (see Rofel 1992). The workers are divided up into groups *(krom)* reflecting the kinds of procedures. The number of workers in one *krom* ranges from five to more than thirty, depending on the procedure. There is, for each *krom,* one or more group leaders, *meekrom* or *prothien-krom,* who oversee the *krom.* The *meekrom* is usually a Cambodian woman who has been promoted from the ranks of the ordinary workers on the basis of her job performance, reading and writing skills, and possibly language skills. Being a Khmer woman and a former worker, the *meekrom* is, for the workers, often a person whom they can easily consult concerning work as well as other problems. Vy, who was working in the factory behind my house, explained to me that: "The Khmer *meekrom* helps Khmer [workers]. For example, if she sees that the trousers I made have a defect, she tells me to correct it quickly before the Chinese [supervisor] sees it. We understand each other, she doesn't tell the Chinese that I did something wrong. And if it is, for example, a bit too short, she tells me to cut it in small pieces and throw it away so that that the Chinese doesn't see it." Vy here referred to the fact that the *meekrom* stands below the supervision of the *meephneak* (section head or line leader), who supervises several groups. Supervision at this level is, in many factories, in the hands of Chinese women. Many factories prefer to employ Chinese supervisors, often from mainland China, because they are considered to be more experienced and better trained than Cambodians, and thus to have the knowledge and skills necessary for such positions. Although the Chinese in Cambodia do not have a particularly bad reputation, the different cultural backgrounds and the language barrier cause many conflicts between Cambodian workers and Chinese supervisors. Workers fear these women for their harsh criticism and for their rude behavior when workers do something wrong. A union representative reasoned that misunderstandings arise between Chinese supervisors and Cambodian workers because, in Chinese culture, people are used to speaking very loudly, as though they were always angry at each other, whereas in Cambodia people tend to speak more softly. Such misunderstandings have led Vy to assert that "the Chinese [supervisors] blame Khmer, they hate Khmer," and that, as Hem Sivorn sings in her song, they oppress *(cih coan)* Khmer workers.

Yet, because the language barrier assures that criticisms by Chinese supervisors are often not fully understood, they can also be easily ignored. Given that messages often have to be translated, workers sometimes criticize their Cambodian translators for being arrogant and siding with the Chinese, instead of blaming the Chinese supervisors themselves. Moreover, not only words but also gestures, such as throwing a wrongly sewn piece of cloth at a worker's head, are more important in provoking feelings of unfair and oppressive treatment on the part of supervisors. In order to overcome such problems some initiatives have been set up to employ Cambodians in line-supervising positions. The Cambodian Garment Training Center (CGTC) has started a program to train Cambodians as supervisors and technical advisors in the garment factories, with the rationale, as an employee of the CGTC told me, that "it is not good for Khmer to be controlled by Chinese."

This remark refers to the conflicts that arise on the work floor, which is dominated by women. The middle and upper management of the factory is predominantly in the hands of men, except for administrative tasks. Whereas at the middle level Cambodians or Cambodian-Chinese are employed in the different departments of the factory, such as production, personnel, finance and shipping, the upper-management levels are in most (especially larger) factories almost exclusively filled by Asian (male) expatriates.

LABOR LAW AND INSPECTION

Treatment of and relations with workers have become important issues determining the image of Cambodia's garment industry among the predominantly overseas investors as well as buyers. The process of globalization requires, as the Ministry of Commerce (2000) put it in their *Business & Investment Handbook,* an adjustment of the Cambodian labor administration to the reality of an economy increasingly dominated by market forces. The challenge is therefore "to introduce innovative labor policies and enforce laws and regulations that strike an appropriate balance between promoting economic efficiency and providing social protection" (Ministry of Commerce 2000: 99). The balance referred to is one between assuring a competitive place among other garment-producing countries and assuring that the working conditions and human rights of workers are respected, since both are necessary to attract producers as well as buyers.

In 1997, the Cambodian government adopted a new labor law introducing regulations regarding wage payment and working hours, defining working conditions, and guaranteeing freedom of association and the right to strike. The labor law includes specific sections regarding employment age and women's work, providing, for example, for maternity leave. The labor law is generally considered to be rather progressive and comprehensive, although some points are not clearly defined and its actual implementation faces problems. These have led to complaints concerning forced and not properly paid overtime, unsafe and unhealthy working conditions, pregnant women who get fired instead of maternity leave, and, despite the freedom of association, easy dismissal of union candidates.

Cambodia's Labor Ministry[8] is in charge of tasks related to labor protection and the effective enforcement of the labor law. A special department is charged with labor inspection and industrial relations services. They provide information to employers and workers regarding the clauses of the labor law, provide conciliation services in the event of disputes between employers and workers, conduct inspection visits, and compile data regarding work establishments and labor statistics. However, lacking as it does the necessary capacity for performing these tasks, the ministry's labor inspection is criticized for being ineffective in contributing significantly to improving working conditions.

Labor inspection has, however, become a major tool in the pursuit to build up the reputation of Cambodia as a country where workers are treated well. The working conditions of factory workers in countries like Cambodia have attracted international attention, as they are producing clothes for the world market, including famous clothing companies. Labor and human rights organizations as well as contracting clothing companies have started initiatives to monitor labor in garment factories, especially exploitative working conditions and the employment of underage workers. In 2001 the International Labor Organization (ILO) started a program called Better Factories Cambodia to monitor and report on working conditions in Cambodian factories in light of national and international standards, with the aim of improving them as well as productivity.[9] The garment industry has thus become probably the most controlled and monitored sector in Cambodia.

Also, international clothing companies are taking part in monitoring the local producers they subcontract. Many of them have been subject to pressure from consumer campaigns and activists regarding the conditions under which their clothes are produced. Bearing in mind consumer interests and criticisms, companies like Nike, Reebok, Gap, Hennes & Mauritz and C&A have responded with codes of conduct for factories subcontracted to produce their clothes. These codes usually contain provisions regarding child labor, forced labor, health and safety regulations, payment and working hours. There are important variations in the emphases and contents of the codes of conduct among clothing companies. This is most obvious in provisions regarding child labor. Some use the ILO Convention on Child Labor[10] or the standards set in the national laws of producing countries, while others have set their own standards. This means that one factory may employ workers of fifteen years and above to work on certain orders, while being required to employ only workers of eighteen years and above for other orders.[11]

How old women are, or should be, to be employed in a garment factory in Cambodia has become a confusing issue for labor inspectors, employers and the media alike.[12] The labor law stipulates that the minimum legal age for workers is fifteen unless the working conditions are harmful to their physical development and their morality. Many factories, however, fearing accusations of using child labor (and thereby losing orders) claim to have set eighteen as their minimum age for employing workers. As a way to control age, factory managers have resorted to asking for family registration papers issued by local authorities in which the date of birth of every family member is noted. Yet, eager to get a job in a factory, women under eighteen years old often fake their family book, pretending to be eighteen or older. Determining the real age of a person is not easy in a country where demographic statistics are not systematically kept, and where falsified identification papers can be easily obtained. Factory managers can thus claim to be innocent of purposely using child labor and point to the ample and ready supply of potential workers, indicating that they do not need to resort to underaged workers. Yet, in actual practice it is not uncommon to find sixteen- and seventeen-year-old, or even younger, factory workers. This is particularly the case among smaller factories and so-called sweatshops, which largely fall outside the scope of labor inspection.

The confusion regarding legal age of employment and codes of conduct has caused some factories to take precautions and dismiss young-looking workers. A program manager of ILO's child labor program feared that such a mistaken refusal by employers to hire workers under eighteen years old could lead desperately poor families to send their daughters to the sex industry until they reached that age (quoted in O'Connell and Vong, 8–21 December 2000). Other factories were cautious only when labor inspectors came to the factory, as in the case of a roommate of Srey who, looking younger than her seventeen years, was told to hide in the toilets until the labor inspectors had left.

LABOR RESISTANCE AND ASSOCIATION

Issues of working conditions and human rights in factories are of concern first and foremost to the workers themselves. Yet, as Mills (1999) also observed in her study on Thai factory workers, coming from the countryside and having little to no education, factory workers' abilities to express their discontent with the working situation and resist unfair treatment are limited. The lack of knowledge of the content of labor law and hierarchical structures prevent young female workers, who are at the bottom of the hierarchy, from protesting openly against violations of the labor law.

Labor resistance can, however, take place in diverse, often indirect, ways that are culturally consistent with the status of female factory workers and their ability to express their discontent. Ong (1987), for example, describes how women in Malaysia indirectly protested against structures of domination in industrial labor through spirit possessions, in which women became violent and screamed abuse, thereby slowing down or even halting the production process until factories were cleared of the spirits. Such spirit possession should, according to Ong (1987: 8), be depicted as a form of protest against the loss of autonomy and humanity in work. Wolf (1992: 128) lists four different forms of labor resistance among female factory workers in rural Java: walkouts, production slowdowns, stay-outs, and visions of ghosts or spirits. Mills (1999) describes how factory workers in Bangkok, although unhappy about the harsh and difficult conditions in which they had to work, rarely felt in a position to challenge these directly, partly because active protest could quickly undermine their economic goals and their abil-

ity to uphold obligations to rural families. Fearing the negative consequences of open and collective protest, workers adopted more individual forms of labor resistance, through withdrawal, seeking work in
another factory, or returning home (Mills 1999: 24–25).

Cambodian factory workers utilized similar individual forms of
resistance against unfair treatment, harsh working conditions and
improper payment. Moreover, the adoption of a relatively comprehensive labor law provides for the freedom of association and the right to
strike. Unlike some other countries in Southeast Asia, Cambodia has as
a result seen an unprecedented development of the labor movement.

UNIONIZATION

On a Monday afternoon in December 2000, when I was driving
home, I ran into a demonstration by factory workers with banners and
loudspeakers on the way to the National Assembly. Manny, a roommate of Srey, came running toward me. She and some of her colleagues
explained that they were in their third day of a strike, which had started
after ten union members demanding an end to forced and unpaid overtime were fired. The protests escalated on that Monday morning, when
factory workers demonstrated in front of the factory, thereby blocking
the traffic along an important northern thruway. Military police and
water cannons were called in to break up the protest quickly and clear
the road for traffic. Protesters were furious about the violent breakup
of their protest and the rude behavior of the police, who hit protesting
women and told the workers to go back to work in the factory or otherwise find work as *srey kouc* (lit. "broken woman," commonly used
to mean prostitute). This behavior of the police only aggravated the
tempers of workers, who saw it as wrong for the police to strike women
and come to the aid of the Chinese owners. Union activists continued
to march toward the National Assembly, with banners demanding a
minimum salary of seventy dollars and respect for the labor law and
code of conduct. When they arrived at the National Assembly, protesters waited until two or three opposition parliamentarians came out,
promised their support in the dispute, and urged the workers to go back
and wait for the results of negotiations with the factory management.
Upon their return to the factory, the protesters found a paper from the
management calling upon the workers—whom they addressed as brothers and sisters *(bong-p'oun)*—to think things over, return to work and
receive their salaries less a deduction for the days they were on strike.

The next day workers went back to work, not really satisfied with the solution that one extra meal, rather than extra money, would be provided in the event of overtime.

Demonstrations like these were frequent. Almost on a weekly basis I observed smaller, and sometimes larger, demonstrations of groups of garment factory workers in front of the National Assembly complaining about their working conditions and payment, and read reports in local newspapers about demonstrations that had gotten out of control and strikers losing their jobs. Indeed, with the increasing awareness of labor stipulations, problems related to forced overtime, nonpayment of the required overtime rate, as well as feelings of solidarity with unjustly treated fellow workers have increasingly given rise to strikes and demonstrations. Such actions, however, do not always arise spontaneously from factory workers, but are often organized and backed by unions.

Unionization has since its onset been strongly politicized. Several labor union federations have been established since the expansion of the garment industry, many of whom have some kind of political or economic affiliation. The different union federations compete with each other for worker membership. The oldest union federation is the Cam-

FIG. 3. Demonstration of factory workers

bodian Federation of Independent Trade Unions, which succeeded the labor union established during the 1980s along the Vietnamese model of mass movement of workers. In 1999, the former union federation was restructured and renamed the Cambodian Federation of Independent Trade Unions in order to mark the break with the connection to the socialist regime of the 1980s.

The first union federation set up since the political and economic reforms of the 1990s was the Free Trade Union of Workers of the Kingdom of Cambodia (FTUWKC). This union is considered to be affiliated to the "opposition party," as it was established by opposition leader Sam Rainsy in 1996. The FTUWKC claims to give a voice to those workers who suffer under the working conditions in factories owned by foreign investors profiting from the systematic corruption and misery in Cambodia (Gorman 1997). It is the most active union federation, frequently calling strikes and demonstrations.[13] In order to counter the influence of the FTUWKC, the Cambodian Union Federation (CUF), considered to be allied to the government, was set up in 1997. The CUF rarely calls strikes, because it seeks, as its leader formulated, not only to protect the workers' interests, but also to promote the garment industry, to stabilize the country and to promote investments.

In 2006 there were eighteen union federations active in the garment and textile sector. Not all of them have such strong political affiliations. The National Independent Federation of Textile Unions in Cambodia (NIFTUC), for example, was established in 1999 with assistance from a nongovernmental organization and with US support. NIFTUC exclusively organizes workers in the garment industry and is staffed and headed by former factory workers. A conflict with the supporting organizations fragmented the federation and led to the creation of the Coalition of Cambodia Apparel Workers Democratic Union. There are, however, some smaller unions, such as the Cambodian Labor Union Federation (CLUF) and the Cambodian Workers Labor Federation Union, that have been criticized for being headed by people involved as factory owners or administrators, and therefore in positions that run counter to the task of protecting workers' rights.

Many workers are unaware of the existence of the unions and their political affiliations. In factories where a union is established, workers are encouraged to become members and participate in the elections of their representatives. As a result of the structure of unionization in factories and their alliances to a union federation, more than one union federation can be represented in one factory—about nine hundred enterprise-based unions were registered at the Ministry of Labor in 2006. Although there are still factories that violate the right to associate, and do so within a climate of impunity, there is a growing recognition among factory managers of the importance of these factory unions and their representatives in labor conflicts. A union representative noted that, a few years ago, factory owners still saw workers and unions as bizarre and as their enemies, and therefore refused to negotiate with them. But she noted that this has changed; unions have become negotiation partners for factory owners. But factories do show differential treatment of the unions and their representatives. The unions considered to be more in line with the government are treated with more benevolence than the so-called opposition union, which makes more use of strikes and demonstrations to force factories to observe proper working conditions and payment regulation laws. Representatives of the FTUWKC within factories are often seen as agitators or troublemakers and are readily dismissed for what is often only a minor mistake.

Given the political affiliations, the political factor in representing workers' rights and in organizing strikes and demonstrations, like the one at Manny's factory, is inseparable from the intentions to improve working conditions and payment for workers. Whereas certain unions believe that factories will only feel forced to abide by the labor law and respect workers' rights when confronted with aggressive strategies, government representatives worry that the growing strength of the labor movement and its actions will lead to loss of productivity and may even scare off investors, who may leave Cambodia for countries whose laws make it difficult for labor to organize. In order to prevent an escalation of spontaneous and violent labor protests, workers and union members are informed by means of leaflets, trainings, and TV soaps about their rights as well as the proper procedures for dispute resolution. A special arbitration council with representations from unions, employers' organizations, and the Ministry of Labor has been set up to resolve collective labor disputes that could jeopardize the operation of the factory or social harmony.[14]

The readiness with which factory workers resort to labor protest is unimaginable to some elderly people, who worry about how young factory workers can engage in actions against their employers. On the afternoon of the aforementioned strike, I discussed the events with some of the workers who had participated. An elderly neighbor, overhearing our discussion, remarked that strikes and demonstrations would only lead to a loss of money and jobs for the workers, and that they would not really accomplish anything since the union leaders were not strong enough. The women replied that the demonstration was the only way they could express their dissatisfaction. It became clear, however, that peer pressure had played an important role in persuading them to participate and set aside their fears of the possible consequences—not only the loss of earnings for each day they did not work, or to the loss of job, but also to more severe ones. A 1997 grenade attack on a pro-democracy demonstration led by the opposition party leader, which killed sixteen and wounded more than one hundred, including factory workers demanding respect for the labor law, still causes anxiety among some factory workers regarding their participation in such demonstrations.

INDIVIDUAL STRATEGIES

Open resistance to working conditions, wages and overtime regulations causes losses to factories in terms of profit as well as their reputation among actual and potential customers. It is therefore not surprising that factories have become increasingly aware of the importance of promoting good labor relations. In some factories, management tries to create goodwill among workers by organizing entertainment activities on holidays. Through parties with live music and food, beauty contests, free cinema tickets and trips to the seaside, factories have brought new dimensions to factory workers' experiences, apparently outside the direct realm of labor discipline and payment. Although such experiences are generally welcomed excitedly by the factory workers, it is questionable that such events contribute to improving worker satisfaction. A general manager was clearly disappointed that the party he organized did not prevent workers in his factory from initiating a strike a month later to protest against unfair overtime conditions and payment delay. He learned that one cannot "buy the hearts of the workers" simply by being friendly and generous at a party.

This does not mean that workers turn easily to aggressive ways of protest whenever they are dissatisfied. Open protest in the form of strikes and demonstrations is dependent on objectionable working conditions, the strength of the unions, and the charisma of workers' representatives in the factories who can make the workers aware of their rights. Since most factory workers are unaware of the provisions of the labor law, they judge exploitative labor conditions, harsh supervision, and violations of payment regulations in terms of their experiences back in the village. As Wolf (1992: 135) formulated in her study of Javanese factory workers, "it is important to understand that workers find factory employment preferable to arduous agricultural labor, to highly controlled and poorly paid positions in domestic service, and to being under the eyes and constant control of parents and other relatives in the village."

In Cambodia, the hard work and strict supervision that women encounter in the factories are also set against the stories they hear from their parents and grandparents about the Pol Pot era. Sophanna noted that even when factory workers are forced to work overtime and produce six hundred pieces in one day, it does not compare to the work people had to do during Pol Pot's time. In the factory, nobody says anything if one can finish only five hundred pieces, but during Pol Pot's era people were not allowed to stop working until they had met their quota. Thus, Sophanna concluded, compared to the old people, young people nowadays "sleep comfortably and eat easily" *(deik sru'el, sii sru'el)*.

Still, factory discipline is undermined in various ways. When workers are lazy *(kcil)* they, as Sophanna described, just sit and talk to each other without taking notice of what the supervisor says; or a factory worker who feels like a break may convince her Khmer *meekrom* to write a note allowing her to take sick leave. And when a worker does not want to risk being docked for such an official absence, she may leave without notice and give her time card to be stamped by a friend who leaves at the end of the shift. This is what a friend of Vy did when she was summoned to work on a Sunday afternoon on which she had planned to go out with friends.

In the case of more open confrontation or dissatisfaction, resistance often takes the form of withdrawal. On an individual level, disputes with supervising staff or dissatisfaction with working conditions are sometimes solved by leaving a particular factory. A roommate of Srey, May, left the factory in which she had worked for more than two years after an argument with a Chinese supervisor. The supervisor had blamed her for sewing the wrong pieces of cloth together. According to May, the mistake was made because the person who gave her the precut pieces was confused about the model of the trousers and gave her the wrong parts. May felt insulted by the way her supervisor had scolded her and quit.

I came across several stories similar to May's, in which feelings of unfair treatment, or of being offended in front of others, played an important role in the strategy of withdrawal. Being scolded in public and gestures such as throwing a wrongly sewn piece at one's head are highly offensive and an open sign of looking down on someone. Not only such offenses, but also information that elsewhere working or pay conditions are better cause workers to change factories. For May, her working experience and the continuous demand for skilled sewers within the factories, means that such moves are not necessarily seen as involving a great risk. May did not fear remaining without a job for long and indeed found a new job in another factory within a few days of quitting. Besides, there was always the village to go back to. It is through this mobility that factory workers resist, challenge and also change their positions on the so-called global assembly line.

The expansion of the garment industry has impelled Cambodia's integration into the global economy and stimulated the integration of rural women into the predominantly urban, industrial workforce. Far from seeing themselves as helpless victims of assembly lines and economic constraints, these women regard their employment in the garment industry as a way to gain new experiences while working and living with other young women, working "in the shade," and being able to earn money. Women like Srey eagerly follow their fellow villagers into the city to seek work in a factory. Finding a job is not always easy, of course, and depends on networks, *ksae,* or funds. This may explain the relatively high degree of tolerance for long working hours, low wages and factory hierarchies, which allow factory workers little opportunity to move up, except for a few who make it as a *meekrom.* Nonetheless, there is resistance to exploitative working conditions. The most outspoken form is union action. Less apparent are the "everyday forms of resistance" (Scott 1985) against long working hours, tedious work, or factory discipline through slowdowns, obstructions, or withdrawal. Women who find no satisfaction may thus choose to leave the factory and look for another job. They can do so because the workforce is based on such flexibility, but also because over time they extend their networks, improve their knowledge of how these networks operate, and can thus more readily turn to them for information, support and security regarding a new job. While most women prefer to remain within the confines of the relative protection of these networks and the factory walls, some also look for an alternative in the world of glamour and sex.

Sex Work

5

Tuol Kork is one of the infamous red-light districts in Phnom Penh. Sex workers with white-powdered faces, red lips, tight jeans, short skirts and tops sit or stand in the doorways of the wooden shacks that are lined up along the main road. With gestures, sweet words and teasing remarks they invite passing men on bicycles, on motorbikes, or in cars to come in. The lights, loud music and bustling traffic add to a mishmash of colors and sounds. When I started my fieldwork the main road was dirt and full of potholes creating chaotic situations when trucks, pull-carts, motorbikes and cars on both sides tried to avoid them. The road has since been broadened and paved, some shacks have disappeared or moved to the smaller streets off the main road, while others were rebuilt and soon functioning again as brothels, some disguised as beer gardens. Although the upgrading of the street was also meant to contribute to a "normalization" of the area, for many Phnom Penhois it still has the reputation of a "hot" place where unlawful and immoral things go on *(tombon kdaw kokuk)*.

Another notorious brothel area was at Boulding,[1] a squatter area in the middle of town that housed, at its high point, an estimated fifty thousand people. Until 2002, brothels, karaoke shops, massage and coin-rubbing *(kohkcol)*[2] places, and "guesthouses" were concentrated especially in the first few alleys off Sothearos Boulevard. Even during the day these alleys were bustling with music and women chatting, putting on makeup, eating snacks from passing vendors and making jokes with shy schoolboys, while young monks on their daily begging round passed by this "place where women sit" (outside their houses waiting for clients) as quickly as possible. After the squatter area at Boulding was torn and burned down to make way for city beautification plans in 2002, the prostitution scene continued in other places or took other forms.

The crowding, noise, dirt and poor conditions in these and other red-light districts in Phnom Penh has contributed to the image of a "gruesome" or "immoral" sex industry in Cambodia. Western media reports portray Cambodia as a country where the "sex trade" flourishes, where one can have easy and inexpensive access to women and child prostitutes, and where the associated AIDS epidemic threatens to result in its "next Killing Fields." Sex work has come into the spotlight of publicity. While ideas about sex workers as immoral, loose women persist among many Cambodians, images of sex workers as slaves, commodities and viruses have come to dominate Western and NGO reporting on sex work. These reports portray young rural women, anxious to do whatever they can to provide financial support for their families, yet finding few alternatives to prostitution, in which they become tricked into a life of debt and virtual slavery (ADHOC 1999: 3). The dominant discourses about prostitution thus ambiguously present sex workers as either "broken" women or as victims. Such presentations also can be found elsewhere in Southeast Asia. They are being perceived as "truth" through repetition, a lack of serious research, and the ignoring of sex workers' own voices (Murray 2001:65). I would argue that these views reveal more about the moral attitudes of observers than about the daily lives, struggles and experiences of the workers themselves.

PROSTITUTION IN PAST AND PRESENT

Prostitution is not a recent phenomenon in Cambodia, although it has not always existed in the same forms and on a similar scale. Lack of documentation regarding prostitution in Cambodia's precolonial times makes it difficult to reconstruct a clear picture of the practice in the distant past. Archival sources indicate that during the early years of the French protectorate prostitution was practiced in several urban centers within Cambodia, though less openly than in other parts of Indochina. There were no specific brothel areas in Phnom Penh. Instead, clients and women were brought together in private rooms through the mediation of local residents. Yet, the presence of French troops contributed to a small but growing local sex industry that also stimulated the recruitment of women of Vietnamese origin (Muller 2006: 140).

French administrators, concerned with public health and morals, issued a number of decrees in order to regulate the *filles publiques* (public women). According to these decrees, all sex workers, whether working in *maisons de tolérance* (brothels) or independently, were obliged to register with the police, where they received a card for identification and for mandatory medical examinations. Special police and medical units were in charge of surveillance of the sex workers. The decrees also regulated the registration and management of brothels. Management was allowed only for women. Brothels were subject to taxation according to fixed tariffs, which were set for the whole of Indochina and based on the ethnicity of the sex workers: brothels with Chinese or Japanese women were taxed higher than those with indigenous (Cambodian) or Vietnamese women. Sex workers were also subject to certain behavioral codes, which prohibited them from provoking attention through inviting gestures or talk and denied them access to bars. When women wanted to stop working as sex workers, they had to change their status at the police station and justify their new means of existence. Although it is unclear to what extent these regulations were followed in practice, they were clearly part of an effort on the part of European countries and their colonies to control prostitution and the associated moral and health consequences (Solé 1993).

The concern over the moral consequences of prostitution continued to exist after independence. The practice of and measures taken with regard to prostitution are, however, strongly related to political developments, most notably the consequences of civil war and social upheaval. The Sangkum Reastr Niyum regime displayed an ambivalent attitude toward prostitution. Members of the government were advised not to frequent "places of pleasure" and the government bulletin reported on the number of prostitutes that were arrested each month. Yet at the same time prostitution was seen as an acceptable form of entertainment and even legalized in the port town of Sihanoukville (Jacobsen 2004: 206–207). During the period under Lon Nol from 1970 to 1975, sex work was practiced more or less openly within various sex establishments in urban areas. It was still widely associated with Vietnamese women (e.g., Tarr 1996), but a growing number of Cambodian women, including refugees from the civil war and bombing in the countryside, resorted to prostitution to earn a living (Shawcross 1986: 223).

This situation changed radically when the Khmer Rouge seized power and emptied the cities, abolished money, markets and any kind of commercial exchange. Prostitution was then banned and "extramarital" sexual relationships were punishable by death (Burgler 1990: 81). However, this did not prevent practices that involved an exchange of goods for sexual services. Some women, desperate for food, offered themselves to DK cadre or agreed to heed their demands for sex (Frieson 2001: 11). During the 1980s, prostitution began to be practiced sporadically again, especially near army bases such as the one in Tuol Kork. The official policy of the Vietnamese-backed socialist regime, however, was to impose measures to control the practice. In order to maintain security and social order, sex workers were occasionally arrested and taken to an island in the Mekong for reeducation and rehabilitation (CWDA 1995).

The repression of sex work was abandoned with the political and economic opening up in the 1990s. Several reports suggest that this opening up was accompanied by an increase in the number of sex workers in urban areas. The increase was partly stimulated by the arrival of approximately twenty-two thousand civilian and military personnel during the UNTAC period in 1992 and 1993. Brothels, bars and nightclubs flourished in Phnom Penh and the major provincial towns. Although the number of sex workers may have decreased somewhat after UNTAC left, the scale of the sex industry has remained considerable in comparison to the years before.

In an effort to deal with problems and "immoral practices" related to sex work, the government tried at times to put an end to it by closing down brothels. At the end of 1997 the government intensified its policy of cracking down on sex establishments. The policy proved to be ineffective. Brothels that were closed in one place opened in another, often as a karaoke shop or a massage parlor. Moreover, corruption and the involvement of the police and military in the sex sector helped many establishments to continue their services despite these measures. The failure of the crackdown policy, and concerns about the alarming rates of HIV, of which sex workers were thought to be the main transmitters, led the government to adopt a more pragmatic approach. At the end of 1998, the government started a pilot campaign in Sihanoukville requiring clients to use condoms with sex workers, with the idea to later extend the policy to Phnom Penh and the rest of the country. This so-called 100 percent condom-use strategy was copied from Thailand, where it had been implemented successfully eight years earlier. Although the strategy is focused especially on countering the threatening HIV/AIDS epidemic through cooperation between brothel owners, police and health officials, and customers and sex workers, it also serves to control sex establishments and the health situation of sex workers and, as such, is not unlike the measures imposed during the French protectorate.

The implementation of the strategy has not prevented authorities from tightening the restrictions on sex establishments. Out of concern for morality and security, Phnom Penh's governor, as well as the prime minister, has at times directed the closedown of brothels, karaoke shops and nightclubs, and the cleaning up of parks from which sex workers started to work after the closing down of sex establishments. It was not only the health, but also the reputation of Phnom Penh and the nation that was thought to be at stake. These concerns were strengthened due to reports about (child) sex tourists coming to Cambodia, who would allegedly move on from Thailand to benefit from the lower costs, weak law enforcement and adventurous thrills that are associated with a country still recovering from decades of war (e.g., Sok Hach et al. 2001; Thomas and Pasnik 2002; von Gyer 2005).

FORMS OF SEX WORK

Although governmental and municipal policies regarding sex work have definitely influenced the practices, it is much harder to estimate how they have influenced the number of women involved in the sex business. The reliability of estimates for the number of sex workers in Cambodia leaves much to be desired. Sensationalism and a lack of clear definitions have given rise to estimates ranging from fifteen thousand to one hundred thousand women involved in Cambodia's sex business.[3] Most of the sex workers and sex establishments can be found in Phnom Penh, where estimates also vary widely. A census conducted by Populations Services International (PSI) in 1998 counted 1,489 brothel-based sex workers in Phnom Penh (Chommie 1998). The Commission of Human Rights and Reception of Complaints counted, a year earlier, 8,022 brothel-based sex workers, while a more recent (and transparent) estimate found 5,250 sex workers in Phnom Penh (not only brothel-based) (Steinfatt et al. 2002).[4]

The enormous variations in the number of sex workers are related not only to sensationalist presentations of Cambodia's sex industry, but also to the ways in which the sex business operates. Sex work takes many different forms and occurs in many places. At the upper end of the scale are the high-class sex workers in nightclubs and bars catering to businessmen, government officials, expatriates and tourists. At the lower end are the brothel-based sex workers and hustlers who try to get some money for food by selling sex to cyclo drivers, construction workers or day laborers. In between there is a large gray area of sex-work practices, with sometimes very thin lines between what is called direct sex work, offered in brothels, and indirect sex work, such as those found in coin-rubbing places, massage parlors, karaoke shops, or under the guise of beer promotion work in restaurants. The measures taken to control or close down the sex business have led to ever-renewing forms and locations in which it takes place. Brothel keepers and karaoke shop owners have recently turned to beer gardens. Public parks have also become favorite spots to pick up clients, not only for the *srey krouc crobac* (literally "orange-pressing women"), or "orange girls" carrying small bags of oranges to sell, with possible additional sexual services, but also for young women working under the guidance of a *meebon* (brothel owner), a *taipan* (Chinese word for pimp), or independently.

Concomitant with the various ways in which sex work takes place are the terms that depict those working in the sex business. While there are also young men and transgenders, so-called *ktuiy*[5] or *srey sroh* (literally "fresh women"), working in bars, parks and brothels, the majority of the sex workers are female. The most common term for women in the sex business, *srey kouc,* is closely related to the moralities concerning female sexuality within the Cambodian context. The term *kouc* means "damaged" or "broken," but is also more generally used for disobedient children as well as for a deceased person. Yet, when applied to women *(srey),* the term *kouc* refers specifically to women who have had multiple sexual partners and is most commonly used for prostitutes. A *srey kouc* is thus a "broken" or "damaged" woman, one who has gone bad and is considered spoiled, physically and socially. Prostitutes are not only considered to be spoiled because of their sexual behavior, but also because they use a language, are active at times, occupy spaces and take liberties that are not open to "virtuous" women.[6]

There is a variety of other terms, such as *srey peesya*—from Sanskrit *vesya; srey sompheng*—"sluttish woman"; *srey pkaa mieh*—"golden flower girl"; *srey rook luy*—"woman who seeks money"; *srey bon*— "brothel girl"; *srey bar*—"bar girl"; *srey roam*—"dancing girl," for those who work in bars and nightclubs; or *srey kaliip*—"high-class girl," for those who are in the "upmarket" areas of the business. The negative connotations of the words used for a sex worker induced NGO workers to use a less stigmatizing term, *srey rook sii plew peet.* The term *rook sii,* literally "to find something to eat," means to do work to earn money, or to do business. A *srey rook sii plew peet* is thus a woman who

FIG. 4. Sex worker preparing for work

is earning money by way of sex. This term comes closest to the English term "sex worker," which came into use among feminists who were analyzing sex work in order to get away from the term "prostitute."[7] I have, however, hardly ever heard sex workers refer to themselves as a *srey rook sii plew peet.* More commonly they call themselves *srey kouc* or *srey luek kluen,* a "woman who sells her body."

SEX WORK AND ETHNICITY

As we have seen, for many Cambodians there is a clear link between prostitution and Vietnamese women. The involvement of the Vietnamese in Cambodia's sex industry is used in daily parlance to perpetuate certain stereotypes in relation to ethnic differences between Khmer and Vietnamese. This is connected to perceived differences in notions of female behavior and sexuality, as Khmer women are believed to maintain certain moral ideals that are considered to be different (or nonexistent) for Vietnamese women. Expectations regarding "proper" behavior therefore lead to the persistent idea that prostitution is "un-Khmer." The rationalization is, as Prasso (1995: 22) writes, that since "all Khmer women are virtuous, all prostitutes must be Vietnamese."

The idea that Vietnamese women are more frequently involved in sex work is also related to their appearance because they are considered to be very beautiful due to their whiter skin, and to their behavior, as they are considered less shy, and therefore more sexually skilled, than Khmer women. Tarr quotes, in her study about sexual behavior among young Cambodians, a twenty-two-year-old student who explained in detail how a Vietnamese sex worker actively seduced him and then noted: "I would never expect a Khmer girl to behave this way. If she did I know that she would be like the Vietnamese [. . .] you know that Cambodian women must not initiate lovemaking or demonstrate they know how to suck your cock or do other things with you. It is not our custom to permit such things to occur" (Tarr 1996: 91).

The common link between prostitution and Vietnamese women is further strengthened by local understandings of historical-political events. As noted before, Vietnamese women were active in sex work in Cambodia during colonial times. According to popular belief, in earlier times Vietnamese women were also used by the Vietnamese to subvert Cambodia. This is what is thought to have happened at the beginning of the seventeenth century when the Vietnamese king used his beautiful daughter to seduce King Chey Chestha II; the king's falling in love with and marrying the Vietnamese woman opened the way for Vietnamese to settle in the Mekong Delta and eventually occupy the area (Phnara 1974; Leonard 1996).[8] This belief in the "sordid use of young girls" by the Vietnamese forms a recurrent theme in visions of how the Vietnamese might try to take over Cambodian territory (Thion 1993: 47). With their seductive skills, Vietnamese women would easily convince border police to let them cross into Cambodia, and their overwhelming presence (especially as sex workers) could, according to some Cambodians, again lay the groundwork for a major Vietnamese takeover, or at least pose a threat to Cambodian culture and society (Chou Kim 1993).

Although statistical information on the number of sex workers and their ethnicity is inconsistent and unreliable, it does not give any support to such a conspiracy theory or fantasy regarding the influx of Vietnamese women as spies of a greater power.[9] In some brothel areas, such as Svay Pak,[10] sex workers are predominantly of Vietnamese origin, but Cambodian women formed the majority of the sex workers in the areas where I conducted my research. These areas had a few Vietnamese brothels operating next to a Cambodian brothel. Brothels in which both Vietnamese and Khmer women worked were exceptional.

This ethnic separation is often related to language barriers and the distinct social networks of which brothel owners and sex workers are part. Many brothel owners consider Vietnamese women not only more beautiful but also more hygienic, less ashamed, smarter and willing to work harder when it comes to earning money. This means that Vietnamese sex workers are ready and able to receive more customers per day and perform more diverse sexual practices than Cambodian sex workers, who are seen as lazy and more concerned about their honor *(ketteyuh)*. A brothel owner interviewed in Svay Rieng in 1997 as part of a study on the trafficking of Vietnamese women and children to Cambodia noted:

> The Vietnamese women don't worry about their honor, because they know that when they go back to Vietnam they will still become wives. It is very interesting, they earn money for a motorbike, or a new house, and when they get married they stop working here. [. . .] The Khmer women can't earn money, whereas the Vietnamese women can earn a lot of money, and after three or four months they go back to Vietnam. When they come back here again, they are refreshed and can receive a lot of customers. They can receive ten customers per day. For them the most important thing is to earn money, and they don't spend it. The Khmer women, after receiving two or three customers, are afraid and don't want to receive any more. The Khmer women spend all their money. In the end, only their body remains.

Vanna, a sex worker in Boulding, noted that, whatever a client wants, Vietnamese women will do it, like *sii caraem* (lit. "eat ice cream"; here meaning oral sex), whereas Khmer sex workers only want to have sex with customers "like husband and wife." She added, "even me, I have been a sex worker for a long time, but I am still shy."

Assertions about the differences between Vietnamese and Khmer sex workers can be heard among Khmer brothel owners and sex workers alike, who say they feel disadvantaged in the competition for clients. Rho, a brothel owner in Tuol Kork, argued that two Vietnamese women can earn as much as eight or ten Cambodian women. This is only partly explained by the actual preferences of customers; Vietnamese brothel keepers are also accused of actively using specific strategies in order to increase their own clientele at the expense of others. I have witnessed several arguments between Cambodian and Vietnamese brothel keepers accusing each other of unfair competition, such as by purposely fencing off the view of a neighboring brothel. Brothel keeper Rho once got into a foul temper when one of the workers in her brothel found a bag full of used sanitary napkins on the roof of the brothel. Rho immediately accused the Vietnamese brothel keeper two houses farther up the row of having thrown it onto her roof to send bad luck and prevent clients from entering her brothel.

These examples of the skills, working spirit and strategies of the Vietnamese are often more related to perceived ethnic differences between Khmer and Vietnamese than to real differences in their sex-work practices. They serve to reinforce the stereotype of the Vietnamese who will do anything for money with a clear goal and without any shame or fear of losing honor. This is related to the dominant belief among many Cambodians that Vietnamese women who were sex workers in Cambodia remain marriageable once they return to Vietnam. Khmer women, on the contrary, are described as victims of deception and exploitation, who have no idea how to get money out of such a dishonorable situation that makes them *srey kouc* forever. Such stereotypes, of course, have little to do with the actual experiences and strategies of the Cambodian sex workers I met in the course of my research.

ROUTES INTO SEX WORK

When I first met Melea in the Boulding brothel area, she took me by the hand to show me the karaoke-shop-cum-brothel where she worked, and "her" room a bit farther down the alley. With her loud and affectionate manner, and her tall, voluptuous body, which she accentuated with sexy clothing, high heels and lots of makeup, she seemed to represent the opposite of the stereotype of an ideal Khmer woman. Even in comparison to the other sex workers in the various brothels around, she stood out because of her outspokenness, a characteristic that made her the most obvious local candidate among the sex workers in her area to become *prothien-srey,* literally a "leader of women," within an NGO-supported effort to organize sex workers.

Melea was born in Kampong Cham during the Khmer Rouge regime after the *angkar*[11] had arranged the marriage of her parents. Theirs, like many other *angkar*-arranged marriages, split up as soon as the Khmer Rouge regime fell in 1979. Both her parents remarried and had children with their new spouses. Melea did not really feel at home in either of these newly formed families. She felt that her father's new wife wanted to separate her from her father: "She hates me because I am the daughter of his first wife." Her mother remarried a poor man who had a liking for gambling and drinking, leading to debts that forced Melea's mother to sell their small piece of land. Although Melea would have preferred to stay with her mother, she was afraid of her stepfather and knew that her mother did not have the means to support her and the rest of the family. She therefore moved on to live with her grandparents, and later with a nearby uncle and aunt, whom she helped prepare and sell rice porridge.

When Melea was about eighteen years old, she ran into problems with her uncle and aunt, with accusations flying back and forth about sexual harassment and stealing money. Melea decided to leave for Phnom Penh, where a friend of hers had found work as a domestic servant. Through her friend she found a family to work for, and earned 25,000 riel (about 6.5 US dollars) per month. When her father found out she had left for Phnom Penh, he came after her and took her back home, where he had arranged a partner for her to marry. Considering the fact that she felt at home nowhere, she agreed in order to establish one for herself: "I wanted to have happiness. Unfortunately, it did not turn out as I had thought." Soon after they got married, Melea found out that her husband had another wife and that she could do nothing to please either him or her mother-in-law with whom they lived. Only a few months after the wedding, Melea and her husband separated. Melea went back to Phnom Penh and visited her friend, who by then had found work in a bar, where Melea decided to work as well. She told me:

> My friend invited me to come and visit the shop where she sells beer. When I came to that place, she told me the real nature of her work. [...] Since I had a difficult time with my husband and since my

mother was very poor, I also tried to get this job. Nobody forced me. Really. I know that others often say that they were sold by someone. But I see that most sex workers here are not sold by their parents or their boyfriends. Out of ten girls, maybe only two are sold. Others are disappointed with their boyfriend and then decide to work as a sex worker. This is how I got involved in this work.

Melea's distinction between free choice and force in prostitution is a recurrent theme in discussions about prostitution. In that sense, sex work stands apart from other categories of work in which no similar fundamental disagreement exists as to the question of whether it can be seen as a job, which women may choose to enter, or whether women's involvement in this kind of work is principally related to force and male oppression. This fundamental disagreement has led to divergent analyses regarding prostitution. Such opposition between forced and voluntary prostitution, as Doezema (1998: 47) suggests, perpetuates the old division between the Madonna and the whore in the figure of the prostitute through a dichotomization between innocent victims (madonnas) and "fallen women," or free whores. In the Cambodian context, this means distinguishing, as one NGO worker did, between those women whose "nature" *(saaraciet)* it is to be a sex worker, such as Vietnamese women; and those women or girls who were unwillingly "sold" into prostitution, and are thus really still "good." While such a forced/voluntary dichotomy is commonly repeated in discussions about sex work, often in connection with trafficking, it does not promote a true understanding of the context or the diverse and, at times, contradictory experiences and interpretations of women's involvement in sex work.

BETWEEN CHOICE AND COERCION

The different routes into sex work are strongly related to many forms of mediation and networks, involving peers, parents or other family members, as well as brothel keepers and other people associated with the sex business. In earlier papers (Derks 1997, 2004), I distinguished among voluntary, involuntary and bonded ways of entering sex work in order to classify various routes. Such distinctions, I argued, make it possible to separate the experiences of individual women while exploring the structures that cause women to enter sex work. However, such distinctions are also hard to draw and may again lead to an undesirable dichotomization between so-called victims and "true" prostitutes. The experiences of Melea, Phea and Khim showed me that the shifting borders between the sex worker as agent, as the "ignorant girl" deceived into prostitution, or as the "sacrificing daughter" brought into debt bondage are related to changing perceptions of their situation.

Such perceptions cannot be detached from the idea that sex work, as the women I met argued, counters the ideals of the proper Khmer woman. Melea was very much aware of the stigma of sex work. She knew of a young woman from her village who worked in a brothel in Tuol Kork long before she came to Phnom Penh herself. She remembered that her mother had warned her not to talk to this person. "My mother told me that she is a woman who sells her body and warned me to be careful, or she would persuade me to do like her." It actually was not this woman but another friend who introduced Melea into sex work.

Melea's voluntary entrance into sex work does not mean that she made a free choice among economic alternatives. Economic opportunities in Cambodia's slowly modernizing economy are scarce, especially for women with little education. Other alternatives, such as factory work and street trade, are dependent on mediation and networks. But this is also true for sex work. Peer association, or relations with others in the sex business, function as important "strings" *(ksae)* through which young women get in contact with, and gain access to, sex work. Thus, "[a]n option not thought of before presents itself and a decision to try prostitution is made" (O'Neill 2001: 78). This decision may be stimulated by stories about the amount of money that can be earned or the "glamorous" lifestyle, with beautiful clothes, makeup and jewelry, which stand in strong contrast to the hard, poor farmer's life in the village, but also by factors such as abandonment by a husband or boyfriend, and economic needs.

As in other forms of employment, mediation and networks thus facilitate women's entry into sex work. In the case of the sex business, however, networks are frequently associated with direct forms of coercion. Forced prostitution, often subsumed under the term "trafficking," has during the past ten years been the focus of various media and activists' presentations on sex work. These presentations usually contain stories of girls and women lured, kidnapped, drugged, raped and subsequently sold into prostitution by brutal traffickers. By stressing violence, rape, drugs and the trade in women as commodities, sex workers are presented as "ignorant victims" forced into sexual slavery. What I often found, however, was a much more complex picture of the notions of force and freedom. Many young women left their homes deliberately in the hope of earning an income elsewhere, because of economic needs or aspirations, or maltreatment by parents, other relatives, a boyfriend, or a husband. Many women emphasize both their drive to escape their present situation and their "ignorance" in order to explain why they so easily agreed to go along with someone promising a well-paid job, a new adventure away from the village.

This is also how Phea explained her involvement in sex work. She was fourteen years old when she went to Phnom Penh with a neighbor from her village in Prey Veng to work in a brick and tile factory. There she met a woman who was "a *meekcol* [mediator] and was the one who cheated me. She told me that she knew a place in Srey Ambil where they needed someone to cook. The salary would be forty thousand riel per month. I agreed to come with her, because I know how to cook and I thought that the work would not be so tiring."

After Phea was brought to the house in Srey Ambil, the woman abandoned her with one thousand baht in her pocket, the fee she got from the house owner. During the first month Phea had an easy life; she had to do some cooking, but could spend the rest of the day sleeping and chatting with the daughters of the owner. She had enough food and fruit to eat. Her face became a bit fuller and her skin turned a little lighter. She was sent to have her hair cut in a more fashionable way and was given powder cream to apply on her face. She remembered, "I was pretty and loved myself at that time." After one month, Phea was introduced to a businessman as the new girl "fresh from the countryside." He was to be her first *pñiew* (guest, customer). She remembered how she was brought to a nearby hotel: "I first didn't know that I was being taken to *khui* [be deflowered].[12] When the client came into the hotel room, I started crying in front of him. He let me out and I ran back to the house where I stayed, but the owner kicked and hit me several times till my face was all swollen. [. . .] I was told that I was a prostitute from now on."

Phea's account of how she was "sold" and coerced into sex work relates to the involvement of the *meekcol,* who earned money by recruiting her, and the brothel keeper, who forced her at least initially into having sex with guests. After a first difficult time, she realized that, having lost her virginity already, she could just as well profit from the relatively high earnings in sex work and decided to "voluntarily" stay in the trade.

In the case of Khim it was her mother who led her into sex work. Khim's entrance was part of an agreement between her mother and the brothel keeper. Khim perceived her situation as the only way to help her mother out of misery and willingly agreed, because she was "broken already" *(kouc haey)*. Khim's mother had had a difficult time with her second husband. After she divorced, she was left by herself to earn money and support Khim and three younger children. She borrowed money to buy lotus and tried to sell it for a profit. The stiff competition among lotus sellers made it hard to make any money, and she fell even further into debt. Seeing no other way, she brought Khim and her other children to Phnom Penh. She negotiated with a brothel owner about the conditions under which Khim could work and earn enough to pay back the moneylender in their village. Khim and her mother saw this as a temporary situation, lasting no longer than two to three months, during which time Khim's mother and her three younger siblings stayed close to her in a rented place near the brothel.

Debt bondage thus can involve parents or associates who bring a child or young woman to a brothel keeper for promised employment in return for cash. Some have related this to a traditional practice in Cambodia in which bonded labor was used to repay a debt incurred either by the laborer or by an associate of the laborer, most often the youngest daughter (Delvert 1961: 518; Reynolds 1996). Muecke sees in this "historical practice of selling women," which can be found throughout Southeast Asia, an important precedent for the current practice whereby adults sell family members, particularly daughters, for economic gain (Muecke 1992: 892). This widespread existence of debt bondage in Southeast Asia is, according to Osborne (1995: 59), often misinterpreted as slavery. In theory at least, the debt-bonded persons had voluntarily given up their freedom and their position was subject to change once a debt had been met or an agreed period had elapsed (Osborne 1997: 8).

Debt bondage in prostitution does not necessarily involve a relative or mediator but is also a common practice in which sex workers engage themselves with brothel owners. Sex work, contrary to most other kinds of work, presents the possibility of getting money in advance, which has to be paid back later through work. The amount of money paid up front may vary from thirty to a thousand dollars, depending on the beauty of the woman and the kind of sex establishment. Melea had to work off a debt of a hundred and twenty dollars. Brothel keeper

Rho often extends smaller loans of about fifty dollars and seldom agrees to higher loans in the fear that she will lose money when women run off. Rho claims that most women in her brothel are indebted to her because they need money up front in order to pay off loans (often outstanding with other brothel keepers), pay the *motodup* or other *neak noam* (recruiter, bringer), and send money back home to support their families. The women usually pay off their debt within a few months, the conditions for repayment being calculated on the basis of a fixed "salary" of around thirty or forty dollars, or one *cii*[13] per month. The duration of the loan may be extended if women ask for additional money for clothes, medicine, or expenses.

Rho, like other brothel keepers, formalizes such loans by means of a contract, which certifies that the woman received a loan and voluntarily agrees to stay and *rook luy* (lit. "find money") to pay back the loan. This contract is a handwritten document with thumbprints, and is kept by the brothel keeper. An example of such a "contract to stay" *(ket-*

Kingdom of Cambodia
Nation, Religion, King

Contract to Stay

I [Ni], twenty years old, asked for a loan of 50 dollars from older sister [Rho] in group [. . .], village [. . .], Sangkat Tuol Sangkeo, Khan Tuol Kork.

I voluntarily came to stay in this house; there is nobody who forced me.

I promise to pay back the loan according to the possibility to earn.

I ask to put my thumbprint for evidence.

Day, 20-10-2000

Witness	Borrower
(thumbprint + name)	*(thumbprint + name)*

FIG. 5. "Contract to Stay"

sanayaa snak-new) is the one I hand-copied from Rho and translated into English as follows:

Contracts like these are morally binding. They declare the amount of money that has been borrowed, and especially the voluntary engagement of the sex worker with the brothel owner, but the nature of the work is not specified. It shows again the complexity in clearly demarcating choice and deception in sex work. These are not clear-cut categories, but subject to different interpretations. That makes it difficult to support any simple dichotomy between victims or agents who actively construct their lives, as it does no justice to the diversity of "worldviews and everyday experiences of Southeast Asian sex workers" (Law 2000: 11).

WORKING IN THE SEX BUSINESS

Sex workers differ in the ways they enter the business, and also in their social and economic appreciation, control over working conditions, individual experiences and adaptation to work among and within the various sex-work categories. Although these cannot be isolated from the moral dimensions, such differences may lie less in the nature of the work than in the social location of the worker performing it and the conditions under which the work takes place (Chapkis 1997: 57). The organization of the sex business, and the different forms in which sex work is practiced, play an important role, as they have a great impact on working conditions, including control by a third party (brothel keeper, pimp), exposure to physical abuse, protection against clients, financial rewards, and health issues that with the increase in AIDS have become particularly pressing.

The organization and forms of sex work, furthermore, play important roles in the social location of the sex worker. As we have seen, the different forms of sex work are hierarchically related. Status is assigned more to what the clients pay than to the amount sex workers can keep for themselves (see also Chapkis 1997). Networks, the manner and length of involvement in sex work, as well as the age and beauty of a woman, all have a great influence on her mobility within and between categories of sex work. Most sex workers, as they grow older, experience downward mobility and move to less prestigious and cheaper establishments, though often with increased control over their working conditions and freedom of movement.

Melea's experiences reflect this pattern. The bar where she started working was frequented by high-ranking officials and video stars who paid twenty or thirty dollars for a night with a sex worker. The money went directly to the bar owner. Every two weeks the manager would split the earnings in two, deducting money for food, telephone, laundry and other expenses, leaving Melea with up to seventy dollars per week. She remembered: "That place was very unlike Boulding where I work now. They gave us injections to make our skin look nice. They bought things for us, like makeup and beautiful clothes. [. . .] They told us to take care of our body. [. . .] It was very different from Boulding, where everything is dirty."

Melea worked in this bar for almost half a year, until the bar was closed by municipal order. Then she went back home and worked as a day laborer on the *chamkar* (garden farmland) of others, earning 3,500 riel (less than one dollar) per day. When there was no more work on the *chamkar*, she tried to make a living selling vegetables at the nearby market. However, profits were small and sometimes she lost money. Melea was unhappy to be back in the village, where some of her friends had gotten married, where she again had to confront her drunken stepfather, and her poor mother who had "nothing but ragged sarongs" to wear. If she started working as a sex worker again, she figured, she would be able to support herself and her family. She went back to Phnom Penh and started working in a small drink shop close to the bar in which she had worked before. She picked up customers in the drink shop and went out with them for sex. Once a customer took her to a "guest-house" in Boulding. This is how she met her next employer, a woman who had several young women under her guidance as dancing girls in a nightclub. Melea worked for about a year in this nightclub until she ran away, without collecting her share, to escape the woman's scolding and abuse. She went to the owner of a karaoke-shop-cum-brothel in Boulding and asked her if she could stay with her.

For Melea, working in a brothel in Boulding meant a drop in status from working in the bar where she had begun. In Boulding, clients pay only five thousand riel (1.3 dollars) for sexual intercourse in a brothel room. In Boulding, Melea also had to receive many more customers per night. These were not high-ranking people but mostly junior officials, students, *motodup* and construction workers. The setting was less glamorous. The room in which Melea performed her sexual labor was much like the rooms in other brothels in Boulding and Tuol Kork.

Typically such rooms are built in houses made of cheap wood with corrugated roofs, often in bad shape. Inside there are rows of small, dark rooms, separated from each other by wooden boards. The rooms have just about enough space for a bed with a red sheet, a small stool with a fan, and a small red light. Clothes, plastic bags with makeup articles and sometimes a mirror hang next to HIV/AIDS prevention posters, Thai film stars and Number One Condom stickers that decorate the thin wooden walls.

Although there are major differences among sex workers in different establishments, all those I met maintain that the economic returns compare favorably to those of other kinds of workers. The amount of money that can be received up-front serves as an important stimulus for women working in the sex industry. Melea pointed out that "As a sex worker, I can get some money, and save some. When I work in a factory and I need money quickly, for example because my mother is sick, I will not be able to get it. I can only get my money at the end of the month. We cannot just borrow money from someone. [. . .] In a factory, I can earn forty dollars per month and give the sum to my mother. Then there will be nothing left for me to buy new clothes or to buy something to eat."

Sex workers in brothels live on the money agreed upon with their *meebon.* They also receive tips from clients. These are used for snacks and other small purchases, so that monthly earnings can be kept as savings. It is on this basis that Lim (1998: 17), in her study of the "sex sector" in Southeast Asia, argued that from an economic perspective the conditions of sex work could be considered reasonably good, as take-home income tends to be higher than what the women could expect to earn in the other occupations open to them.

The share of earnings women can "take home" is dependent on the agreements between a brothel keeper and her sex workers. Many sex workers are in some way indebted to their brothel keeper, and the ways of paying back may differ even between sex workers within the same brothel. In some cases, a fixed amount of "salary" is agreed upon, *sii khae* or *prak-khae.* This fixed amount was, for most of the sex workers I knew, set at the value of one *cii,* and then they received food and lodging without charge from the brothel keeper. For this "salary," women are expected to receive at least three customers per day. The days when they entertained fewer customers were not counted, so that monthly calculations could extend into the next month for those missed days out. The pressure to receive a certain number of customers per day is somewhat less for those who rent a room *(cuel bantup)* inside a brothel, or who split the earnings *(way-ceak)* with the brothel owner. In the latter agreement, the brothel keeper and the sex worker may both keep account of the daily earnings. At the end of the month the total amount of earnings is split into two. The advantage of a "salary" over renting a room is that the brothel keeper provides a room and food for free. The sex workers remain, however, under the strict control of the brothel keeper.

Sex workers who rent a room inside a brothel are under less strict control and are called "independent women" *(srey 'aekariec)*. They usually remain in a brothel area, through which they can take advantage of the protection they can expect in such an environment. Yet they work more or less for themselves and have more freedom to move. This may allow for a certain degree of independence regarding the organization of work, but does not release them from the pressure to receive a sufficient number of customers to cover their daily expenses for living and the rent of five-to-six thousand riel per day. Although only a minority of the women in brothels work independently, brothel owners have now turned increasingly to renting out rooms in order to circumvent the policies regarding the closing down of brothels as well as demands of police and local officials who cream off much of the profit they receive from running a "regular" brothel.

COMPETING FOR CUSTOMERS

Brothel areas like Tuol Kork and Boulding cater for customers throughout the day and night, and sex workers are expected to be available. This means that they may work long hours, much of it spent waiting for customers (see also Lim 1998). The evening is the most active part of the day. Preparations start after an afternoon nap, when the *meebon* orders the women to get up, wash and prepare for work. A real metamorphosis takes place when the women start putting on makeup, exchanging creams, colors and small hand mirrors among themselves.

The clothes and makeup are a major source of investment that sex workers have to make in order to achieve a "professional" appearance. Sex workers often buy these items themselves with extended loans from brothel owners, but the brothel keeper may provide some essential makeup and clothing, which has to be shared among women in the brothel. This sharing applies in some cases also to the rooms in which women rest and work. For example, brothel keeper Rho for a while had six women share four rooms. The women had to take turns using these rooms and, as Mom, a sex worker, stressed, "agree with one another that, after having sex, we should not make the mattress dirty." She explained that "sometimes customers wash themselves after having sex and then sleep on the mattress, making it wet. When another customer comes, he cannot know it is only water, but thinks it is sperm."

Sex workers in the same brothel cooperate in attracting customers, for example by jointly calling out to customers, but they also compete over them. More customers mean more earnings, but also entail a loss of energy. Mom noted about her colleague Peou: "Peou gets a lot of men, but she always complains that she has lost her strength. I told her that it is because she receives so many men. I told her not to be so ambitious *(looplen)*."

While Mom was concerned about rather than envious of Peou, competition over customers, especially regular ones *(mooy)*, can sometimes lead to arguments. Sex workers often have one or more *mooy* with whom they build up an intimate relationship and from whom they expect an extra tip or gift. A *mooy* who goes to another sex worker in the same brothel can become a continuing cause of jealousy and fights. This enmity may be expressed in various ways, such as throwing away another's makeup or refusing to talk, but also in more direct acts of aggression. Melea, for example, once stormed out of her room where she had had an argument with her *sangsaa* (boyfriend) and shouted at the women in front of the brothel that she wanted to know which of them had told him that she had many boyfriends. She threatened that if she found out, she would take a razor blade and cut out the guilty person's clitoris.[14]

Such arguments among sex workers not only affect their interrelationships but also the atmosphere in a brothel. Brothel owners want to maintain harmonious relations among their workers in order to assure the flow of customers and income; but they may also use other means to influence this flow. This is especially apparent during the late afternoon, when the sex workers prepare for the evening while brothel keepers spray some water or scatter some rice in front of the brothel and into its doorway to attract customers for the night. Also, incense sticks are burned and leaves of tamarind attached to the doorway, while sometimes even more powerful measures are marshaled to increase the number of customers. Brothel owner Rho, after several quiet days, decided to visit a *kruu Cham* (Cham traditional healer) and ask him to increase

FIG. 6. Sex workers waiting for clients

her success in business. He prepared several papers covered with magical signs and arcane writing for her to take back home. One of the papers was folded and tied with a thread, and Rho stuck this inside a fissure between the wooden planks above the doorway of the brothel. She distributed the other papers to each of the women, who burned them in their own rooms, wafting the smoke over the bed and leaving the ashes underneath. The final two papers were burned and the ashes put in water, which was then sprinkled in front of the house, and from there leading into the house toward each room. Finally, Rho burned incense sticks and placed them at several spots inside and outside the house, after which all the necessary preparations were made for the evening, and the women from her brothel were summoned to sit outside and call out to potential customers driving along the road. When asked a few days later, Rho claimed that she had seen an increase in the number of guests visiting her brothel. This was also confirmed by some of the sex workers who, convinced of the efficacy of the ceremonial papers prepared by the *kruu Cham,* later went to visit him on their own.

MATRON–CLIENT RELATIONSHIPS

Although there are women who work independently, the organization of the sex business is to a great extent dependent on the involvement of a pimp *(taipan)* or brothel keeper *(meebon)* who controls the sex workers and receives the major part of the earnings from their work. Brothel keepers are usually referred to as *mcah pteah* (house owner), *mcah haang* (shop owner), or *thawkae* (boss; owner of a store) and are mostly women. The relationship between the brothel keeper and the prostitutes is one of mutual dependency. A *meebon* cannot earn money without the women who work for her, and she uses many different ways to make them dependent on her. The dependency is clear from the term used in employing them, *ceñcem,* "to nourish," which implies almost a parent–child relationship. The brothel keeper does indeed provide food and shelter for the women in her brothel and refers to "her" women as *srey ceñcem,* a phrase similar to *koun ceñcem,* or adopted child. In addition to the loans made in advance, the brothel keeper may provide money for medicine, clothes, and police protection, which add to the financial obligations of the women toward her. In some cases, brothel keepers can "rescue" women who have been deceived or mistreated by other *meebon,* or by clients, or for those who have fallen into the hands of police. In such cases the *meebon* becomes a kind of matron figure, which is also expressed by the familial terms that sex workers use for their *meebon,* such as *bong* (older sister) or more commonly *mae* (mother). Mom refers to Rho as her *bong:* "It is not very difficult to live with *bong* Rho, but her speech is sometimes very harsh. She sometimes scolds and blames, but afterwards it is okay again. [. . .] Sometimes she asks us to call out for customers when she sees that we are chatting and not calling customers. Then she tells us to get to work. When we have customers, we also get money. If we don't call customers, we get nothing to eat." Whereas Rho uses harsh language and restricts food to discipline the women in her brothel, these are other brothel keepers who do not allow their sex workers to rest until they have received at least five customers. Some, as in the case of Phea's first brothel owner, may resort to violent means to assure obedience.

The control that brothel keepers exercise also extends to determining workers' freedom of movement more generally. Indebtedness leads to sex workers being kept under strict control, especially in the first weeks after their arrival. It is not uncommon to see brothels with newly acquired women locked in from outside during the quiet noon hours, to prevent their running away. Brothel keepers also hire people, usually men, to hang around and keep an eye on the women.

In Rho's brothel, women change about every two months. Although this also served the purpose of providing variation for customers, not all the women left in agreement with Rho. Thierry, for example, ran away two and a half months after she arrived. The immediate cause was an argument she had with Rho, who accused her of keeping the money from the customers she had entertained during one evening. Thierry had borrowed two *cii* of gold when she arrived, and later took on another, smaller loan to buy some clothes. Rho claimed that Thierry was still in debt to her and went looking for her to take her back. When I met Thierry by coincidence in Boulding, she told me that she had worked so much that she had already paid back all her loans. She was sure that her new brothel keeper in Boulding would protect her if Rho ever dared come to take her back, because she knew that "the *meebon* here are very strong."

The "strength" of brothel keepers does not refer to physical force, but to the kind of protection they can rely on to maintain their business. Most brothel keepers can "rely on the skin" *(aang sbeak)* of police or military officials, whereby the "skin" symbolizes their uniform and concomitant position of authority. The more stripes, or the higher the rank of the "skin" of such a protector, the better chance a brothel keeper has of remaining in business even when a crackdown threatens to destroy it. These relationships between brothel keepers and local or higher authorities—like the *ksae* bringing young rural women into urban work—rely on village, marriage, or family ties, or on gestures aimed at assuring good terms with them, such as an occasional box of beer or free sex with one of the sex workers in their brothel.

VICES, VIRUSES AND VOICES

In a speech prepared for the Cambodian Prostitutes' Union for the

National Conference on Gender and Development in Cambodia, Chan Dina, a sex worker from Tuol Kork, addressed the most pressing issues that she saw confronting herself and sex workers like her:

> I am a post Khmer Rouge child
> But was a slave
> I was forced to work against my choice
> My body is tortured
> I am full of pain
> I am not a citizen
> I am not a person
> You see me as a virus
> I am invisible
> Your eyes do not see me
> You hate me
> You blame me
> Some of you pity me
> I do not want your pity
> I do not want your charity
> I want my rights
> Not your lies and abuses
> (Chan Dina 1999)

The urgency of issues like trafficking, sexual exploitation, and AIDS has caused the government and local authorities, as well as local and international organizations, to focus on prostitution in Cambodia. The sex workers I talked to, however, did not necessarily identify the sex trade or health concerns as most disconcerting to their daily lives, but police harassment and disrespect.

SEX AND THE STATE

The official treatment of prostitution in Cambodia is strongly related to the political history of the country, with different regimes applying different approaches to the existence, regulation, or suppression of prostitution. Moral concerns have played a consistent role, and still do so today. Prostitution, according to Mop Sarin, assistant governor of Phnom Penh, is a vice that has no place within the precious culture and tradition of Cambodia. In 1999, he stated that "[c]itizens of the Royal Government of Cambodia have a precious culture and tradition and

they regard prostitution as a crime which [. . .] society hates very much"
(Mop Sarin 1999).

Some years earlier, the government adopted a law on the "Suppression of the Kidnapping and Trafficking/Sales of Human Persons and
the Exploitation of Human Persons." The law largely follows the provisions set in the 1949 UN Convention, which prohibits pimping and
other forms of profiting from prostitution, but not prostitution as such.
Thus, although sex workers are not criminalized, procuring, debauch-
ery, benefiting from prostitution, or the exploitation of the prostitution
of others, as well as child prostitution and forced prostitution, are all
criminal offenses, punishable by imprisonment of five to twenty years.
The orders of Phnom Penh's governor to crack down on brothels and
immoral acts committed by teenagers selling sex in parks are presented
as part of an effort to enforce this law. Melea recalled how the drink
shop in which she worked was closed down by the police: "They said
that if we continued running this shop, they would arrest the shopkeeper and send her to prison for ten to fifteen years. They would take
the girls and put them on display for all to see that they worked in this
service. In reality, the police just wanted to have money, thirty dollars
per girl." As Melea points out, the crackdowns often mean that in practice sex workers are arrested and kept in custody until they pay a fine,
while the brothel keepers get away.

Earlier raids and crackdowns led many brothels to function as karaoke shops, massage parlors, or coin-rubbing places. This induced the
prime minister to attack the vices and crimes that take place in these
establishments. His interventions, together with the complete destruction of the squatter area at Boulding, including the various brothels
inside and around the squatter area, contributed to a major increase in
the number of sex workers who look for customers in Phnom Penh's
public parks. The nightly raids that police conduct, driving with pickup
trucks through the parks, catching as many "suspected" sex workers as
possible and taking them to the police station, do not seem to be very
effective in suppressing sex work. As long as the various actors continue
to benefit a great deal from the incomes, profits and services offered
in Cambodia's sex business, new forms and places will continue to be
found.

SEX WORK IN A TIME OF AIDS
Another policy directed at sex work is linked to the spread of HIV/

AIDS. After the first zero-positive case was detected in 1991, the spread of HIV/AIDS increased dramatically, leading to concerns about an AIDS epidemic threatening to decimate Cambodia's population. With 42.6 percent HIV zero-prevalence among brothel-based sex workers in 1998 (UNAIDS 2000), sex workers in Cambodia, as elsewhere in Southeast Asia, became designated as "victims and agents of the spread of HIV/ AIDS" (Law 2000: 33).[15] For this reason, a majority of the efforts to interrupt the high levels of HIV transmission focused on sex workers. The declining percentages of HIV-positive sex workers (20.8 percent in 2003) does indeed suggest that this group has been well covered by interventions (National Aids Authority of Cambodia 2005).

One of these interventions is the above-mentioned 100 percent con-dom-use policy, which aims at the regulation of sex work by stimulating cooperation between brothel managers and health officials and promot-ing education and mandatory monthly sexually transmitted infection (STI) checkups for sex workers. Critics have pointed out, however, that a government policy based on cooperation with brothel keepers will be counterproductive if the government at the same time cracks down on their establishments. Such measures encourage brothel keepers to move into indirect forms of sex work, thus withdrawing from the regulations and cooperation that are necessary for a proper implementation of this policy.

Several local NGOs and international health organizations have developed initiatives regarding HIV/AIDS awareness and condom dis-tribution, reaching out directly to sex workers. Educational sessions in which groups of sex workers are informed about the ways in which HIV is transmitted and how to use a condom, complete with a wooden penis onto which a few selected women are, with much giggling, invited to put a condom, are part of the HIV/AIDS-awareness strategies aimed at sex workers. After one such session, a sex worker explained her understanding of AIDS by referring to the colors purple and blue. First one contracts *svaay*, meaning "mango" and also "purple," a term that in Khmer is commonly used to refer to any sexually transmitted dis-ease. When one does not cure *svaay*, it will start to itch, and then one can contract *khiew*, meaning "blue," which she had deduced from the notion of *hiew*, as HIV is pronounced in Khmer. In her own way, she had adapted the terms and associations of AIDS to her own understand-ing of sexually transmitted diseases, in which local concepts play an important role.[16]

The many HIV/AIDS prevention and surveillance initiatives caused sex workers and their managers to lose sight of the objectives and benefits of the different groups and activities. One brothel owner expressed frustration with the organizations that come to the brothels asking the same questions about condom use, even though the sex workers have the feeling that these add nothing more to what they already know. Although the intensifying of these activities may well have contributed to an increased awareness of how to prevent HIV, health officials and other involved parties recognize that actual behavioral change is more difficult when sex workers do not possess the negotiation skills and conditions necessary to convince customers to use a condom.

The non-use of condoms can, however, as Law (2000) argues, not be simply attributed to a lack of negotiation power and the oppressive nature of the business. As has also been pointed out in many contexts, sex workers do not always insist on using condoms with regular customers or boyfriends. This may be even more likely when HIV/AIDS campaigns, such as those in Cambodia, have successfully connected AIDS as well as condom use with prostitution. This has not only changed sexual practices, as clients now more often turn to women other than brothel-based sex workers, but also has affected the meaning of condoms. Through its association with commercial sex, the use of condoms is considered to impede feelings of intimacy and trust that sex workers seek to create with some of their *mooy*, and that may ultimately lead to an opportunity to exit the sex industry (Law 2000: 53). It is therefore differences in the meanings attached to personal and work-related sexual relationships, not frequency of sexual encounters, that play a role in considerations regarding condom use (Zalduondo 1999: 316).

CHANGING SEX WORK(ERS)

The measures taken in relation to sex-work practices rest, on the one hand, on the image of the sex worker as an immoral person who poses a major threat to public health and, on the other hand, on the concept of sex workers as victims of patriarchal and capitalist structures, risking an early death due to HIV/AIDS infection for profit. In general, less attention is focused on the impact such measures have on the actions and reactions of sex workers themselves.

Due to the crackdowns on sex-work establishments, sex workers have been forced to adapt and find ways to resist the new conditions. After the demolition of the Boulding squatter area, sex workers turned

to the parks, and confronted a new set of problems. The immediate
protection by brothel keepers and guards against clients who use force,
refuse to pay or use condoms had fallen away. Several sex workers from
Boulding who had resorted to working from the park near the independence monument had experienced how this made them more vulnerable
to exploitation. They told me about customers who took one of them
to a guesthouse where ten or more friends were waiting to have sex
with her for the price of one,[17] or customers who did not even bother
to rent a room in a guesthouse but forced them to have sex in a park or
an open field. Yet, over time, the sex workers started using tricks when
they thought they were unsafe. They would, for example, let a shoe
fall when sitting on the back of a motorbike of a customer heading for
an unknown direction in order to force him to stop and be able to run
away. Or they would refuse all along to go to places that their, especially
young, customers nicknamed "moonshine guesthouse," "banana farm
guesthouse," or "landscape guesthouse," but are in fact open spaces
outside Phnom Penh.

Sex workers have also learned to deal with police raids. Although
simply running away is still the most common reaction to the sight of
a police car, some women carry a sarong that they can quickly put on
over their work clothes in order to look like "normal" women. Vanna
referred to such tricks for dealing with the police as *kruu kaac, seh
kouc,* "when the teacher is strict, the student becomes naughty." Sex
workers struggle to adapt to and deal with the difficult circumstances
under which they practice their work, and which determine the profits
that can be made. As Phea noted: "This job is not permanent. We can
only earn a lot of money when we are still young and pretty, but when
we get older it is less than nothing. But the job is not worthless, because
I use my own energy and labor to earn money. I am just very angry with
the police, because they always come to arrest us and release our names
to the media. Why do they do that? It is only because they want money
from us. If we give them some money, they let us go." Phea points
toward some important factors that condition prostitution in Cambodia. The temporariness of work in the sex business is related to ideals
of youth and beauty, which also determine the profits of a sex worker's
"energy and labor." Obviously many interested parties demand a share
of the profit.

The question of who profits and in what way from prostitution
underlies diverse positions regarding the interconnections between

prostitution and exploitation. The question of whether to see sex work as work or not also has consequences for the possible ways to address exploitation in prostitution, either by improving conditions within existing structures or by eliminating these structures altogether. The latter calls for raids and rescue operations of underaged and trafficked sex workers. Such operations have, however, been strongly criticized by those working to improve conditions within existing structures while aiming to put an end to exploitation and coercion. The process requires carefully building up relationships with brothel keepers; these fall back into the sphere of mistrust and noncooperation after raids have taken place, and concern not only efforts regarding HIV/AIDS education and the provision of medical services, but also empowerment activities for sex workers.

The concept of "empowerment" plays an important role in international and national initiatives regarding sex workers' rights. It also guides the initiatives taken by some NGOs in Cambodia that try to organize sex workers to allow them to "speak out," take more control of their lives, and resolve problems regarding their individual situations as well as their position in Cambodian society. To do so, these organizations set up sex workers' meetings and engage in activities regarding HIV prevention, negotiation skills with clients, solidarity among sex workers, and saving schemes to accumulate capital for the future. These initiatives thus aim to introduce prostitute networks based on new social and economic principles.[18]

In one such initiative by a local NGO, Melea was elected as *pro-thien-srey* of the sex workers in Boulding. She saw it as her task to explain to newcomers about AIDS and condom use, and to show the facilities available to sex workers if they get sick. The meetings also inspired her to think about the agreements with brothel keepers regarding the earnings from sex work. As most women in brothels get a fixed amount per month, *sii khae* or *prak-khae*, sex workers lose much of the money they earn to the brothel keeper. Melea thus tried to convince her colleagues to share the actual earnings with the brothel keeper.

Although Melea wanted to improve the conditions of sex workers, including herself, her case shows how initiatives that try to organize the workers are also hindered by the women's own capacities for negotiation and self-determination. Melea's own plan, to pay off her loan with the brothel keeper as soon as possible and then rent out rooms herself to sex workers who, after the payment of a fixed room rent, could work independently, was never realized. Before having paid back the loan, Melea ran off with her *sangsaa,* and although the brothel keeper went to look for them in several brothel areas in Phnom Penh, Melea and the money she had borrowed remained lost. Maybe Melea had decided to move on to a better situated and serviced establishment. Maybe she had gone back to her village. Or perhaps Melea and her *sangsaa* left for somewhere else, trying to make a living together and settle down as husband and wife. I never found out what had happened to them.

As we have seen, the experiences of sex workers are more diverse and complex than the stereotypical presentations that are dominant in the media, organizations, and most literature about prostitution. Sex workers have come into contact with different and changing forms of sex work due to their own mobility as well as the influence of national policies and the spread of AIDS. They have also encountered different forms or degrees of coercion as they have entered the business through various routes led by peers, family members, or middle(wo)men. Their diverse experiences also influence their self-presentations, as either self-conscious sex workers like Melea, ignorant girls deceived into prostitution like Phea, or sacrificing daughters brought into debt bondage like Khim. Women's perceptions of sex work, however, are fluid and change as they move between establishments, extend their personal networks, and become older. Faced with a downward mobility, with matrons and others skimming off their profits, as well as with the temporary nature of and stigma attached to prostitution, sex workers seek to maximize their situational advantage in ways that may run counter to the efforts of organizations to set up new networks and introduce new economic principles but that may, at the same time, defy victimization.

Street Trade   6

The sounds, smells, colors, tastes and bustle of city life in Phnom Penh owe much to the activities of traders vending their products in markets, small shops, stalls, and on the streets and sidewalks. Already by early morning, calls of *numpan* (bread) can be heard in the quiet streets as vendors with baskets full of fresh bread cycle through the city. By then, small breakfast places also appear at the sides of streets selling *bobo* (rice porridge), *baay-moan* (rice with chicken), or *kuy-tiew* (noodle soup). The stalls disappear when urban residents start work, but a whole range of snacks, meals and other food remains available throughout the day. Sellers offer their products at strategic locations, many of them by walking along the streets in residential areas, at bus and taxi terminals, the riverfront, Wat Phnom and other tourist or leisure destinations. Here one can see children pushing small, colorful carts loaded with sugarcane or cool boxes of soft drinks; young women balancing large plates of fruit, sweets, lotus beans, fried crickets and other snacks on their heads; and other, mostly female, traders carrying baskets filled with noodles, cooked eggs, or coconuts on shoulder poles. Besides different kinds of food, mobile vendors also peddle sunglasses, caps, scissors, newspapers and books, hammocks, or doormats along the streets. Those with a fixed location spread their goods—from clothes and household items to vegetables and fruit—on mats or in baskets on the streets outside markets and factories. In early evening, when regular markets and shops close, the streets remain bustling with life, with vendors offering a variety of street foods to hungry urban residents. Among those are the famous *tik-kralok* sellers, who prepare fresh fruit-shakes until midnight. By then, most residential areas have grown quiet again, only to be disturbed by the approaching sound of the wooden *tok-tok* announcing the noodle cart bringing a late evening meal.

Although men as well as women engage in these forms of trading, women clearly dominate as vendors in the streets, markets and shops. With the recent demographic and economic developments in Phnom Penh, the possibilities and locations for these activities have increased considerably. This is especially important for female migrants from the countryside, for whom trade is often the most accessible niche in which they can generate an income.

TRADES AND TRADERS

The involvement of women in trade in Cambodia is not a new phenomenon. Trade, especially small-scale trade, in both urban and rural areas in much of Southeast Asia has been an activity through which women traditionally contribute cash to the household economy (Boserup 1970; Heyzer 1986). As early as 1296–1297 the Chinese envoy Zhou Taguan (1993: 43) noted that "in Cambodia it is the women who take charge of trade." For this reason, he noted, a Chinese immigrant should lose no time in getting himself a Cambodian wife in order to profit from her "commercial instincts."

This pattern continued for centuries. Trading activities in Cambodia were predominantly in the hands of female vendors and Chinese or Sino-Khmer merchants. Whereas small-scale trade and small markets in the countryside were largely dominated by Cambodian women, Chinese traders—often with the support of their Cambodian wives—were active in a broader range of trading, from wholesale and intermediary forms to market trading, shopkeeping and the running of food stalls (Ledgerwood 1992; Edwards 1996). During the French colonial time, Chinese were even actively welcomed to Cambodia in order to compensate for the "obvious disinclination" of (male) Cambodians to engage in commerce (Osborne 1997: 251–252). Commercial activities came to a temporary halt after the Khmer Rouge took power and abolished markets and money, but trading structures were rebuilt during the 1980s: observers found markets that provided, besides basic elementary items such as foodstuffs and household goods, all sorts of consumer goods smuggled in from Thailand and Vietnam (Vickery 1984: 255; Thion 1993: 114; Gottesman 2003). Trade became an important means for enabling urban households, especially new settlers and low-salaried officials, to survive (Martin 1994: 267). Trade has by now become the second largest employment category in the country, after agriculture. Women predominate, about twice as many as men working in trade.

In the urban areas this is even more apparent, as almost one-third of the women in urban areas are involved in trade (National Institute of Statistics 2005b).[1]

This is especially visible in Phnom Penh. Within its markets *(psar)* various traders and forms of trading come together, connecting traders to each other and to buyers within a range of social and economic practices. Alexander (1998: 206–207) speaks in this respect of a *"pasar* system," which is not necessarily confined to the market space itself.[2] While the market symbolizes the center of this *pasar* system—or, in the Cambodian context, *psar* system—many other forms of trade radiate from it, involving a broad spectrum of products and people. In Phnom Penh's markets, one can observe how markets connect farmers bringing their fresh products with wholesalers, who then resell to retail traders, who are again connected with urban-based stallholders as well as migrant street traders. The hustle and bustle of these layers of buyers and vendors also attracts people not directly involved in trading and buying, such as young people who spend their free time hanging around in the markets, or war-affected amputees begging for money. The market space, as Banwell (2001: 15) observed, forms, in a way, a "microcosm of life in Cambodia."

Phnom Penh has thirteen major markets and several smaller street markets. Psar Thmey, or New Market (also known as Central Market), is the most distinctive one. The yellow dome with four wings was built between 1935 and 1937 under the French protectorate according to an architectural design adapted to the rationalist, hygienic standards of the time (Blancot and Hetreau-Pottier 1997: 38). The market, then the largest market in Indochina, was built at the center of Phnom Penh's commercial quarter (ibid. 1997: 33). The area around Psar Thmey is still the center of commercial life. The shops located around the market, decorated with Chinese and Khmer signs, specialize in electronics, gold, and more recently in mobile phones and computers. The market itself offers a broad range of products, from meat, fish, vegetables and ready-made meals, to clothes, shoes, and jewelry, and from books, household utensils and flowers to electronics, silk and souvenirs. The market is divided up into different areas, each of them dominated by specific smells, sounds and colors. Mobile vendors move between these different areas, offering snacks, hammocks, or old Cambodian coins to vendors, buyers and tourists alike.

Within large indoor markets such as Psar Thmey, Psar Olympic, and the more recently renovated Psar O'Russey, vendors have their own, rented or purchased, stalls from which they sell a variety of goods directly to buyers. Psar Tuol Tumpong, or Russian Market, is well-known among tourists because, besides the sections with regular goods and foodstuffs, it has a large section with souvenirs, silk, and bootleg movies and CDs. The big outdoor markets of Psar Damkor and Psar Chbah Ampeu function especially as wholesale and resale markets for fresh foodstuffs. These markets are active throughout the day and night. Farmers or middlemen bring their products there in the middle of the night, which are then purchased by vendors in the early morning to sell during the day. Psar Tuol Sangkeo—also called Psar Touc, or Little Market—is a smaller market on the fringes of the city, close to where I lived. This market has a roof of corrugated iron and tent material under which the owners or renters of stalls and small shops sell food and household items throughout the day. Market activity extends, in the mornings, to the surrounding streets where vendors spread their products on the ground. Most of these vendors are not able to afford to rent a stall inside the market and sell small quantities of vegetables, meat, fish, or fruit from a basket *(kañcraeng)*.

Entrepreneurial activities also take place on the streets. Street traders offer gasoline, cigarettes and toys, but also meals, snacks, fruits and vegetables from almost every street corner. Much of this street trade is small-scale, but it forms an important source of income for those engaged in it and provides urban residents with an array of products, including nutritious and affordable meals. While women's involvement in trade extends well beyond such small-scale street trade, their obvious dominance in these activities is considered to be a "distinctive feature of the [Southeast Asia] region" (Yasmeen 2001: 92).

This gender distinction also relates to the types of traders.[3] Khmer distinguish between *neak cumnueñ*, middlemen who are involved in wholesale and distribution of goods, and *neak luek-dou,* those involved in more direct, localized trading. The former functions are usually associated, especially when conducted on a large scale, with Chinese or Sino-Khmer merchants; whereas women's involvement in trade is more commonly associated with *luek-dou.* The term *luek-dou* literally means "sell-change" and also indicates barter. Money is now commonly used in trade, but this has not always been the case, and until relatively recently, especially in the countryside, rice used to be an important measure and means of exchange in daily interactions. The term *neak luek-dou* usu-

FIG. 7. Street market in Phnom Penh

ally refers to independent traders with a relatively small capital outlay, but as such does not indicate the scale or value of trading. Besides differences in scale, differentiations between *neak luek-dou* also relate to the forms of trade, as they differ for market traders, stallholders or street traders, traders with a fixed location or itinerant vendors, and seasonal or regular traders.

In her study on female retail traders in Phnom Penh, Kusakabe (2003: 32) links such differences to ethnic and social characteristics.

She found that the kinds of trading in which female traders engage can be linked to differences in family backgrounds. She distinguishes among female traders from "business families," mostly Sino-Khmer, who sell nonperishable goods such as watches, shoes and clothes in shop-houses or market stalls; female traders from "government officers' families," whose trading activities resemble those of business family traders, but for whom trade is a subsidiary activity, as more importance is attached to maintaining the social status gained by their husband's occupation; female traders from "small vendor families" who sell perishable goods such as vegetables, fish and meat at markets and conduct business as their way of life; and, at the lower end of the scale, the traders from "manual labor families," who are mostly street traders or itinerant sellers with a farming background, many of them new migrants to the city. This last group is the focus of my study.

WOMEN IN TRADING

The dominant role of Southeast Asian women in trade has been discussed in the literature as an indication of their relatively autonomous position, their lower spiritual potency and status, as an indication of their entrepreneurial skills and domestic responsibility as well as of their relegation to the informal sectors of the economy for survival (Brenner 1995; Yasmeen 2001; Seligmann 2001). These contradictory positions are related to interacting spheres of life that are affected by gendered ideologies, economic structures and political processes, and also by women's own agency.

The important economic role played by women in the household as well as in trade has contributed to the view of Southeast Asian women as relatively autonomous and holding high status. Yet several authors have pointed out that this dominant role in economic-entrepreneurial activities does not necessarily bring the greatest "prestige" (Errington 1990). As Kirsch (1985: 303) argues, women's specialization in economic-entrepreneurial activities can be related to the idea that women are perceived as being more deeply rooted in worldly attachments, which does not have positive value in Theravada Buddhism and would thus explain the lower position assigned to them within the moral and social hierarchies in countries like Thailand or Cambodia.[4] Such an interpretation would also fit the case of traders from government officers' families, where family status is dependent on the usually poorly paid civil service jobs of men, while their wives engage in trade to earn money to support the family. But, as Ledgerwood (1994) points out, it is precisely women's engagement in such economic activities, and their important role in creating family wealth, that in fact influence the status of men. It would therefore be inappropriate to draw simple conclusions by connecting women's involvement in trade to women's position more generally.

Moreover, most of the traders I encountered referred to actual skills and needs when explaining women's dominance in trade. Trade is seen as an appropriate domain for women, who are thought to possess better negotiation and bargaining skills than men (Sok Hach et al. 2001: 30). Women are "stricter in calculations" than men in selling as well as in buying. According to a female official of the Ministry of Commerce, this is because women have an eye for even small pieces, women "think in cents" *(kit cen)* and do not throw anything away. Yet, at the same time as being tough in business, they are believed to form better contacts with buyers than men because they know how to communicate and relate in a "sweet and soft way." Men, I was told, lack the communication skills as well as the patience required to sit for a long time and wait for customers. Men would never be able to make much profit and would soon lose the regular customers that are so important to any trade. Furthermore, the argument goes, men go out to work, whereas the wife stays at home, takes care of the children, does housework and, besides these domestic activities, gets involved in small-scale trade.

The argument that trading is compatible with domestic activities is often found in the literature. Women become involved in trade, Seligmann (2001: 3) argues, "as an extension of household tasks they perform as well as to make possible the economic survival of those households and, particularly, to secure the survival of their children." While this reference to household tasks and needs is an important argument explaining women's involvement in trade, it does not properly address the diversity of female traders and trades. Trading differs from other types of work in which women dominate, such as factory and sex work, in that the latter types of work employ mostly young single women, whereas trading absorbs a far larger spectrum of women from different socioeconomic and age groups. I quickly found out that market trade at Psar Tuol Sangkeo, for example, tends to be dominated by mostly adult women in their forties and older, while young women—the focus of this research—were more often involved in itinerant trade, at small stalls along the streets, or at night stands.

This reflects the fact that domestic responsibilities are linked to a woman's life cycle and the influence of marriage and childbirth on their social and economic responsibilities. Young unmarried women with few domestic responsibilities can more easily engage in forms of trade or other activities that are not tied to specific working and household arrangements, such as itinerant or night trading activities. Maybe even more important than age and marital status, however, are social networks, which determine access to specific trading activities and, at the same time, play a role in, for example, child-care arrangements for mobile vendors with children who, like the children of factory or sex workers, are usually left in the care of family members back in the village.

A too narrow focus on the appropriateness of women's involvement in small-scale trade as a result of specific women's tasks and skills thus obscures the fact that these are not essential traits, and that trading women bear the social and economic responsibilities of the household in different ways. Furthermore, women are not automatically equipped to engage in trade. In fact, many newcomers to trading still have to learn skills related to the preparation of products, including the cooking of street food, as well as regarding the process and selection of locations for selling. In this they often rely on networks of family members or other former villagers who have found a niche in the urban economy. Although many street traders operate on their own, they are dependent on these social networks to learn about a trade as well as to acquire the skills and facilities, such as credit and information, necessary to start up a small trade (see also Krisnawati and Utrecht 1992: 49–50).

Despite these facts, street trading is relatively easily accessible to poor and illiterate women. This is especially true for small-scale trading activities on street corners, lucrative roadsides, marketplaces, or night markets (Heyzer 1986; Alexander 1994). Such informal economic activities are therefore often regarded as a refuge for women who are unable to partake in "formal" economic activities and as a way of servicing the "formal" sector with cheap food and services. Yet informal trading activities can just as well function as a refuge from the "formal" sector due to the better incomes and more independent working conditions they offer (Yasmeen 2001: 94). Further, the relative independence, working without a boss and being able flexibly to organize working times, places and products, means that young rural women's engagement in street trading should not be considered merely as an issue of gendered appropriateness or sheer survival, but should also be related to their own preferences among the available alternatives.

STREET TRADERS AT WORK

Dha came to Phnom Penh when she was sixteen years old with a group of eight young women, all of whom wanted to find work in a garment factory. A distant relative of Dha was working in a factory and helped her find a job soon after she arrived. However, Dha found the long hours of work boring and the pay low. After four months, Dha returned to her village in Kampot. She got married and stayed in the village to grow rice with her husband and, after their son was born, to take care of their family. When I met Dha, she had returned to Phnom Penh about three months previously and had recently separated from her husband. Their son was now four years old. While Dha ventured back to Phnom Penh to earn money for her son and herself, she had left him with her grandmother. Dha had come to the city with a relative from her village who sold *num-bancok* (rice noodles with a special curry-like sauce and fresh vegetables) and was willing to introduce her to the trade.

The *ksae* that Dha used to sell *num-bancok* in Phnom Penh reached far beyond her relative. Dha came to live in a house in Tuol Sangkeo, the northern part of Phnom Penh, along with about thirty noodle sellers aged between sixteen and fifty years, all from Kampot. Other *num-bancok* sellers, including those living in other houses in Tuol Sangkeo, were also from Kampot. This apparent monopoly of sellers from Kampot in selling *num-bancok* may, as a Cambodian friend of mine noted, be related to the good reputation that curry from Kampot has among Phnom Penh residents. Sellers themselves thought connections, including those to the house owner *(mcah pteah)*, who is also from Kampot, more relevant than reputation.

Dha spent her first days in Phnom Penh with her relative and some other experienced vendors to watch them make the sauce and to walk along with them to get to know the streets. She was taken along different routes in residential areas in the northern part of Phnom Penh, at Preak Leap on the other side of the Tonle Sap, and around Wat Phnom. After three days, Dha decided to go and sell noodles for herself. This meant that Dha, like the other women, had to adjust to the routine of getting up at about four o'clock in the morning in order to make the necessary preparations. At that early hour the house is already full of life, as all thirty women somehow have to clean up their mosquito nets, get dressed and prepare the curry and vegetables for the *num-bancok*. Every seller has her own cooking stove and pot lined up along the wall in front of the house. They usually have prepared the paste of spices and coconut the day before. Some of the ingredients for this paste, such as coconuts, come from Kampot and are brought to the city by the women themselves. Other ingredients, such as vegetables and spices, are bought fresh every day at the market or from the landlady. The *num-bancok* sellers are dependent on the landlady for buying the fresh rice noodles, which are every day delivered to her house in huge baskets.[5] She divides the noodles among the sellers, weighing out three, four, or five kilos—depending on how much a seller can carry and how many regular customers she has—while the grandfather of the house assists in noting down the quantity each person has bought.

Dha and the other *num-bancok* sellers usually go out with their noodles on a shoulder pole twice a day; from about half past five till nine in the morning and, in the afternoon, from half past two till five or six o'clock. In between, the sellers go to the market to buy fresh vegetables, take a nap, and prepare the curry paste for the afternoon and the next morning. Dha makes her morning round along streets where she has regular customers. In the afternoon she either stays in the area around Wat Phnom or takes a motor taxi to Preak Leap, on the other side of the Tonle Sap. At the end of the afternoon, if she has not sold out, she goes to one of the factories close to her house to sell what is left over to factory workers coming out of work.

This kind of itinerant street trading is a common strategy for young women from the countryside who use public spaces to sell their products. Mobile street traders like Dha, or Thea, who sells pickled fruit carried on a plate on her head, and Chanda, who pushes a cart with sugarcane pieces, go to meet their potential clients at specific locations, such as Wat Phnom. They also serve customers as they pass along a more or less regular route. Stationary street traders, on the contrary, wait for customers at a fixed location and at a particular time, such as the food and drink stalls that appear on the pavements in the evening. Trading at a fixed location requires not only access to capital but also to connections with people who can help to introduce a newcomer to a site or trade, since local authorities or other traders restrict access. This is what Lim experienced for herself.

When Lim first came from Kampong Chhnang to live with relatives in Phnom Penh, she started out as an itinerant trader, selling cakes and pineapples at factory gates. On some days she could make a profit of three thousand riel, but there were also days when she could not sell all her cakes or pineapples and sustained a loss. With the support of a neighbor, she was introduced to a location on the street outside Tuol Sangkeo market where traders sell vegetables, fish and other food and household items from a basket or mat on the street. Lim encountered several obstacles when she tried to establish herself as a vegetable seller in this street market. Already the first day Lim ran into difficulties with a market official who demanded two hundred riel "hygiene tax," instead of the usual one hundred riel for basket vendors *(neak luek kañcraeng)*. He threatened to confiscate her vegetables and ban her from selling at that location. Fortunately, her neighbor intervened. She was allowed to sell again, but ended up paying the market official to keep a place reserved for her. She had gained informal permission from the local market authority to sell at the site, but she still had to find a niche in the highly competitive arena of vegetable sellers. In the beginning she lowered the price of her vegetables to about one hundred riel under the going rate. This aroused the anger of the traders around her, who accused her of taking their buyers away. Yet, with time, she has been able to secure her place and gradually increase the number of regular buyers.

Lim's day starts early. At around four o'clock in the morning she goes to the wholesale market at Damkor to buy ten kinds of vegetables, depending on the season. She has a regular driver of a *remorque* (motorbike with trailer) who brings these vegetables to her selling spot on the street outside Tuol Sangkeo market. Lim sells from about seven until noon, after which market activity calms down. In the afternoon, when selling along the street is not allowed, Lim takes a rest or, especially in the period before festivals, buys (on credit) a stock of shoes or clothes from a neighbor to sell outside factory gates.

Lim's story shows that it is not easy to secure a niche for oneself within the competitive segments of street trading. Social networks, socioeconomic status, and age are important factors in determining the kind of trading activity that is available to a newcomer. Many young women from the countryside who become involved in street trading in Phnom Penh do so with the support of relatives, friends, or neighbors who have moved to the city and can help to make them streetwise.

These networks are therefore of importance for getting introduced to a trade and the specific conditions of the urban context, such as knowing the way around the city, how to talk with people, and how to deal with local authorities demanding money. Becoming a successful trader requires not only an entrepreneurial spirit but also the necessary resources and connections to gain access, permission, cooperation and trust, and the skills needed to create and sustain networks of relationships with suppliers, *motodup* drivers, steady customers and other traders. It is not surprising that many prefer to stick to their specific trade. While traders require the flexibility to adapt to changing circumstances, they tend to do so within the framework of their own networks, skills, and knowledge. It is much more difficult to change to a completely different type of trading—for example, from itinerant noodle selling to selling meat at a market stall—that would require new skills, access to new goods, and building up relationships with new customers (see also Evers 1994: 73).

INVESTMENTS AND PROFITS

In order to start trading, an initial investment, or *prak-daem* (lit. "original money") also shortened to *daem,* is necessary. The amount required for the basic investment or working capital depends on the kind of trade. The investment that Dha had to make in order to sell *num-bancok* included buying the baskets, shoulder pole, cooking pot, plates, and other utensils, which added up to 40,000 riel (around ten dollars). On top of this are the costs of the ingredients necessary to prepare the *num-bancok,* which can amount to 10,000 riel (2.6 dollars) per day. The starting capital needed for itinerant vendors selling from a basket, like Thea selling pickled fruit, is much less. She only had to buy a basket and a knife, and spends about 10,000 riel per day on fruit and spices. The more permanent a selling place, the more vendors are subjected to additional payments for rent or tax. Lim calculated that her daily fixed costs, including hygiene tax, security tax, rent for the selling spot (4,000 riel), and transport (4,500 riel) amounted to more than 10,000 riel per day. On top of that she has to buy the vegetables she sells, for which she typically pays around 100,000 riel (twenty-six dollars) per day.

Making a return on such investments is not always easy. Obviously, there is no fixed income in street trade. As Dha once casually said to me, "On some days we sell well, then we make a profit; but on other days we cannot sell well, then we lose." Most street traders calculate their profit on a day-to-day basis and few of them keep a written record. This, combined with the fluctuations that exist between days and seasons, makes it difficult to assess their incomes. Especially with regard to street foods, the seasons influence the buying patterns of customers and thus the earnings of the traders. Selling *num-bancok,* for example, is much more profitable in the rainy season, when people prefer to stay home and wait for someone to come by and bring them something to eat. In the dry season, on the other hand, people tend to buy fruit and sugarcane juice. Such fluctuations are also visible during holidays such as the Khmer New Year, when the streets and markets seem strikingly empty and quiet in the absence of the usual bustle of traders and buyers. Then again, festivals like the boat races in November offer ample opportunities for sellers to sell more than double the amount of a normal day. Vendors selling fruit and flowers also anticipate more buyers during holy days *(tnay sel)* when such wares are in great demand for offerings at home or in the pagoda. Flexibility is therefore necessary in order to change quantities, and sometimes also products, according to season, availability and fashion.[6]

In order to make a profit, women new to trading need to find a lucrative trade and become accepted. Itinerant street trading is relatively accessible due to the low capital investment required and the fact that urban space can be used freely without the need to find and pay for an unoccupied space. However, these are also conditions under which the possibilities of increasing profit from a street trade are limited. On a typical day, Dha sells about six kilos of noodles, which means that, after subtracting the costs for housing (1,400 riel per day), noodles and other ingredients, she can make a profit of 5,000 to 6,000 riel. Since she is physically unable to carry more noodles on her shoulder pole, it would be very difficult for her to increase her profit as a *num-bancok* seller. Fixed or roadside trading activities are usually easier to expand than itinerant street trading. This is what Lim achieved by changing from itinerant selling, where she earned 3,000 riel per day, to selling on the street outside Tuol Sangkeo market. Over time she gradually extended her network of buyers at her fixed place and with this raised her profit to 10,000 riel per day.

Lim's earnings are above the average daily earnings of small vegetable traders, which according to a recent survey (Cambodia Development Resource Institute 2006: 19), fluctuated between 6,500 and 7,300 riel per day between 2000 and 2005. Most street traders remain within the lower levels of earnings in comparison with garment workers and other unskilled workers (Rao 1996: 24; Pon and Sarthi 2001). This is especially true for street traders from poorer households who lack the financial means to make major investments, a situation that in turn, leads to small returns (see also Krisnawati and Utrecht 1992: 62). Further, many migrant street traders remain oriented toward the rural areas they come from and do not typically reinvest their profits in trade, using them, rather, to support rural households and the education of kin or children (see also Yasmeen 2001: 95; Kusakabe 2003).

Heang, Peou's older sister, is a good example of someone who has been successful in upgrading her business. She is from a poor farming family in Prey Veng, and came to Phnom Penh several years ago to work as a domestic servant. There she got to know a neighbor woman who was in urgent need of cash and offered to sell Heang her fruit-shake *(tik-kralok)* stall. Heang used some of her savings and contacted a better-off relative in her village to borrow the rest of the capital necessary to purchase all the equipment, including glasses, shaker, tables and chairs, and the place to set up the stall in the evening on the sidewalk along one of Phnom Penh's main parks. Her business went well, and soon she brought her younger sister from the village to help out. On a regular-to-good evening, Heang was able to count on a profit of twenty thousand, and sometimes even forty thousand, riel. Some of the profit she used to invest in a telephone booth, which she is now operating next to her fruit-shake stall. Her most recent investment was in a cart with a cooking stove for preparing fried noodles.

Not everybody can rely on a better-off relative to obtain the necessary *daem* for starting or upgrading a business. Credit schemes in the private banking sector are either nonexistent or not targeted at this trading segment, while private moneylenders offer loans with interest rates as high as 20 to 30 percent per month. Traders usually turn to more informal credit mechanisms that are often based on relations of trust (Banwell 2001: 99). The most common way is *tiñ-cu'e,* or "buying on trust," whereby the buyer takes possession of the goods and pays the lender at a later time, usually after acquiring profits from reselling. This could be the same day, but might also take several days or weeks, depending on the agreement that has been reached. It is a common practice between traders and regular customers. Another way of arranging credit is *luy-roap,* meaning "to keep count of money." Here the loan is paid back in installments, whereby the terms and the amount of the repayments, including interest, are established up front between buyer and lender. In a similar way, arrangements for the payment of goods or tools of production can be arranged in what is called *roap-roboh* (lit. "to keep count of property"). Chanda's mother bought the pushcart that Chanda uses to sell sugarcane on this principle. A first installment was paid up front, while later installments had to be paid back over time from the profits made from vending. *Luy-roap* or *roap-roboh* are common among those traders who do not have enough money of their own and therefore have to depend on a moneylender—who may be a neighbor, a nearby shopkeeper, or a relative—to obtain start-up capital.

Another widely practiced credit mechanism is a rotating saving and credit scheme, known as *tontine,* which is organized by a group of friends, neighbors, or coworkers (see also Ledgerwood 1992: 87; Banwell 2001: 99).[7] The members of the group contribute a set amount of money to the kitty every week or month, which is taken in turn by members of the group and used for investments or major purchases. While the "leader" *(mee)* of the group takes the first kitty, the subsequent order in acquiring the kitty depends on the highest bidder in terms of "interest" *(prak-kaa).*[8] The *tontine* has the advantage that individual members of the group who do not have much capital of their own can obtain a larger amount of money for investment. It is important, however, that the group members (*koun,* meaning "children") and the *mee* trust one another, since there is always the risk that one (most notably the *mee*) might run off with the kitty before the *tontine* round is completed. Market traders can participate in this form of credit or saving mechanism because, as an itinerant vendor pointed out, they have fixed stalls and therefore see each other on a daily basis, which leads to relationships of trust and control similar to those that exist among family members or fellow villagers. Mobile vendors, who live and work in a more scattered way, have to rely on other ways and people for accessing credit.

Although capital is indeed important, traders may also call upon more spiritual means to deal with the quest for buyers and growth in business. Some of the larger markets have their own altar where traders offer fruit and burn incense to pray for greater profits and increased luck in business. Street traders more often burn incense or offer some fruit at their altar at home. Some also use *tik mun* or holy water (that is, perfume blessed by a monk), which is put on the face before going out selling, to attract buyers. More extensive ceremonies are performed after sudden downturns in business. These can be relieved through a *sraoc tik* (lit. "spray water") ceremony at a pagoda.[9] These ceremonies are costly, as they involve offerings of fruit, betelnut, incense, candles and money, which few traders can afford to pay for on a regular basis.

TRADING PRACTICES AND CONNECTIONS

For many traders, whether in markets or on the street, the first customer of the day has symbolic value. The term used for first customer, *kaw-chae,* comes from Chinese. When the day starts with a *kaw-chae* who refrains from bargaining too long and readily accepts the price proposed by the vendor, it is a good sign for a profitable day, or *tnay heeng.* When, to the contrary, a *kaw-chae* bargains to below the market value or does not buy at all, it may indicate that the day will be no good, *tnay sooy.*

The symbolic value of the *kaw-chae* also influences bargaining patterns. Lim, for example, refrains from long bargaining, even if the profit is very low. "When the first buyer comes to buy my vegetables and she gives me a price that is just above the cost price, I will sell for this price, so that I can open the day. I sell immediately. They bargain quickly, I sell quickly." This kind of bargaining is less relevant for food sellers who have fixed prices. Here the quality of the food, communication skills, and discounts for regular customers play important roles. Dha considered communication skills especially important for successful selling. Back home she used to be rather shy, but she has learned to be more talkative and to address people politely, such as by calling women respectfully *bong* (older sister) even when they are younger, or *mae* (mother) for women of middle age. Her trick is to make the people feel sympathy for her so that they feel inclined to buy. Dha here points to the fact that trading involves alternative styles of behavior, which, although not condemned, are at odds with the shy and quiet "daughter" from the rice field.

Interactions with customers are even more an issue of moral concern for female traders who work at nighttime, such as fruit-shake sellers along the main streets. As Peou noted, many people associate fruit-shake sellers with beer promotion girls, who are "no good" because their customers are mostly men. When Peou started working at her sister's fruit-shake stall, she first had to overcome her shyness in her interactions with customers: "My sister blamed me for not being friendly with customers, because I am not so talkative and am shy. [. . .] Yet, I learned by watching my sister Heang. Now she sometimes lets me sell all by myself. When I see a customer who looks easygoing I feel confident enough to welcome him and invite him for a drink at my stall. But I feel nervous when a person looks hard to get along with." By the time I came to know Peou, she had overcome her shyness. Due to her friendly ways and delicious fruit-shakes, I became one of her regular customers long before I started my fieldwork among other street traders.

Profitable trading depends on selling techniques and bargaining skills, which may bring a profit in the short term, and also—as in the case of sex workers—on the regular customers with whom traders have been able to establish fairly stable personal relationships. Murray (1991) therefore calls personality and a distinctive way of working crucial in a system of trade that depends on personal loyalties. Geertz (1978: 30) calls this system clientalization, or the tendency for habitual buyers of particular goods and services to establish continuing relationships with particular vendors rather than search widely through the market, or vendors, on each occasion.[10]

Personalized relationships between traders and regular buyers *(mooy)* can extend along the chain of buyers and sellers, producers, wholesalers, retail traders and consumers. Take the case of Lim. She prefers to buy her vegetables, early in the morning at Daem Kor market, from a wholesaler she knows and trusts. This wholesaler may in turn have obtained the vegetables from middlemen or farmers with whom she has established personal relationships. Although selling a major part of her goods to occasional buyers at Tuol Sangkeo market, Lim can also count on seventeen or eighteen *mooy,* or regular customers, every day. Among these are women who come early in the morning to get the best fresh vegetables, which are then turned into meals at the food stalls outside factories, and finally eaten by a regular group of factory workers during their lunch break.

This system of personalized relationships is advantageous to the trader and benefits the customer: by showing loyalty the customer can get a fairer price with less haggling and, when the trust has built up, will be able to get credit when money is tight. Buying on credit *(tiñ-cu'e)* may be done informally by letting a regular customer pay for vegetables or a plate of noodles the next day, or more formally by noting down the client's name and amount of money. Most street traders, fearing loss, are wary of selling on credit, since "it is difficult to trust someone when

I don't know their house," as Lim put it. There is always the danger that buyers won't pay for what they have obtained, and traders who find themselves under pressure to extend such credits may, in the end, have to end their trade. Yet, as Lim added, "if I don't allow them to buy on credit, it is not good for my relationship with my regular customers. I am afraid they will go to another vendor, so I have to do it."

It is indeed not always easy for a trader to find a proper balance between risk and trust, which determines profit or loss. Dha has learned to be extra careful with groups of teenage boys *(stiew)* since the time when four such boys each demanded two orders of her *num-bancok* without paying for them. Although she regretted the loss, a friend of hers had experienced more serious problems with a group of young men. After eating her noodles, they left without paying, taking with them the knife she used to cut vegetables. The knife was found later as a weapon that had been used to kill someone in a fight. This incident afflicted her so much that, fearing that the suffering relatives of the deceased man might blame her, she stopped selling and went back to her village in Kampot.

Such incidents raise questions regarding the solidarity among street traders. Although most work individually, feelings of solidarity are

FIG. 8. Noodle seller at Wat Phnom

shown in many ways, ranging from more experienced traders introducing newcomers to the trade, but also in watching over the stall of another trader who is taking a break, or helping with a few words to reason with annoyed customers. At the same time, competition among traders is high, sometimes giving rise to arguments between traders about potential buyers, price settings, and selling locations.

BETWEEN CONTROL AND INDEPENDENCE

The small-scale nature of most street-trading activities usually implies that a "business" is run by one person or with the help of family members. Enlarging a business means more investment, which many lack, as well as more people involved, who have to be paid when there are no family members available. These factors help to explain why most street trade remains small-scale.

The small-scale trade and the individual responsibility for running it has also clear advantages as it allows for a great deal of flexibility and independence. Though it is physically exhausting to walk around with loads on a shoulder pole, *num-bancok* sellers have much more freedom than they would get in other jobs. They repeatedly told me that they can take a rest whenever they want because they have no supervisor or boss who can order them around. Dha, for example, goes home each month for a few days to take her earnings and visit her son at her grandmother's home. Many traders take a break from work for longer periods when agricultural labor is in high demand, for example during the transplanting and harvesting seasons. Traders emphasized that they can decide for themselves when and for how long they go back to rest or help at home. This cannot happen when one works under a *thawkae* (boss) in a garment factory, where workers have difficulties asking for a day off even when they are sick. Street trade is therefore viewed as a relatively independent way of earning a living in which those involved can attend to their job as they wish without being answerable to anyone (Rao 1996: 12; Bijlmer 1989).

But how justified is this view of street traders as independently operating, self-employed micro-entrepreneurs? Certainly not all street traders have the flexibility to organize work any way they like. This is most obviously the case with employees or family members who help out. Peou complained that her older sister, Heang, is hot-tempered and "openly shows anger at her in front of other people" when she does something wrong at their fruit-shake stall. Besides, Heang is the one who pays the rent and controls the earnings. When Peou asked for her share of money to buy jewelry, Heang told her to sell more or to "earn money by yourself, so that you can buy whatever you want." Their mother talked to both of them and helped calm their frustrations. Peou went back to the village for a while, but returned to help out, knowing that her sister's street business is of major importance for the financial support of the whole family. This case illustrates that, although not characterized by the kinds of restrictive control found in more formal employer–employee situations, the reliance upon unpaid family labor nonetheless involves clear hierarchical relationships.

Yet, not only unpaid family members but also individually operating street traders are subject to varying dependencies. These dependencies concern, as Bijlmer (1989: 148) argues, especially the means of production and the associated appropriation process of surplus value. He distinguishes among the "dependent street worker," the "disguised wage-worker," and the "true self-employed."[11] The true self-employed street worker is the only one who does not rely on the means of production owned by someone else to run his or her business. This pertains in particular to those engaged in very small-scale activities, such as mobile traders like Thea who are involved in selling unprepared or pickled food, fruit, or vegetables from a basket. The disguised street worker, on the other hand, does not own the means of production but operates on a commission basis. The vendors pushing Coca-Cola carts along the river boulevard in the late afternoon and early evening are representative of disguised workers. Many of them do not own the cart or the products they sell but get a share of the money they make by selling soft drinks, the greater part of which goes to the boss or manager *(thawkae)* who provides the products.

The last group of dependent street workers covers a broad spectrum of traders who rely on others to keep their trade going. This dependence may relate to a supplier, financing of supplies, start-up capital, or ownership of equipment (Bijlmer 1989: 150). Noodle sellers like Dha, who possess their own tools for the production and sale of *num-ban-cok,* but are dependent on the landlady *(mcah pteah)* for the supply of rice noodles and other ingredients, fit this category of dependent street traders. The landlady plays an important role in providing essential raw materials. As Dha noted, it is difficult not to buy these ingredients from the landlady since she provides shelter and the opportunity to trade in Phnom Penh. When she was young, the landlady used to help her own mother to sell *num-bancok*. She later used her experience and connections to board and supply other *num-bancok* sellers. Even though these noodle sellers control the production of curry, their selling route and customers, there is some question as to what extent they can be considered truly independent street traders. But then again, the question is whether such "truly independent" street trading makes sense to the street trader whose success in trading depends on creating and sustaining client relationships with suppliers, transporters, customers, money-lenders and other traders.

Besides, street traders, due to their specific use of public space, are exposed to controls exerted by local authorities. Although policies have so far been lenient, the unruly use of urban space and associated concerns regarding disorder and pollution have led to new initiatives to increase control over those involved in street trade and services. A municipal government official complained during an interview that the fact that street traders sell "wherever they feel like" causes chaos and problems with hygiene.

Unlike market traders, who have fixed stalls, are registered with a market committee and the municipality, and have to pay daily fees for taxes, security and sanitation, street traders operate "outside the law" *(kraw chbap)*. Their "informality," however, is not absolute in all aspects (Cross 2000). Street traders, especially those with a more fixed location such as along the river boulevard, major streets and market areas, may not be registered or have a permit, but they are often subject to daily payments of "tax" *(pahsii)* and other fees for garbage collection and security collected by local authorities, which may vary from several hundreds to several thousands of riel per day, depending on the kind of business, the location and the authorities concerned.

Dha usually tries to evade such charges, but she was nevertheless subject to rebukes and expulsions. Municipal authorities have resorted to the stricter enforcement of security rules in public spaces such as those around Wat Phnom, intending to keep it a clean tourist spot; and as tourists do not eat Khmer noodles, sellers have been prohibited from entering the park around Wat Phnom. Experiences of being scolded by security guards, who sometimes confiscate a plate or other utensils, have led several of these traders to wander farther afield. Dha has become more careful and remains with her basket and shoulder pole just outside the park, bringing in a single plate of noodles when someone (often a security guard) calls out for something to eat. Other public parks and street borders are regularly "cleaned up" of street traders, especially when the "public face" of the city is on show, such as during international visits, conferences and other events. The city beautification project includes the building of new markets and designated areas for food stalls along the river boulevard. The rents of these stalls are, however, far too expensive for an average street trader, who continues to use the remaining public space in order to earn a living.

This mobility in relation to changing location or trading patterns and products in adjusting to capital and available opportunities is characteristic of informal street trade (Murray 1991: 57). The fact that a business can be started with relatively little capital investment means that it can also be abandoned without losing much. Street trade can easily function as a form of interim activity for young women who come from the countryside. While some, like Dha, value the relative independence and flexibility in street trade if they have found the work in a factory too hard and long, others use street trade as an income-earning activity until they have established the contacts necessary to get a job in a garment factory in which they hope to earn an income in a more regular modern setting.

Unlike factory and sex work, trading involves women of a variety of ages, at different stages of life, and from diverse socioeconomic backgrounds. Young, poor women from the countryside are generally involved in street trade, either as itinerant street traders or as small-scale vendors with a fixed location. Their success in establishing themselves in a competitive arena is dependent, besides start-up capital and entrepreneurial skills, on village-based networks and their capacities to extend these in the city through clientship relations *(mooy)*. The diverse forms of trading make it difficult to generalize about their conditions, strategies and profits. While often portrayed as independent entrepreneurs, street traders are often dependent on others for the use and ownership of tools, products and profits, as well as for gaining access to urban space. Street traders nevertheless demonstrate and appreciate their flexibility in the organization of work through their dealings with seasonal variations, household affairs, village concerns, and also economic and political changes.

One may argue that the flexibility and mobility that I found among street traders as well as among sex workers and factory laborers predominantly serve the interests of factory managers, brothel owners and local authorities by assuring cheap, controlled and easily disposable labor and services. While this is indeed crucial, flexibility and mobility are also part of the women's own strategies for dealing with exploitative conditions and new opportunities in the city. Women build upon networks to move to more profitable or exciting activities, even if alternatives usually remain within the limited range of options open to young, low-skilled women from the countryside. Hence, if we want to understand women's agency in migration and urban employment we need to go beyond analyzing socioeconomic conditions and constraints, and explore the ways these are reworked through social interactions, cultural symbols and women's own aspirations and creativity. The following chapters will consider the symbolic meanings, the joys and risks of life in the city, and how these are balanced against the expectations and ideals shaped by the young women's rural backgrounds.

City Life and Modern Experience   7

For many young Cambodian women who come from the "rice field," Phnom Penh is, to use Chambers' formulation, the "chosen metaphor for the experience of the modern world" (1994: 92). This modern urban world is very different from that of their rural background. Although the urban and the rural are not, and probably have never been, isolated separate spaces, the stories of fellow villagers who work and live in Phnom Penh, as well as the images of urban life and people that reach the countryside through television and other mass media, bring the city closer than ever to the world of Cambodian villagers.

Migration and mass media are, as Appadurai (1996) argues, central forces in the "work of imagination." Flows of people and images, Hodgson writes, "enable some people to experience, albeit unevenly, new ideas and practices and thereby imagine (if not realize) new ways of being" (2001: 6). For the young people who live in Cambodia's countryside, imagining new ways of being is strongly related to their ambition of finding work in the city. Moving to the city to work gives young women an experience of modern urban life and, with it, an independence that their mothers never had. Such experiences involve the highly desired "modern" consumption and behaviors, but at the same time are marked by ambiguity, contestation and negotiation. In their struggle to strike a balance between what is acceptable or desirable modern behavior and what should be cherished as so-called village values, young rural women living and working in Phnom Penh variously explore the new opportunities open to them and thereby shape their self-presentations as *neak srae* and *srey samay* (modern women).

This chapter will explore the urban experiences of several young rural women working in Phnom Penh—experiences that are often defined by contrast with the traditional village life these women have, usually temporarily, left behind. Almost all the women I met aspired to "be modern," but they lived out their aspirations in different ways. The perceptions of, and participation in, the modern urban world vary among the women in their different kinds of work, partly—though not solely—because the work experience itself is connected to aspirations of modernity (Mills 1997: 44; 1999: 129). The chapter will analyze the connections between urban employment, living situations, and modern experience. The different perspectives that I found suggest also a "fluidity of urban life," or the potential for personal change in the city (Hannerz 1980). Such a change is not without problems, as it involves moral dilemmas, predominantly those regarding the need to uphold ideals of parental authority, proper behavior and sexuality, and the desire to participate in modern urban life. Nor is such change uniform or unidirectional, because it is also marked by women's mobility in relation to rural and urban geographies as well as to different spaces in the city, social worlds, employment and forms of self-presentation.

CAPITAL AMBITIONS

Srey, a factory worker, explained to me why she was so eager to come to Phnom Penh: "They said Phnom Penh is a happy place, not quiet like *srok srae* [countryside]. They said it is happy to *dae leeng* [walk around] at Wat Phnom, in front of the palace, to the new park and river boulevard. When I heard about this I also wanted to come and see."

Like those of many young rural women, Srey's "capital ambitions"[1] became stronger after hearing stories about the city from friends working in one of the city's factories. The attractions of the city for people like her are obvious. Ebihara (1968: 569) describes how the younger generation of the 1950s and 1960s saw Phnom Penh as "the epitome of excitement, sophistication, and glamour, the symbol of wealth and escape from peasant life," and how they used to "visit the city eagerly and describe its sights with glowing eyes." The same could be said of today's rural youth who have visited or moved to the city and enthusiastically describe to those remaining behind in the village the lights, parks, high buildings, traffic, noise, music and markets full of food and commodities. Through such lively stories of friends and other villagers, as well as the pictures in the media and, sometimes, also their own experiences with work and social life in Phnom Penh, rural youth appreciate the differences between the city and the village.

Much of this fascination stems from Phnom Penh's role as Cambodia's capital and as the center of the country's political, economic and cultural developments. The *srok srae* overwhelmingly lacks such marks of development. Dha, a street trader, was particularly impressed by the houses and hotels, especially the tall brick buildings with fancy entrance halls to which people are delivered in shiny, air-conditioned cars. By contrast, she described the village where she comes from as consisting of a grouping of small wooden or straw houses lining unpaved, bumpy roads along which people walk in the burning sun to their rice fields. For Dha it was indeed not just the rural and urban landscape, but also work and class that constituted important differences between *neak srae* and *neak krong*. Nary and Saw, two young factory workers, related such differences to education when they compared themselves with city girls their age: "Girls in Phnom Penh and girls from the countryside are very different. [. . .] Girls from the city have access to better education. They can obtain jobs and a high rank. We are farmers' daughters, we only learned at a low level. [. . .] After we get married, we'll just do farming."

The contrasts between the allure of city life and the marginal position of the village crop up in many spheres of life. Most obvious are the kind of indispensable material aspects of life, which are scarce for many people in the countryside. Young women repeatedly pointed out the fact that in Phnom Penh people pay, and are paid, in dollars, whereas in the village "Khmer currency" (the riel) or gold is much more common. And for those who have money, Phnom Penh's many markets and restaurants offer different kinds of food prepared with ingredients that are not available in the village, where rice and *prahok* often prevail in the diet.

Young women speak about the city as *sapbaay,* a "happy" place, which they contrast to the hard and uneventful life in the village. In Phnom Penh, Melea, a sex worker, noted, "people go out every day; it is just like Khmer New Year every day." Compared to the city, life in the countryside is quiet *(sngat),* as Mom, another sex worker stressed: "Phnom Penh is a happy place. In the *srok srae* it is so quiet. In Phnom Penh there are lots of parks, one can buy anything to eat and ride a dodgem car at the funfair. In the *srok srae* there is only the festival time during which we can have fun and go out with friends. But after the festival is over, it is quiet again. So boring *(opsuk).*"

These views are related to different rhythms of life. Life in the village is determined by the agricultural calendar and the sequence of the seasons, in which Buddhist celebrations provide the main occasions for going out and dressing up. In Phnom Penh, however, time is organized by the clock and a weekly rhythm. Sophea, a beer promotion girl, remarked that "here in Phnom Penh we have Saturday and Sunday. In the village there is no Saturday and Sunday. Monday and Sunday are the same in the village." Also Vy, a factory worker, remarked that Sundays are happy times, during which she feels like visiting "east and west" after a week full of work. The regularized free time that is part of most urban workers' week, in other words, is a much cherished time for pleasure, consumption [2] and also relaxation. While the agricultural calendar in fact allows for much more free time in the countryside, that time is much less fun and exciting.

The women further emphasized the differences between city and countryside in terms of appearances and styles of dressing. City people "have modern clothes, maybe hundreds of clothes, whereas a woman in the countryside has only one set of clothes." Clothes are probably the most desired consumer items for young rural women in Phnom Penh, especially skirts, jeans, T-shirts, blouses and shoes, which are considered modern compared to the old sarong and the loose clothing women wear in the village. Differences in appearance relate furthermore to the skin complexion, which is an important sign of beauty.[3] Since the life and work of *neak srae* is mostly outdoors in the sun, they generally refer to themselves as "black" *(khmaw)*. City people, who spend their days indoors in houses, schools, markets, or offices are, as a consequence, considered to be "white" *(soo)*. We thus see how the stereotypical contrasts between *neak krong* and *neak srae* are put on par with oppositions between rich and poor, white and black, fun and monotony and, related to all this, modernity and tradition.

Notwithstanding the allure of the city and its appealing modern features, the city has its dark sides. Many rural young women and their families view Phnom Penh, at least initially, as a dangerous place, where crime, AIDS and immoral activities are rife. To most of them, the capital is an unknown, wild place and resembles their perceptions of the wild and unknown in the forest *(prey)*. The forest is the space inhabited by spirits and ghosts, or malevolent creatures that can harm people by causing them to become sick (Ebihara 1968: 433; Ang 1986; Forest 1992). The perceived disorder in the city is equally dangerous and can be harmful to unguarded young women. As Srey noted when she had just arrived, "back in the village I am afraid of *khmauc* (ghosts); here in Phnom Penh I am afraid of people." She explained: "I am afraid of people who say that girls from the countryside are easy to cheat. City people are smarter than us. They can lead us into a bad job." Contrary to the village, where people know and trust each other, women like Srey, as well as their families, perceive the city as consisting of a large variety of people, unknown and unrelated, and, as such, potentially untrustworthy and inclined to do bad things *(baap)*. To support this perception, parents, as well as young rural women themselves, readily refer to the stories about violent fights, robberies, deadly diseases, and young women who were raped or sold into prostitution.

Such views of the differences between the city and the village, in which the village is seen as backward but also as a model for moral unity and trustworthiness in contrast to the city as a model of development, modernity, and fun but also immorality, has often been repeated in literature.[4] Yet, whereas village life is not necessarily as harmonious and unchanging as depicted, so also city life is not as modern, fun, or impersonal as is often assumed. The stereotypical images of modern urban life that rural youth imagine have little to do with the reality of urban dwellers living on the streets or in squatter areas, struggling to survive in a highly competitive environment. What is more, the essential distinctions between "rice people" and "city people" do not hold water in Phnom Penh, which now consists predominantly of migrants. Thus, it makes more sense to explore the ways in which young women try to bridge the differences they encounter in their move from countryside to city.

FOOD, SLEEP AND AIR CONDITIONERS

For many young rural women in Cambodia, the real and imagined distinctions between the city and the countryside, on the one hand, enhance the attractiveness of working in Phnom Penh and its enticing prospects regarding beauty, consumption and lifestyle while they also reinforce identification with their rural background due to the gap between the lives of *neak srae* and *neak krong*. And many women find that this gap is difficult to cross.

Dha, like many other young women, had high expectations of life in the city—expectations fuelled by the suggestions of urban possibilities that dominated the stories told by fellow villagers who lived and worked in Phnom Penh, as well as in the glorified pictures of urban life and people that dominate in commercials, karaoke clips and other media messages. She remembered how fellow villagers tried to convince her to come to the city by telling her about easy food *(sii sru'el),*[5] comfortable sleep *(deik sru'el),* and air conditioners *(masin trociek).* These suggestions did not, however, correspond to the realities she found once she came to Phnom Penh. The range of jobs available for young rural, poorly educated women is confined to those on the bottom rung of the service and manufacturing sectors.

Such experienced inequalities, according to Appadurai, make the harsh lot of these women an "ironic compromise between what they could imagine and what social life will permit" (1996: 54). Although Appadurai (1996: 55) goes on to argue that the link between the imagination and social life is increasingly becoming a global and deterritorialized one, for young Khmer women this link is highly localized. Not only do local villagers' stories play an important role in the work of imagination, but also the social conditions of migration and work in the city are very much determined by local village networks. Thus, structural determinants and individual motivations mutually interact with women's diverse positions in and reliance on webs of social relationships as they move from the countryside to the city.

We have seen young rural women move to the city with the help of networks of relatives and friends, often from the same rural area, which provide, at least initially, shelter, employment information and start-up loans, as well as social companionship and moral protection. A clear example of this is Srey, who rents, along with about twenty women from the same district in Battambang, the upper part of a stone house in the Tuol Sangkeo district of Phnom Penh. Each tenant pays five dollars' rent per month, and about five thousand riel for water and electricity. The house has a front room with two wooden beds, a bedroom with a bed, and an upper floor where the remaining women sleep on the floor under the iron roof, which heats up under the sun and leaks when it rains. In contrast to most houses where factory workers live, the house has a bathroom with running water. Cooking is done downstairs next to the house in order not to blacken the walls with the smoke from the clay cooking stoves. The last time I visited the house, I was proudly shown the newest acquisition, a small television set. All the women living in the house had pooled some money so that they could afford to buy the set and did not have to disturb the neighbor down the alley anymore in order to watch their favorite soaps or live music performances.

Other factory workers commonly live with two, three, or more other women in a rented room in a housing compound. Local house owners in Tuol Sangkeo have benefited from the factory boom and built small chipboard rooms with corrugated roofs to rent to factory workers; the landlords earn ten to twenty dollars per room per month. Such rooms provide space for three or four women to sleep together on a wooden bed or on mats on the floor. The walls are often decorated with posters and clothes hanging on a string. Many house owners forbid cooking in the room and provide food for which the women have to pay extra. Some factory workers get food in their factory or eat at one of the food stalls by the factory, where they can choose from a range of foods.[6] Factory workers thus spend a lot of time among their peers, sharing not only spaces for eating and sleeping but also social activities.

The living situation of street traders is less oriented toward peer companionship and more directly attached to the family or work situation. Dha, for example, sleeps on one of the long wooden beds under and behind a wooden two-story house. About thirty women find here, for 1,400 riel per night, a sleeping place under a row of mosquito nets. They also share the toilet and water jug *(piing)* behind the house. The house, though crowded, is well-situated for those who sell noodles, because the house owner is involved in the trade and allows her tenants to use the area behind and in front of the house for the clay stoves they need to prepare the curry for their noodles.

Around the corner from Dha is the main road of Tuol Kork, where the brothel of Rho is located. At the time of my research, Rho was living in a stone house on the other side of the street, from whence she could keep an eye on the wooden shack in which chipboard walls separated six small spaces serving as the rooms in which her sex workers received their clients. Although Rho complains frequently about the lack of order and hygiene of the women in her brothel, she cannot say this of Mom. Mom's tiny room has no window to admit fresh air and contains not much more than a bed with a thin mattress and, on a small board next to the bed, a small fan, which in order to save electricity costs is used only when clients stay in the room. Despite its small size, Mom made an effort to give the space a personal touch. The walls are decorated with old newspapers, pictures of Thai film stars, modern houses, and photos of herself (dressed as a high school student) and friends. Her spare clothes are neatly packed in a small suitcase, which she keeps under her bed with a few utensils for washing herself and her clothes. Since Rho provides food for her sex workers, Mom does not have to cook for herself. Yet, the food provided is not always enough, and generally not very tasty, so Mom and the other women often buy snacks from mobile traders or a nearby food stand.

In other words, living situations are largely related to differences in employment. Those who are living with peers, away from parental authority, experience a level of independence unmatched in the village. Still, the village remains present due to the women's continuing embeddedness in, and attachment to, its networks and notions of morality in the city. One can still claim, as Delvert did in the 1960s, that many rural migrants retain a strong rural outlook. Yet, as Hannerz (1980: 261) rightly points out, we must be aware that these "villages in the city" are open to other facets of urban life. The city embodies a potential for creating new social relationships, environments and identities. This is perhaps most obvious for sex workers, who, due to the nature—or rather the stigma—of their work, are highly mobile and often prefer to keep their urban lives, as much as possible, separate from their rural background. The creation of new social relationships, environments and identities is also relevant for women in factory work and the street trade who, over time, may expand their social networks and change living and working environments in the city.

Such changes are important insofar as urban work and life form a central part in young migrants' urban experiences. The urban experiences of factory workers, street traders, and sex workers seldom correspond to the earlier images of ease and comfort, such as those expressed by Dha regarding food, sleep and air conditioners. Instead, factory workers, sex workers, and street traders often find themselves confronted by conditions that are abusive, unhealthy, or marked by eviction and low returns, while their living situations in the city are determined by the demands of work, and are often crowded, hot, lacking hygiene, controlled by a *thawkae* (boss), or absorbing a major part of their monthly earnings. Such economic and social constraints thus affect women in different categories of employment. They are, however, "widely mediated by aspirations for and participation in new patterns of commodity consumption" (Mills 1997: 37). I found, as Mills did in the case of Thai migrants in Bangkok, that participation in modern consumption and social activities opens an arena within which young rural women "may confront and attempt to rework the tensions and contradictions that underlie their status as urban wage workers" (1997: 41). Yet, I would argue, it is not consumption as such, but as part of young women's enhanced social life in the city that provides young Khmer women with a creative basis on which they try to make sense, in their own ways, of the tensions and contradictions they encounter when their "traditional" village values come up against their "modern" urban aspirations.

BEING MODERN

During an interview, Nary and Saw, two factory workers, disclosed to me how they saw the distinctions between *neak srae* and *neak krong* inscribed in the body:

> They see us with our black skin, whereas they have a white skin. They know we come from the countryside, because we are black and we don't wear similar clothes to them here [in the city]. Also the way we walk is not similar. They know their way around, so they go anywhere quickly. We wait for something, for cars, motorbikes to pass and we are hesitant to cross the road. They can know our characteristics from their observation. [. . .] They know it by our timid way. We are reserved in talking to someone when we go anywhere. When they call us, we don't respond because we don't know them. Then they say, "Hey, this black girl is from *srok srae*, she is a farmer's daughter."

Underlying these evaluations of differences between rural and urban people are feelings that urban dwellers look down on the backward ways of dressing, behaving, and living of the *neak srae*. Young women who have come from the countryside to the city are therefore eager to lose their "provincial image" and change to more modern styles and attitudes. In the minds of rural women, the stereotypical distinctions between urban and rural, *neak krong* and *neak srae,* are often put on a par with the equally stereotypical opposition between modern and traditional. However, such dualisms do not reflect the social realities of everyday life, in which the supposed opposites of modern and traditional are in fact interconnected, complex, ever-changing, and contextualized in time and space.

This has become increasingly emphasized in recent ethnographic literature. Just as most anthropologists now agree that "tradition" is not an authentic and static state but more a process that is constantly being created and historically resituated (Ledgerwood 1996a), so some authors now also speak of the "production of modernities" (Hodgson 2001: 7). It has even become fashionable to talk of "new, local modernities" (Pred and Watts 1992), "alternative modernities" (Appadurai 1996), and "multiple forms of modernity," taking into account "the different pre-histories, the different 'routes to and through modernity' [. . .] taken by different cultures" (Tomlinson 1999: 65) and stressing the creative processes in which people engage in global/local interactions (Hodgson 2001: 7). Mills speaks, in the case of Thailand, of a specific modernity, one that is, according to her, "a powerful field of popular discourse and cultural production." These ideas of modernity are "linked to an increasing global capitalist political economy that manifests itself in different forms and provokes varied responses across time and space" (1997: 42). From this it follows that Khmer ideas of modernity should be understood within the specific historical context of Cambodia as well as in light of its changing relationships to the global political economy.

"Modern," in Khmer, is translated as *tumneup,* in the sense of "newly created" (Headley 1977: 411). Other oft-used concepts for the meaning of modern are *toan samay* or *samay thmey. Samay* comes from Pali *(samaya)* and is translated as "time" or "period," but also as "style" or "fashion" (ibid.: 1081). In combination with the word *toan,* it is also translated as "to be up-to-date" (ibid.: 1081).[7] In combination with *thmey,* meaning "new," it can be literally translated as "new time" or "new period." For many Cambodians this "new time" signifies the period following the end of the country's destructive years of war and isolation and new hopes linked to the political and economic development of the country. These new times, it is hoped, will bring peace, social progress and material well-being. Cambodia, I was often told, is hopelessly behind in terms of modernity. Other nations, be they in the West or in neighboring Southeast Asia, are all considered to be more up-to-date, or *toan samay.* Thailand clearly stands out as the closest model of modernity, not least because actual pictures of this modern Thailand can be seen in Thai programs on Khmer television. In the wake of the anti-Thai riots in Phnom Penh in 2003, the dominance of Thai programs has diminished, while Indian and also modern Chinese soap operas have become increasingly popular.[8] Young people are fascinated by such programs because they show, as a market trader noted, how people "dress in modern clothes, live in modern houses and do modern things."

Although Cambodia may be a long way from Thailand's or other Asian forms of "modernity," not all of Cambodia is equally "non-modern." Phnom Penh stands out in terms of progress and modern styles. This has been the case since the 1890s and developed further after independence. Ly and Muan (2001: vii) speak of an emerging urban elite that, at the time of independence, undertook the task of conceiving, defining, and building a "modern Khmer culture." These aspirations for modernization would affect, it was hoped, the entire population. The Cambodian "whom novelists used to see as lazy, laid back and backward" is, as a French language newspaper wrote in the 1950s, becoming "a myth"; yet, it continues "[w]e are sure of one thing, namely that once plunged in modern life, he will maintain his benevolence and his smile" (*Cambodge d'Aujourd'hui,* quoted in Ly and Muan 2001: xvii). The civil war, and especially the Khmer Rouge regime, had temporarily destroyed this view of a modernizing Cambodia—as well as of its gentle, smiling population—and brought an abrupt halt to the modern ideals that existed among the urban elite. Yet this halt was only temporary.

As we have seen, Phnom Penh is the "chosen metaphor of the modern world." The visions of this world contrast sharply with life in the village, which is often depicted as being *boraan*—"ancient," "old," or "from former times" (Headley 1977: 540)—with regard to appearances, ways of life and behavior. The oppositions between *boraan* and *toan samay* are not merely a substitute for categories of time—old versus new—or for geography—urban versus rural. They are also, perhaps even more so, a function of class. Being modern costs money, something the majority of the Cambodians, living from rice farming and earning an average income of 357 dollars per year[9] do not possess. As a mother of a factory worker wondered, "How can we be modern, if we don't have the money to change our *mode* [Fr. fashion]?" She added that rice farmers only earn cash when they sell paddy after harvesting, and can therefore buy something new to wear only once a year, customarily before the Khmer New Year, whereas people in Phnom Penh earn money all year round and therefore can afford to be modern. Although this woman, like many others, easily identified Phnom Penh with wealthy traders and the countryside with poor farmers, those who had been in Phnom Penh for any length of time were usually more aware of the nuances of stratification. And just as there are different classes in Phnom Penh, so are there also differences within villages that are easily overlooked when focusing solely on those between the city and the village.[10] Melea, after first emphasizing the outdated styles of village women, added that "also some women from the countryside can have long fingernails and *toan samay* clothes as long as their parents are rich; but poor women have black hands and legs."

Melea's remark also suggests that participation in modern life is possible through fairly simple changes. Modern styles include up-to-date clothing, motorbikes and mobile phones. The allure of this kind of commodity consumption is based in the fantasy of the rest of the life that would appear to go with the way people dress, move, communicate, or work. Working indoors in a factory with machines and earning a monthly income, or selling something in a shop with daily profits is considered *toan samay,* but rice farming, as a highly manual activity performed outdoors under the burning sun, is not. Therefore, not only urban wages as such but also the ways these wages are earned contribute to rural women's aspirations for modern consumption and experiences (see also Mills 1997; 1999).

The terms *boraan* and *toan samay* also relate to behavior, such as that between parents and children or between men and women. The discourses of the international and nongovernmental organizations have clearly influenced perceptions of the roles of respect, obedience and authority in parent–child relations. Elderly people complained to me that whereas respect traditionally marked the relationship between parents and children, these times of modernity have brought things like children's rights. During a visit I made to the village of a factory worker, a few elderly neighbors recalled that in former times children needed only to see the face of their mother and they would leave obediently when guests were present. Nowadays a mother can look at her children "until her eyeballs fall out" but her children won't obey her. In former times it was also normal for parents to strike their children in order to make them listen. In these modern times, parents are not allowed to do so, because "children now have rights." These elderly women complained about how youth nowadays contest the authority of elders by telling them that we are now living in the new millennium and that things are no longer as they were in the old days. Elderly village women therefore thought that the "youth of the year 2000 are modern youth" and that these modern youth change according to the television that they "watch and copy accordingly."

The examples of modern behavior that are widely broadcast in soaps, commercials and other programs on television and subsequently imitated by "modern-day youth" include more innocent practices, such as the way they "dance and move like a snake." More worrying, for those of the older generation, are scenes showing how women kiss men and "go into the bedroom together." Such open displays of affection or sexual relationships are considered to have negative impact on youth behavior. A representative of the Ministry of Social Affairs, Labor, Vocational Training and Youth spoke about the need to prevent—though it was unclear how—young people behaving *koh propeinii* (not according to tradition). She argued that "our society is changing fast, especially in the city. In Phnom Penh young people behave as in Europe, especially relating to relationships between boys and girls. In the rural areas young people behave still according to tradition *(taam propeinii)*." The concern for loss of tradition has even led to some government interventions. In 2000, songs about young women's involvement in extramarital affairs were banned from radio broadcasting (*The Straits Times*, February 25, 2000). That same year, Prime Minister Hun Sen issued a warning that the nation's values were being eroded by the short skirts and skin-tight styles worn by female singers in television shows and demanded that program managers lower the skirts of their stars and return to modesty (Nov 2000). Although it is questionable if, and for how long, such measures were obeyed, the concerns underlying them show the degree to which modernity in the behavior and appearance of women stands as an important symbol for the preservation or erosion of Khmer culture in general.

These views about modernity also reveal how the older generation and state representatives worry about possible implications for parental authority and ideas about sexuality. These worries are reflected in the attitudes on the degrees of acceptability of modern behavior among younger generations. This arose very clearly in a discussion between a few rural and urban women working at a local market about the meanings of *toan samay* and *boraan*. They all agreed that when people do not go out but stay at home, they are old-fashioned and boring. When, to the contrary, people do go out *(dae leeng)*, have fun and are happy *(sapbaay)* or wear new-styled clothes, they are *toan samay*. However, when women go *dae leeng* and do not come back at night, when they flirt with men, or when they wear short shirts showing their navel they are *toan samay peek* (too modern), or *toan samay cruel* (beyond modern).

Young rural women living and working in Phnom Penh thus struggle to find a balance between what is acceptable or desirable, and thus not too modern, behavior and what should continue to be cherished as so-called village values. Peers play an important role in stimulating one another to participate in common "modern" activities such as outings and buying things, as well as in judging each other and preserving certain values. For example, when I visited the house of Srey one Sunday afternoon, Manny, Sophal and May had just returned from the market. They had gone to buy new clothes for the free open-air concert they wanted to attend later that day. Each of them came back with a pair of long black trousers and a white T-shirt, which they proudly showed to their roommates. When Sophal tried hers on, the trousers appeared to be tightly cut, especially in comparison with the loose trousers she usually wears. This caused a discussion among her roommates about whether the trousers were still decent or, as was finally concluded, too tight (and thus too sexy). Sophal was left to consider losing weight or giving the trousers to her younger, slimmer, sister.

The distinction between what is acceptable and what is too modern is drawn most sharply in images of women. Munshi (2001: 6) notes how views of the "modern woman" in Asian contexts are often underpinned by ideas of social progress and improvement and "acceptable modernity." Mills (1997: 44) refers to the darker side of modern womanhood, where the "prostitute stands as a reminder of the disreputable consequences that being too modern and too up-to-date may entail for the unwary." This suggests that the traditional-modern border is related to work itself, and that women migrating to the city explore this border between being modern and being too modern in various ways, partly as a consequence of the differences within work and living experiences. Yet, as we shall see, it would be premature to reach easy conclusions regarding "being modern" and "working identities."

Most migrant women emphasize, in different ways, their desire, need, or struggle to maintain the so-called village morality with regard to seemingly superficial issues like clothing, makeup, going out, and having fun. This should not be equated with a resistance to change. On the contrary, young women who go to the city are known to, and are also expected to, become *s'aat* (beautiful) and enjoy their leisure time. This is what women migrating to the city, as well as their families who stay behind, consider desirable, if only within limits.

COMMODITIES AND CONSUMPTION

Part of being modern is being able to participate in "modern" forms of consumption. Several authors have pointed at this connection between consumption and the maintenance or establishment of identities (e.g., Bourdieu 1984; Friedman 1994). Consumption cannot be merely regarded, as it used to be, as an erosion of culture, but is itself part of the creation of "social and cultural identities" (Miller 1995: 156). Consumption, as Stivens (1998: 5) points out, is central to the "constant search for and the construction of the 'new,' including new identities, that is the hallmark of modernity."[11] With the proliferation of commodities and the new forms of fashion and practice produced by capitalism and circulated in mass media and advertising, people are offered new ideas about self-expression and self-display (Hodgson 2001: 10).

We have seen that commodity consumption plays a central role in the motivations to migrate and ideas about self-display among young migrant women in Phnom Penh. Women performing different kinds of work wanted to buy things for themselves and to show them off back in the village. May, a factory worker, explained that she had come to Phnom Penh to "earn money to buy clothes for myself." Rha, working in a karaoke bar, remembered how she—like many other young women—was convinced to follow the women from her village to Phnom Penh after admiring their newly acquired possessions—because "they wore a necklace, earrings, ring and a watch, worth at least two *cii*. They also had modern style clothes and nice shoes. They looked rich. They could pay for all this, and I could not."

Jewelry is a sign of wealth used for personal adornment, which serves at the same time as a relatively inflation- and flood-proof investment. Gold and jewelry keep their value and can be easily converted into cash. This is possible if women lose their jobs or get sick and have to pay for treatment. Sophea, for example, saved some money while working as a factory worker and used some of it to buy jewelry. After she quit the factory and could not find a new job immediately, she had to sell it in order to pay for rent and food. Living expenses consume a major part of urban earnings. Besides, urban existence proffers new opportunities for spending money. Be it a snack during a work break, a poster of Thai pop stars to hang on the wall of one's room, or a pair of trousers from the nearby market, in Phnom Penh, I was often told, one can spend *men-chup,* or "ceaselessly."

The actual desires, patterns and possibilities for urban consumption vary among, and also between, those engaging in different types of employment. Differences in job-related appearances, earnings, and social life influence the consumption patterns of young women.

A young female street trader drew distinctions in the appearances of women in different types of work as follows: *kaliip*, or "sexy," for sex workers; *lmoom*, or "nice" and "decent" for factory workers; and *srae*, or "farmer-like" for herself and other street traders. Whereas makeup and sexy clothes are the standard outfit for sex workers, but not necessarily worn outside work hours, street traders who work during the day make sure to cover their bodies with wide, long-sleeved clothes to protect themselves against the sun. This does not mean that appearance does not play a role in their work. Street traders often put on a bit of lipstick in order to "attract buyers," and many factory workers claim that "only women who look nice, with nice clothes and makeup are selected for factory work." Differences in styles also reflect differences in spending patterns.[12] Sokha, a sex worker in Boulding, spends about half of her monthly earnings on clothing and borrows money from her brothel owner if she does not have enough. A factory worker like Meng only spends money on herself if there is any left after deducting the amount that she sends home, and after paying for rent, water, electricity, and food. Peou, a fruit-shake vendor, is completely dependent on the goodwill of her sister if she wants to buy something for herself.

Notwithstanding such differences in styles and spending patterns, clothes and appearance are the first and most easily observable changes that migrant women undergo when they become influenced by city life. As noted before, enhancing one's beauty, being *s'aat*, is a strong desire among young rural women working in Phnom Penh and is considered to be an important part of the urban work experience. Within this enhanced preoccupation with appearance, a great deal of value is attached to the skin. Working in the city, especially in a factory, is associated with working "in the shade," and thus with enhanced beauty in the sense of a lighter skin. Lim noted that older vendors working alongside her advised her to find work in a factory "so that I would get a nice skin." A mother of a factory worker referred to factory work as a way to *coul mlup* (enter the shade), which—not unlike the old custom[13]—allows her daughter to stay inside, and thus become pale and beautiful.

Urban earnings and shared working and living situations also enable young rural women to devote more attention to their appearance than they would be able to do back home. When visiting sex workers during a normal afternoon, it was not uncommon for me to find them with faces covered in some sort of cream, in the attempt to make their skin look whiter or smoother without pimples. On one such occasion, I met Vanna and two other sex workers with egg yolk on their faces, which, as they explained, would give the skin a very smooth appearance. This preoccupation with the skin is not new as such, but its commercialization is. Whereas egg yolk is still a cheap alternative, high prices have to be paid for the creams and powders that promise to deliver the highly valued smooth fair skin. Although the beauty industry may not yet be as prominent as in other Asian countries (cf. Van Esterik 2000; Munshi 2001), Cambodia's television-watching population is now also flooded with commercial breaks during favorite soap operas that promote whitening creams for the *srey robiep samay,* or the "modern fashionable woman." Not only urban middle-class women, but also young women working in factories are inspired to use part of their wages to buy these whitening creams and try them out with their friends at home or during their short morning break.

This attention to beauty is directly linked to work motivation. To satisfy their desire for such beautifying products and other commodities, young women are impelled to increase their commitment to waged work (Ong 1991: 292). In that sense, it may be not that surprising that

FIG. 9. Legendary female figure (Nieng Rom Say Sok) and shampoo ad

the quest for beauty is openly displayed and supported at the workplace. This may be obvious in the case of sex work, where beauty is directly related to earnings. It is, however, also true for factory work. Some factories organize beauty contests among their workers. The contests reaffirm the factory as a place where beauty and modernity are celebrated, while such occasions at the same time serve a purpose in keeping the workers entertained and disciplined. This may also explain why such beauty contests often take place on the first of May, International Labor Day, when labor protests for better working conditions might be expected to occur.

Beauty is also celebrated in the migrants' urban living quarters, where posters of pop stars and models decorate the walls. Alongside these celebrities often also hang one or several framed pictures of the women themselves, dressed up and made up, in front of spectacular landscapes or interiors. Such pictures are produced in specialized photo-cum-wedding clothes rental shops, where a photo of oneself, fully decked up as a star or princess, costs about three thousand riel. Some women keep a special photo book with pictures of themselves and their friends in front of special sights in Phnom Penh, which are, of course, impressive to display back home.

Visits home are indeed perfect occasions for showing off some of the women's urban sophistication. When I accompanied Sophanna and some friends from her factory on a visit to her family, they all had red-and-orange-painted finger- and toenails, makeup and a small suitcase of clothes. Back home, they continuously occupied themselves with their appearance, changing clothes, combing hair, or putting on creams or makeup. With their clothes and makeup, the Walkman they had borrowed from one of their friends (and me, the *barang*—foreigner—they had brought along), they clearly went out of their way to distinguish themselves from other village girls. Their behavior was also a source of concern and criticism to Sophanna's mother. When Sophanna and her friends dressed up in, according to Sophanna's mother, too tight trousers and shirts to visit the Kathen festival at a nearby pagoda, she warned Sophanna that she might be raped—a clear warning to think of her own as well as her family's reputation.

Women not only show off their own "modern" style, but also make efforts to enhance their family's status by letting them share in urban consumption. On their trips home, young women bring food, clothes, household items and other more-or-less useful items from Phnom Penh's markets. On this trip, Sophanna brought a plastic tray to put glasses on, fruit—the expensive sorts such as apples, grapes and mangosteen—cakes, and some toys for younger siblings and cousins. Picture frames and the blue, flowered plastic floor covering in the house evidenced Sophanna's earlier trips. However, not all parents appreciate the money their daughters spend to enable their family to participate in and "taste" a bit of their newly acquired experience. As Melea noted, her mother made it clear that she preferred to receive money to buy essentials for farming and feeding the family instead of "luxury" foods. She remembered: "I brought her special rice noodles. She had never eaten them before and I wanted her to taste them. Once, when I went to Kampong Som, I brought back sea crabs and octopus for her. She said 'My child, what did you bring, this is very expensive!' She told me not buy such things again."

Urban living and work also offer new occasions for consumption. These include such traditional ones as the Khmer New Year and other Buddhist festivals when many women visit their families, but also those that arise from their urban living situation, such as outings and new forms of celebration such as Bon No'ael (Christmas), Bon Sangsaa (Valentine's Day), and Bon Set Neary (Women's Day). During these times market vendors offer plastic roses for five hundred riel or real ones for one dollar, cards with winter scenes, colorful boxes and nicely packed gifts of towels, creams, makeup, or cheap rings. Such gifts are exchanged between friends, *sangsaa* (sweethearts), and also supervisors at work. The factory workers in Vy's working group, for example, all contributed five hundred riel to buy a Christmas present for their Chinese *meekrom* (group leader). Vy explained that this gift was meant to please their *meekrom* and let her know what Christmas is about, since "they don't celebrate Christmas over there [in China]." While Vy and her colleagues used Bon No'ael to smooth relationships with their supervisor, others use Bon Sangsaa as an opportunity to show their love for someone. Sophanna, for example, received on Valentine's Day a pullover, nicely wrapped in a colorful box, from an admirer who worked in the same factory. When she told me about it a few days later, she wondered whether she had done the right thing in accepting this gift, as she already had a *sangsaa* and was not interested in the person who gave her the present.

Such exchange of gifts is above all an urban phenomenon observed by those who have the money to demonstrate their modern way of life.

Older people, like a neighbor of mine, expressed reservations when "the Khmer see how they do it in Europe and then follow whatever they do in Europe." Especially Bon Sangsaa stirred opinions about the possible meanings of the apparently harmless exchange of flowers and love letters, and how this might relate to the erosion of traditional values concerning proper behavior for women and their virginity. Such concerns were recurrent themes in discussions about young rural women's experiences with diverse aspects of urban life, such as *dae leeng*, or going out for pleasure.

EXPLORING THE CITY

On one Sunday afternoon, Srey and five of her roommates came to visit me at my house. They told me that they planned to go *dae leeng* to Wat Phnom, and asked me to come along. Before we could leave, we had to pass by their house to pick up a few other women. The house, in which about twenty women live together, was full of life, as it always is on Sundays. Laundry was hung to dry outside, women were sitting, talking, knitting, sleeping, or eating, and in turns taking a bath. A few women were absent; they were working overtime and would come back only in the evening. The others were enjoying their day off, either resting at home or out exploring the city. Srey and the other women started to prepare themselves to go to Wat Phnom. The newest clothes, shoes and sunbonnets were put on, borrowed, and critically evaluated on their suitability for the occasion. The little mirror, comb and lipstick passed from hand to hand until they finally reached me. By then everybody looked fine enough to go out.

We proceeded on foot to Wat Phnom in order not to spend money on *motodup*. As we walked hand in hand, Srey told me about how she used to walk like this back home across a landscape of rice fields, trees and cows, where it is quiet without cars and motorbikes passing by. Back home she would walk alone, but in Phnom Penh she and her friends felt much more at ease in a group. When we arrived at Wat Phnom the women selected one of the many photographers there and negotiated about the price and locations for taking pictures. The first photo included the whole group standing in front of the flower clock, and several pictures followed of individual women as we walked around Wat Phnom and picked out spots in front of a tree, or the guardian lions, or on top of the hill with a view of Norodom Boulevard.

While the photographer went off to develop the pictures, we entered the pagoda in order to pay respect to Buddha and burn incense. We all had our fortunes told by a local *achar* (lay Buddhist specialist) known for his skills in interpreting a manuscript of sacred texts, out of which one randomly selects one by inserting an incense stick between the pages.[14] Most of the women were happy to have selected a good story after the first or second try; only Saw and I were less lucky, with three stories about difficult situations or deep waters that had to be crossed. Uncertain what to do about it, we quietly strolled down and sat on one of the benches to look at the people walking around and the elephant taking tourists for a ride. Wat Phnom is a favorite place for *dae leeng* on a Sunday afternoon, especially for factory workers who, like Srey and her friends, walk in groups, dressed up and having their pictures taken. Srey and her friends took pleasure in commenting on people passing by, especially the women. The way they dressed or behaved was either admired or disapproved of. A woman with a tight shirt was heavily criticized, as was another woman in a tight dress, which made her look like a "fat pig." Even stronger criticism was uttered when a group of women flirting with young men walked by. Chatting and watching, we ate some snacks until the photographer returned with the pictures and we went home again.

Other alternative outings on Sundays are visiting the palace, walking on the river boulevard, shopping at a market, or attending a free concert at a broadcasting station or a park. The free concerts attract a huge crowd of young people eager to see their favorite artists perform. Those who do not like crowds may stay at home and watch the concert on television, if their landlord or a friendly neighbor owns one. With the recent reopening of cinemas, going to the movies has become another option for spending free time (and money). More and more of Phnom Penh's cinemas[15] are now being renovated and showing Cambodian, as well as Asian and Western, productions. Although the two-dollar tickets are too expensive for many, factory workers may still get a chance to watch a movie, as some factories hand out free tickets to their workers on special occasions—such as Labor Day—through which largesse factory managers hope to create goodwill among their workers when facing union-led demonstrations for improvements to working conditions.

Although the typical places for *dae leeng* are open to all, they are used in distinctive ways by the women I met. Factory workers enjoy their work and leisure activities in a group, dressing up in a similar style and spending time together during their days off. Friendships often date back to the village of origin, which means that many women remain in a social environment that relates strongly to their village. Still, these networks are extended as new friendships develop on the work floor, allowing some women to break away once they find new friends and workplaces. Like factories, also housing and roommates can be easily exchanged when other, more convenient or appropriate rooms become available, when quarrels between women in the same accommodation arise, or when the social control becomes excessive.

A combination of these reasons made Sophanna and Sophiep, two sisters from the same district in Battambang as Srey, to move house. Before I met them, it was hinted that they were "no good," which referred to their way of dressing and their behavior toward men. The younger sister, Sophiep, went a few times *dae leeng* with the son of the house owner, but then she met another man who intended to marry her. This made it difficult for her to stay in the same house, and so they found a room a few blocks away. For Sophanna and Sophiep it meant that they could also escape close contact with, and thus control of, other women from their home area. In contrast to these other women, both sisters enjoyed going out in a group with their boyfriends and got to see places they would otherwise have never entered. Sophanna once noted how she enjoyed the freedom she had in Phnom Penh: back in the village, people would say behind her back *(niyiey daem)* that she was bad because she goes *dae leeng* a lot, but here, in Phnom Penh, nobody says anything. She is aware that people in the village still speculate about her appearance and behavior, but takes cares not to forget her rural origins. She exemplified this by telling a story about a neighbor man who took her out one day to a place "with many colored lights," which, she thought, was not an appropriate place for "normal" women. She thus demanded to be brought back home. Her neighbor did so, but accused her of being a real *neak srae* and never took her out again.

The place "with many colored lights" was a bar or nightclub, associated with the "bad girl," or the "broken woman," and thus inappropriate for a "proper woman" (see also Law 2000). A sex worker once remarked about Tuol Kork, the area where she lives and works, "Good women don't come here." Tuol Kork and other red-light districts are inhabited by women subverting stereotypical images of ideal conduct, and from which other women better stay away, lest they be "confused with prostitutes." The spaces associated with sex impose identifications on those who inhabit or move in there. Sex workers are aware of this stigma and accordingly move between appearances, behavior, and urban spaces in their daily life. They make a point, for example, of wearing "normal" clothes (as opposed to their sexy work outfits) when they leave these areas to go to the market or to visit other places or friends.

The sex workers I knew were mostly brothel-based and at the lower end of the scale. Their movements were more restricted because they were still in debt to their brothel owner, and also much freer as concerned going out with men and to places and at times considered unsuitable for "proper" women. For sex workers, staying out late as well as visiting places is part of their work. Sometimes clients take them out at night to sing at a karaoke bar, have some fun at the new roller-skating platform, or have sex in a hotel. Sex workers often stressed the happy side of working in Phnom Penh through these possibilities for going *dae leeng*. For Mom, going *dae leeng* is a welcome diversion from her life and work in the brothel. "Sometimes I think it is so unexciting to stay in, and then I worry a lot. But when I go *dae leeng* with others, it makes me happy again." She and her friends visit the usual places: markets, the river boulevard, the palace, parks, or a concert at a broadcasting station, which is allowed as long as they are back in time for work. Melea made a point that besides these usual places there are also many others, also outside Phnom Penh, that she and the other sex workers explore, often with their clients or *sangsaa*. "In Phnom Penh, we go on one Sunday to Kien Svay[16] and a week later we go somewhere else. During a month we visit various places."

The places that are frequented by urban residents during their free time form the working space for many street traders. Selling fresh coconuts in front of the palace, pickled fruit along the boulevards, noodles at Wat Phnom, juicy pieces of sugarcane along the brothel streets, or mixed-fruit drinks along the main streets at nighttime, street traders are mobile in space and in time. This does not mean that the young rural women working as street traders never explore the city outside the areas of their work. On Sundays, or special holidays, Dha and her friends work in the morning and then take the afternoon off to visit a live music concert or the boat races during the Water Festival.[17] Street traders, however, are a much less distinctive group than the factory workers or sex workers in the sense of displaying particular appearances or occupying specific spaces during work or leisure time. Street traders are more independent in the organization of their work and free time and are usually not subject to the kind of control and supervision found in factory and sex work. Probably even more important is the fact that many street traders do not live and work with peers. Several of the ones I met lived in Phnom Penh with their families, who had also moved to the city, or otherwise in an environment of fellow villagers and relatives of different age groups. Although friendships sometimes evolve between street traders in the same urban space—like Mao and Thea, who come from different provinces and live in Phnom Penh in different social settings, selling different kinds of food at Wat Phnom—these are not as intense as those between women who work and live together.

Comparisons between the young rural women show how work and social practices influence their explorations of the city and the urban spaces they inhabit, and those they do not. These spaces therefore reveal something about the people who do or do not use them and, as such, also stigmatize, impose norms of behavior and appearance, and hence influence the ways in which young rural women view themselves and others in the city.

WORKING IDENTITIES AND MOBILITIES

For *koun neak srae,* or "rice farmers' daughters," the conditions of work and life in Phnom Penh offer opportunities for self-presentation, involving patterns of consumption, appearance and social activities that help them to feel "modern." What this means, in reality, is dependent on young women's own desires and on the position they must take within the urban context. Although women like Dha have high expectations when they come to the city, they soon find out that their backgrounds and education determine their access to certain jobs in Phnom Penh and limit their opportunities for "being modern." And thus, while young women are often eager to shed their provincial image when they come to Phnom Penh, they usually soon become aware that a gap remains that cannot be bridged. This is regularly confirmed in their daily interactions. Thea, selling pickled fruit, recounted how a "rich kid" *(koun neak mien)* once asked her whether she was not ashamed to be selling while others had a happy time going *dae leeng* at Wat Phnom. She answered that if she didn't sell, she wouldn't have money. For her, such encounters reinforced the idea that "once born a *neak srae,* one remains a *neak srae.*"

There are, however, marked differences in the extent to which young rural women retain their "provincial image" or change to more "modern" urban styles and attitudes. Some women, their heads filled with alluring images of the city when they first arrived, soon lose that fascination once they confront exploitation at work, fears of crime, nostalgic feelings for rural landscapes, and yearnings to be living with relatives. Other women, on the contrary, fully engage in urban life and, as Peou commented, keep their "high ambitions": "They want to have fun and adventure. They see others having fun and want to be like them: they get crazy for the money and are overjoyed. [. . .] By this I mean that they have high expectations, they just want to have fun and adventure, and thereby forget what they are." When asked if she did not want to have fun like them, Peou answered that she did, "but different from them, not in the way they do. I just want to have fun when I go out with my female friends. I do not want people to judge me for my bad behavior." For Peou it was important not to forget that she was a Khmer woman from the countryside, and thus needed to behave accordingly.

Work and life in the city allows and compels women to learn a new repertoire of speech, behavior and styles. Yet, not all behavior necessarily fits within a repertoire that can be considered as "socially acceptable" (see also Mills 2001). Vy complained about women who turn their backs on their rural background: "Some women are crazy with dollars. They forget everything. They forget their homeland, the countryside. [. . .] Some people who come from the countryside like the tap water very much. They come to Phnom Penh, they have a *sangsaa,* they are too happy. [. . .] In the countryside they drink water from the well [. . .], but once they come to Phnom Penh they prefer tap water and forget about the well water." Here Vy uses an often heard expression regarding the changing attitudes of some migrants who move to the city: Namely, they *chlo'ek tik machiin,* or are "extremely enthusiastic about machine [i.e., tap] water" and think that the water—symbolizing the way of life—is better in the city than it is back in one's own village. I heard this expression repeatedly in relation to women who had moved to the city and changed their appearance, behavior, and way of talking into too urban, or too modern, styles. They are considered to have ceased identifying with the rice field or countryside *(leing srae haey).*

We have thus seen that young rural women differently explore and live out their desires to participate in modern urban life, and with it their self-presentation as *neak srae* and *srey samay.* Urban employment constitutes the foundation. While work in the rice field is hot and hard, urban employment for young rural women means working in the shade, according to the clock and a weekly rhythm, and earning their own money. This applies especially to garment factory workers, who like to present themselves as hard-working, dutiful farmers' daughters in a modern, urban environment. In Cambodia, unlike in Europe, factory work has a modern image and is associated with the pleasures of peers working together and dressing up beautifully, but modestly, when they go *dae leeng*. Migrant women working in other jobs in the city are often either eager to become part of this peer-oriented workforce or envy the good reputation of factory women. A sex worker noted: "When we work in a factory, we are good. We get up in the morning, comb our hair, and go to the factory." Yet the long working hours, and concomitantly less leisure time for *dae leeng,* the strict supervision by a Chinese *thawkae* resulting in limited freedom to organize one's own work, as well as other working conditions, mean that factory work is not necessarily an attractive alternative for all. Rha, a sex worker, commented: "It is hard to work in a factory. You have to sit for a long time and there are some chemicals that affect the ears and eyes. It is really hard. When I work in a karaoke bar, I have to sit as well, but I'll have a happy time. I can walk around and talk openly with anyone I want. There is no way a factory worker can do that." It may seem appropriate at this point to conclude that young rural women's urban experiences are most immediately affected by the kinds of jobs they enter (e.g., Mills 1999: 113). However, such a conclusion does no justice to the "chaos of everyday life" (Law 2000: 61) that I found among the women I met.

While different kinds of employment result in differences in earnings, urban living, how free time is spent, and relationships with peers as well as with the other sex, individual variations and patterns in mobility prevent me from making broad generalizations. In fact, during the course of my fieldwork, I became increasingly convinced that the mobility I found among young Cambodian women was relevant, not only in the geographical sense in that young women move between the rural areas and Cambodia's urban center, Phnom Penh, but also in relation to labor, behavior and self-presentation.

Geographical mobility connects stereotypical rural and urban spaces as well as concomitant perceptions of morality, authenticity, anonymity and modernity. This geographical movement between the rural and the urban is not fixed in time and direction, since young women, as well as their relatives, come and go. It requires renewed adaptations according to location, and thus a change in behavior as women move back and forth. Such changes often have a practical relevance: as a sex worker noted, it is not easy to climb up the narrow and steep stairs of her family's house in tight dresses and high heels. Besides clothing, these changes, according to Rha, concern "walking, talking, and working, we change everything." She explained, "When I am in the countryside, I behave like a farmer, but when I am in the city, my attitude is city-style." This form of geographic mobility and adaptability is, as shown above, also relevant within the city itself, as urban spaces, filled with their own meanings, constrain and enable the movements of women and thus play a role in creating identities.

Even more striking than mobility in geographical space is the mobility in social spaces. As we have seen, moving among factory, brothel, and market according to perceived advantages is common. Similarly, changing houses, either to join new friends made at the workplace (as with Sophea) or to avoid undesirable contacts (like Sophanna and Sophiep), involves new social settings and interactions. These forms of mobility are directly related to the maintenance and creation of the social relationships and networks in which women engage and that are crucial in the analysis of the kinds of resistance, adaptation and initiatives young women practice within their working and living situations.

This holds also for the mobility between forms of employment. The categories of sex work, garment factory work, and street trade were not always clear-cut. Apart from the fact that the women working in these forms of employment face similar kinds of problems, many of them were occupied in overlapping forms of employment. There are street traders, most commonly the late-night stall fruit-shake vendors, but also certain mobile traders, who earn extra income by occasionally having sex with customers. Among the garment factory workers there are some who manage to work in the factory during the day and as *srey bar* (bar girls) in the evening. Others, garment factory workers as well as sex workers, earn some extra money by selling food or secondhand clothes in their free time. Piseth, for example, with the help of the sister of her brothel keeper, regularly prepared sweet potatoes, which she sold in the afternoon in front of the factories.

Not only can these occupations be combined at the same time, they are frequently consecutive. Some young women who used to be involved in small-scale trading in their village came to work in a factory or, like Melea, in the sex business in Phnom Penh. Others came from the village with the intention of working in a garment factory but ended up in a brothel. Garment factory workers, bored with the long hours of work for a small salary, sometimes switch their working careers to become street traders, as Dha did, or become sex workers, as some of the sex workers I met in Boulding had done. Then again, a sex worker like Thierry wants to abandon sex work, and she hopes her cousin will find her a factory job, like some "rescued" sex workers who receive training in a shelter in order to earn an alternative income in garment factories. A common goal for many young women, whatever their occupation, is to be able to *luek-dou* (trade) either small-scale once they get back to their village or, for the more ambitious, on a greater scale in one of the larger markets of Phnom Penh. The example of Sophea's mobile behavior described in the Introduction, switching between jobs, places, and styles, as she proceeded with her career from domestic servant to market trader to factory worker and finally to beer promotion work, shows how a young woman from the countryside can accommodate her urban life to the possibilities and constraints she finds in the city.

Given this mobility between forms of employment and the associated lifestyles, it would be hard to claim that these women's identities are derived from, or determined by, their work (see also Law 2000: 79). Similarly, while self-presentations are, as shown above, strongly related to perceived differences between *neak srae* and *neak krong*, the meanings of these differences are neither the same for all nor fixed and stable. The city entails a potential for personal change, not just between roles, but also between relationships and networks. Working and living conditions in Phnom Penh also foster new relationships between peers and, as I will explore further in the next chapter, between young women and young men. Such processes, though given meaning in localized ways, also involve global dimensions, as influences from abroad are used and adapted to give such relationships new dimensions. Celebrations like Bon No'ael and Bon Sangsaa, unheard of in the village, stimulate an exchange of gifts between friends and also with boyfriends. Furthermore, friends made in Phnom Penh are also taken along on home visits and to weddings. These, like the modern consumption and other social practices young rural women engage in, are all important occasions for the self-presentation of those who are trying to give meaning to their lives while finding ways to move between different social worlds.

Dutiful Daughters, Broken Women

8

> She is the one with the looks, I'm realistic. She is just a little mad, my head is on straight. We're really undivided, even though you see two of us. And both of us are Anna. Together with but a single past, a single future, one heart and one savings account and we only do what is best for one another.
> —Kurt Weil, *The Seven Deadly Sins*

Kurt Weill's opera *The Seven Deadly Sins* [1] tells the story of Anna, who works as a dancer in order to earn money for her family's eagerly desired new house. As she moves from one American city to another, she struggles not to commit the seven deadly sins or to give in to her own desires and thereby frustrate her efforts to save money. Her personality is split between Anna I, who is rational and determined to reach her goal, and Anna II, who is inclined to follow her own feelings and desires, thus endangering the new family house.

The story reminded me of those of the women I met during my study, as it points to the centrality of desire, sin, and sex in the phenomenon of rural-urban movements of women. Like Anna, young women from Cambodia's countryside migrate to the city primarily to earn money for their families back home. Yet, as we have seen, the issue of economic gain from work in the city is also related to desires for personal consumption. Urban experiences to some degree also involve participation in "modern" city life. This, of course, costs money and leads to the need for a delicate balance between spending on personal pleasure and beauty, and family obligations. Women variously evaluate this balance through their own conceptions of being traditional and boring, being "modern" *(toan samay),* or being "too modern" *(toan samay peek* or *toan samay cruel).*

Notions of being "modern" or "too modern" pertain most prominently to rural young women's consumption and sexuality in the city. As dutiful daughters, they are often expected not only to contribute to their family's income but also to maintain its honor, expressed by their virginity. Those not living up to these expectations are considered "broken" *(kouc):* physically because of their loss of virginity, and socially because of their improper behavior. Yet, as young women with their own needs, desires and understandings, they differently live up to, struggle with, and negotiate these expectations, and challenge the meanings of "broken women." Not all women live up to parental expectations and feminine ideals, not only because the desire to participate in "modern" city life may conflict with financial obligations toward the family, but also because earning the money to fulfill these obligations may involve activities that run counter to these ideals, as in the case of sex work. Indeed, those most commonly stigmatized as broken women *(srey kouc)* are at the same time those who are generally best able to support their families financially. But also street traders and factory workers, who do not bear a similar stigma, still struggle to keep up moral standards—or at least maintain the appearance of doing so—in terms of financial obligations and sexuality in an environment where all this is challenged. In such a context, the picture of hardworking migrant women struggling to fulfill the expectations and obligations ingrained in certain social, cultural, or religious values is easily transformed into a view of young unsupervised rural women who have either lost or commodified their sense of obligation and sexuality.

When we examine negotiations between dutiful daughter and broken woman it is important to recognize women's capacities and increasing skills to move between the roles of farmer's daughter and streetwise modern woman through speech, comportment, and sexuality. These capacities and skills may be compared to what others have referred to as "code switching" (see Roseman 2002: 22).[2] Whereas "codes" are often described as if they were fixed societal norms, I found that young Khmer women strategically use, interpret, and switch between them in order to deal with, create, and negotiate their position in different social situations and contexts. This is expressed in concrete actions including behavior, speech and appearances, but also through silence and disengagement within specific contexts. Such actions allow women to move among different positions without succumbing to either side of Anna I or Anna II.

TIES WITH HOME

Most migrant women maintain ties with their family and village while they move to the city. These ties are manifest in the rural-based social networks that women can count on for support, but through which they are also subject to control with regard to their living and working situation in Phnom Penh. Migrant women further sustain ties with their family and village through regular visits back home. Home visits are ideal opportunities for the display of "modern" urban appearances and the presentation of new friends made on the work floor or in communal housing. Migrant women thus bring the city, or at least their experiences with it, and new ideas back with them to the village and allow those who were left behind to admire and participate in their urban "sophistication."

Whenever possible, the women with whom Srey shares a house make the trip back home, usually in a group in the back of a pickup truck. For Khmer New Year, for example, they traveled together. They invited a new friend living with them to come along. They had agreed to use part of their urban earnings to contribute to the rental of a hi-fi unit, which, on the second night after their arrival, was set up in the backyard of one woman's house. The women invited relatives, neighbors and other villagers, and they danced, in their newest outfits, until two o'clock in the morning.

Home visits usually last from two to four days. Factory workers are dependent on the holidays granted by the management. Most factories allow a few days off during Bon Pcum Ben (Buddhist festival of the ancestors), the Water Festival, and the Khmer New Year, but only when there are no urgent orders to finish. This means that factory workers can visit their families and villages for a few days on two or three occasions per year. Sometimes additional visits back home are granted, for example when someone is severely ill, or when there is less work due to a lack of orders.

Sex workers are similarly also limited in their opportunities to travel back home. They are dependent on their brothel owner's permission. As long as a sex worker remains indebted, she may find it hard to leave. Brothel owner Rho once gave in to the tears of a newly arrived young woman in her brothel who had just heard that her mother was severely ill. Rho allowed her to travel back home, but under the condition that the woman would go in the company of a *motodup* driver whom Rho knew and trusted.

Street traders face no such restrictions in their movements between the city and village. They are much more flexible and able to go home more regularly and for longer periods than those working in factories or the sex business. Some noodle sellers, especially those with children back home, stay in Phnom Penh for two weeks to a month at a time and then return home for several days.

Though differing in frequency and length, home visits are important occasions to see and reaffirm contacts with family. For some, such visits require an adjustment between the way in which they experience the life in the city and the way they present themselves at home. This is especially true for sex workers, whose position in the family and in the village could come under attack if the nature of their work ever became known. Melea, for example, did not tell her mother about working in a brothel but told her that she was working in a factory. If her mother were to know about her real work, Melea thought: "I would not go home, but instead I would only send her money with the taxi driver [who lives near my house]. I could not go home until she allowed me to enter the house. And if so, I would only arrive in the evening, so that I could enter the house when it is dark. I'd be ashamed, that's why." Melea also imagined how other villagers would talk about her; they would joke behind her back about her working in Tuol Kork and ask her, "Hey, did you have a happy time in Phnom Penh?"

Women not only go to visit their families back home, but also receive regular visits from them. Family members, curious to see the city and how their daughters or sisters are living, come for visits, bringing rice and other products from the countryside and taking part of the urban earnings back home. Srey and her roommates receive visits from relatives on a regular basis and are thus provided with bags of rice that last for another month or two. Lim's mother regularly comes to visit her daughter and helps her to sell vegetables on the street outside Psar Tuol Sangkeo. However, not all women welcome such parental visits. Mom, who had not told her mother that she works in the sex business, found it a painful experience when her mother found out and came to Phnom Penh: "When she came, she said nothing. She only said: 'You have to return home.' I didn't respond to that. Then a customer came, and I had to enter the room and have sex with him. In the meantime, my mother asked the brothel owner to let her take me home. I was so ashamed for my mother, and I didn't want to go. But she said, 'You have to come home for a while.' So I agreed to follow her. At the time, the brothel owner gave me 200,000 riel [fifty dollars]."

Mom's mother did not comment on the situation; she only remarked on their arrival home that Mom should not have been cheated. Her reaction seems surprisingly calm and evasive. Such silence may, however, be her means of expressing discontent, as well as a way of dealing with a situation that could bring shame on the family: as long as Mom and her mother remain silent, there will be no reason for others to criticize them.[3] Mom clearly felt ashamed for her mother, and she also felt that she should obey her mother's wish and go home with her. Mom stayed at home for a while to help with the rice harvest, but soon left again to return to the brothel. Her mother's pursuit to remove her from the brothel and take her home was thus overturned by Mom's determination to continue to earn money in the city to send to her mother.

The views and expectations regarding the moral and financial implications of work in the city may, as in Mom's case, differ between parents and children, but this does not necessarily mean that ties are severed. On the contrary, continuing connections with the family and village of origin often remain of major importance for many rural women working in the city. For many migrant women, the family back home still forms an important basis of support and care, such as in the event of sickness. Since the costs of housing, living, and medical care make staying in the city too expensive when a woman falls ill, recovery from illnesses often takes place back home, under the caring hands of family and trusted neighbors. These family members and trusted neighbors are also indispensable in taking care of the children of divorced or widowed women who work in the city.

However, there are women for whom life and networks in the city have become more important than the ones in the village. Piseth, for example, lives with her "husband" and still occasionally works— although she is over thirty years old now—for the brothel keeper from whom she rents a room. Piseth does not keep in touch with her family, seldom visits her village, and has never been visited in the city by family members. She does, however, feel responsible for her younger siblings who, after the death of their parents, were brought up by their poor grandparents. Piseth has used some of her urban earnings to contribute when her younger siblings were building their own houses and house-holds, because "I don't want them to say that I work as a sex worker, have much money, but that I am stingy." And, in return, she hoped "they will provide offerings for me. [. . .] They can hold my funeral when I die."

REMITTANCES

Nary was very motivated to find work in a factory in Phnom Penh because she thought, "When I work in Phnom Penh, I'll have money to feed my mother." Although she admitted that part of her motivation was also her desire to earn money so that she could buy jewelry, she was determined to send part of her earnings home. Her mother, she thought, deserved her pity and support. She explained:

> After my father died, my mother had to plow the rice field all by her-self, from dawn until late at night. She came back home in between to breastfeed my youngest brother, but then went back to plow again. [As the oldest daughter] I stayed at home to take care of my younger siblings and to cook rice. But I was still young, and did not yet know how to cook. I once had to cry when I saw my mother's face when she tried to eat the rice I'd prepared, which was still hard inside. But she told me not to cry and helped me to prepare soup for us to eat instead.

Many women told me about the economic hardship back home and their aspirations to relieve some of it through urban earnings. Although such aspirations and expectations are clearly formulated, it is less evi-dent the extent to which their urban earnings are used and, given the level of earnings, can contribute to the family economy.

In the literature about female labor migration in Southeast Asia most authors agree that although women name economic necessities, for themselves as well as their families, as an important reason for their migration, the financial returns are not as clear-cut as one might expect.[4] The images of newly built stone houses, televisions and shiny motor-bikes, so often linked with female labor migration in Southeast Asia do not correspond to the reality of most female migrants, and certainly not of those women I met during my fieldwork. The marginal earnings of street traders, the low wages of factory workers, and the small share of money that sex workers actually can save from their monthly earn-ings do not allow them to remit much to their rural homes. The flow of money from urban-based working daughters to their rural families is even less straightforward when the costs for travel between Phnom Penh and the village, the fees for getting work, other work-related expenses, the costs of housing and living, as well as the bags of rice brought from the village are all taken into account. With the costs of transport to, and living in, Phnom Penh, women and their families may, in the short term, actually lose money. As a result, loans incurred before leaving for Phnom Penh may have to be extended, or paid back by selling a carefully raised pig.

Still, most women do manage to save some money to send home. Many of the ones I met claimed to remit on average twenty to thirty dollars a month.[5] Some sex workers managed to save up to three hundred dollars in half a year, but others sent nothing back at all. The amounts vary because earnings differ, and also because remittances depend on the relationship with home. The street traders who live with their parents usually hand over all their daily earnings to them, occasionally keeping one or two thousand riel to put in their clay piggy banks. Other street traders, working away from their rural homes and families, take between 80,000 and 120,000 riel back home on their monthly visits. Factory workers often preferred to send home larger amounts in one go, which they had saved up over several months. Kunthy, for example, saves money by participating in *tontine* and plans to take the whole amount to her mother once it is her turn to receive money from the scheme. The monthly savings of many factory workers depend upon the amount of overtime they work, which varies from month to month. While sex work may allow some women to send more substantial amounts back home, this is certainly not the case for all. As long as sex workers are young and working in an upmarket establishment, their earnings may well bring the family a regular and welcome source of income. This, for example, was the case with Phea, whose mother came regularly to the brothel in which her daughter worked in order to borrow money from the brothel owner. Phea calculated that, during the first sixteen months or so of her career as a sex worker, her mother had borrowed 480 dollars. Sex workers who want to conceal the nature of their job from their family and the villagers back home refrain from sending large amounts of money back in order not to arouse suspicion. Melea, for example, noted, "I don't dare to send a lot [of money back home], because if we send a lot I am afraid my mother will say that I have a lot of money like

[. . . a sex worker]." Every few months she sends forty or fifty dollars with a taxi driver who lives near her mother's house.

The amount of money and frequency with which it is remitted home is, therefore, only to a certain extent related to the kind of employment, but is more directly related to the family situation and the life cycle of the women. The earnings of women who came with their parents to Phnom Penh are usually directly used for the benefit of the household economy, with only a small part kept for personal use. Women who have children from a former marriage that are taken care of by parents or other family members try to save as much money as possible to support their children. Single daughters living and working with peers in the city, away from their parents, are more inclined to use part of their earnings on personal consumption. They are differently subject to the expectations regarding the financial benefits of their work for the family. A factory worker complained: "My mother only thinks about money. [. . .] If the children give her money, she says that they are good children, but if the children have no money, she says that they are no good." Other parents, because they are financially relatively well-off or supported by one of their other children, do not care as much about the remittances of their daughter, and may, for example, save the money she sends to finance her future marriage. Lim's mother made it clear that she was not that interested in the money from her daughter, saying, "I don't want her to send me money; I want her to be well." Some parents also acknowledge their daughter's needs and desires to spend some of their earnings for expenses in the city and on themselves. May, for example, was told by her mother that she could spend her whole salary for March, the month before the Khmer New Year, on herself. This allowed her to celebrate Khmer New Year at home with new clothes and gifts for her younger siblings and other family members.

Even though the amounts of money sent home by women working in the city are not high in absolute terms—and thus dispensable for some families—they do provide rural families with highly valued cash contributions. The money is used mostly for day-to-day living, extra food, or expenses that come up regularly such as school fees and equipment for younger siblings, medicine, fertilizers, rice seeds and other farming equipment. These contributions may help younger siblings to continue their education or prevent their families from falling into debt. Some women clearly showed an awareness of the role they play in the family economy. A sex worker stated, "I am not proud of myself, but it seems that they would lack someone important if they didn't have me, because no one else could earn money like I do."

The various expenses associated with day-to-day living, or even survival, make it difficult to save enough money for major investments in prestigious housing or expensive luxury articles. With some long-term vision, families of working daughters in the city may at best use remittances to upgrade their living conditions. Meng's parents, for example, use the money she sends to buy timber to build a house. So far, they have bought six supporting stilts, while the materials for the walls, floor and roof are still awaited. Meng hoped that next year they would be able to dismantle their small thatched house and build a more stable wooden one. In order to reach that goal, she was determined not to spend much on personal consumption, but save the money and send it home instead. This, indeed, is how dutiful daughters like to present themselves, though it is not always easy to hold to such intentions once confronted with the seductions of urban consumption and lifestyle.

DUTIES AND DEBTS

I came to earn money to build a house for my parents. I wanted to support my parents because they raised me and are old already. I thought like that. But when I came to Phnom Penh I saw the happy life and forgot all about it, about the idea from back home. I forgot about it, did not think about it. I had money to spend easily. When I earned fifty thousand riel in one night, I spent fifty thousand riel. When I earned thirty thousand riel, I spent thirty thousand riel. I did not buy gold or something to keep. I just spent easily, and everything. I played cards and lost. I played every day, did not sleep. When I did not play cards, I went to drink coffee at Chbah Ampeu [a market south of Phnom Penh]. I went at night, at two o'clock and came back only at seven in the morning. [. . .] I just thought about being happy.

Like most rural women who come to work in Phnom Penh, Phea intended to use part of her urban wages to support her family back home, as her earnings had done when she started working as a sex worker. Yet later on, instead of sending money home, she spent her earnings on a "happy life" in Phnom Penh, and "by the time I started to think about my life, everything was gone."

For young migrant women, whose mobility and lack of supervision offset certain ideals of proper behavior, financial contributions to the household become increasingly important in their presentations as "dutiful daughters." In that sense, expectations differ clearly between sons and daughters.[6] Thiep, Srey's roommate, noted that, although she and her older brother both earn the same amount of money in the factory where they work, her brother spends much more of it on himself, because "after receiving his salary, he immediately takes a *motodup* to *dae leeng* and spends money." Her mother does not comment on this, because she is afraid that "he will become angry and stop working." The little amount he sends home is better than no money at all (and an extra mouth to feed).

Curran (1996) observed similar differences in filial obligations in Thailand and connects these with the relative importance of kinship relationships for sons and daughters. Daughters have more to gain by maintaining close ties to their households because they are likely to inherit parental resources in a matrilocal family system. In the Cambodian context, a similar preference for matrilocality and female ultimogeniture can be observed in which actual patterns depend on the relative family situation. Yet migrant women did not explain these filial obligations primarily in terms of the future gains from family ties, but more often in terms of specific cultural and Buddhist values that have different meanings for men and women.

Women often explain their motivations for remitting earnings to the family using the concept of *sang kun*, or "returning (repaying) a good deed" (Headley 1977: 1039). The word *kun* means "kindness," "goodness," or "merit" (ibid.: 125). A person who has *kun* is someone who has done something to be respected, such as a parent, relative, teacher, or patron (Hinton 1998: 355). Those who benefit from a good deed will acknowledge that they "owe" *kun* and have a "debt of merit."[7] One of the greatest virtues in Cambodia, according to Hinton (1998: 355), is repaying the "kindness" of others. Parents, who raise and nourish their children and give them love and support from birth until they are grown up, get married and inherit property, confer *kun* on their children, who are thus "in debt" to their parents. The *kun* of parents is, I was often told, so great as to be impossible to repay completely. Pheng Criev (1963), writing about the importance of *kun*, refers to a Buddhist canon stating that the *kun* of parents is wider and deeper than the ocean, thicker than the earth, higher and heavier than Mount Meru.

Similarly, an *achar* noted that it is impossible to return all *kun* to parents because their *kun* is as high and full as the full moon.

Not only the various religious teachers, monks, and specialists I consulted to learn more about the concept of *kun* emphasized the importance of the *kun* of parents and the moral obligations children have to return their "debts of merit." Migrant women told me of the value and weight of *kun,* especially in relation to their mothers. Since their early youth, their grandparents and other elders in the village frequently had reminded them that children have to recognize (and respect) the "kindness" or merit *(deng kun)* of their parents, and therefore have a moral obligation to return this. During a discussion among sex workers, a woman noted that her mother's life is larger than that of the Buddha, larger than the world. Her mother had a great deal of *kun* because she had raised her and her other siblings and lost "containers full of blood" during their birth.

Although Ebihara does not mention the concept of *kun,* she describes that, in return for their efforts and concerns, parents must receive "obedience, deference, and devotion" from their children in the form of "respect for and submission to parental authority, as well as heightened solicitude for the welfare" of parents and other family members (1968: 116). The examples Ebihara (1968: 116–117) lists of how children obey, respect and devote themselves to their parents are the same as those described by the young rural women to whom I talked: namely, earn money to supplement family income; (for males) become a monk to earn merit for their parents and themselves; marry with the approval (or according to the arrangements) of the parents; support parents in their old age (whether by remaining in residence with them, taking them into one's home, or sending contributions for their maintenance if one lives separately from them); and giving them proper ceremonies upon and after their death.

Children thus can repay their "debts of merit" to their parents in various ways, which differ for sons and daughters. Sons return their "debts of merit" especially when they are ordained (albeit temporarily) as novices or monks. This way of returning *kun* has a strong spiritual meaning, as the monkhood of a son will bring merit to his parents, especially his mother, and will thus contribute to her being reborn into a better next life. The story of "Soben Komaa" (Dream of a child) illustrates this.[8]

The story is about a hunter and his wife, who live their life without following the wisdom of the Buddha. One night the hunter and his wife both have a dream predicting that they will have a child. Soon after, the woman becomes pregnant with their only son. After the child is born, it grows up under the loving care of his parents. When the son reaches puberty, he tells his parents that he wants to become a monk. This comes as an unpleasant surprise to the parents, who initially refuse to let their son go. His mother, however, realizes that her son is determined. She sees that in order to make him happy, she should allow him to be ordained. Her son hence becomes a diligent and exemplary novice.

When the mother dies, she is faced with the demons of the under-world who accuse her of failing to perform acts of merit in her life. They decide to put her in a big pot with cooking oil. Yet, when they try to do so a lotus appears and protects her from burning and drowning in the cooking oil. The servants of the underworld wonder what this means and take a closer look at her list of merit. They then see that this woman has a son "who was very wise and entered the religion in the footsteps of the Buddha." By becoming a novice, the son had stored merit for his mother. As a result, the mother got upgraded to the middle level (earth) and did not have to suffer in hell.[9]

As women cannot be ordained, they do not have the same oppor-tunities to earn merit for their parents—and themselves—as males do (Ledgerwood 1990: 35). Yet, they can show their thankfulness and sup-port their parents in various other ways. Sophoarn, a factory worker, commented that sons do not serve their parents as daughters do. For example, when her mother is sick, her brother tells her to go to the doctor, but he does not wait on her and does not bring her hot or cold water at night. Daughters, she concluded, help with practical support; sons never do. Most women agreed that daughters take care of their parents when they get older. This can be explained, as Curran did in the Thai context, by the fact that a son usually goes to stay with his wife's family, so he becomes more oriented toward his wife and his wife's par-ents. A street trader similarly remarked that sons do not think as much about their parents as daughters do because, when he gets married, he will follow his wife and stay with her family. Similarly, Vy argued that:

"Sons, when they are growing up, grow wings and fly away from their mother. But daughters have to stay at home. [. . .] Daughters take care of the household; they clean the house. But sons don't think of this. They always go out to dance and have fun. Daughters cannot behave like that, because they are afraid of their mother."

It is thus not only out of respect and affection, but also out of apprehension that children, especially daughters, care for parents when they get old, as the consequences of not doing so are considered to be harsh. Thea's mother told her that if she did not support her when she had grown up and married she would cast a spell on her so that she will not be able to earn a living. Children who do not show their respect and gratitude are accused of not fulfilling their moral obligation to their parents, or being ungrateful children *(koun 'akateñu)*. The very negative connotation of such accusations, and the consequences of this for the next life, strengthens the value attached to the concept of *sang kun*. Kunthy explained: "We'll be born in our next life as an animal. We will not be able to be a person. We have sin and will be born as a worm or something similar. [. . .] So we have to do well and contribute some money." Remittances are understood in the context of *sang kun*, as expressed in such common remarks as "the *kun* of my mother is very strong and thus I have to send [her] money" and "I want to return *kun* by trying to earn money."

Women also repeatedly referred to *kun* when trying to explain their reasons for coming to work in Phnom Penh and remitting some of their income to their family. However, a representative of a Buddhist organization in Cambodia thought that such explanations were based on misunderstandings of the concept of *kun*. She argued that women use the concept in an attempt to rationalize what they are doing. Nowadays, she stated, the consumerist ego interferes with the concept of *kun* and everything is put in terms of making money. As a result, she argued, *kun* has become a commodity. Girls who come to the city come for the "gold rush," and they see *kun* as something that can be paid back with money. But, she concluded, *kun* can never be measured in money.

Even considering these differences in the understandings of *kun*, the concept is part of a cultural repertoire in which women try to make sense of their lives, and it may thus also function as a kind of moral support for young women who, besides their financial obligations toward their family, also pursue personal and material aspirations. Local understandings of *kun* are important in relation to women's uses of such concepts in order to sustain their pursuits regarding employment, life, and experiences in the city. It would therefore be wrong to explain rural-urban migration among young Cambodian women simply in terms of such moral obligations. As we have seen, actual practices in relation to filial obligations and personal aspirations differ between migrant women who are strongly embedded in rural-based networks and are therefore more oriented toward ties with home, and those, like Phea, who have, with time, severed these ties to become more oriented toward personal pleasures and urban concerns.[10]

SEXUAL VALUES AND EXPERIENCES

The balance between filial obligations and personal aspirations is not only relevant in financial terms but also in relation to values concerning female sexuality and parental authority. The link between *sang kun* and issues of sexuality and marriage was a recurrent theme in my discussions and interviews. Oun, a sex worker, explained that for Khmer women "[t]he wedding party is the most important event because it can raise merit for our parents. And as long as we are not married, we give honor by remaining virgin." However, these values regarding virginity and marriage are considered to be increasingly problematic as women move to and work—not just as sex workers—in the city.

Young women are very much aware of the importance of virginity *(prummecaarey-phiep)* in Cambodian society. Virgins, I was told, have "value," are "pure" *(borisot)*, because they "have never been touched by anyone." "Virgin" is translated into Khmer as *srey kramom prummecaarey* (Headley 1977: 675) or, for short, *kramom*. As described in Chapter 3, in former times a special ritual, the so-called entrance into the shade, marked the transition from child to *kramom* from the moment of the first menstrual period. This ritual, however, is no longer practiced, and menstruation is now "observed with secrecy rather than celebration" (Ebihara 1968: 460). Ledgerwood (1990: 141) also writes about the innocence and ignorance of many Khmer women with regard to sex and their own bodily processes, such as menstruation. This was also the case for Phea when she had her first menses: "I was *kramom*, but I didn't know. When they said that I was *krup kaa*, I got angry because I thought they wanted me to get married. But *krup kaa* actually means having reached the age of puberty, to be *piñ kramom* [full virgin]. When they say *krup kaa,* the breasts are a little bigger. I used to put on an elastic brassiere in order to conceal my breasts, and like that I went to cut wood. When I menstruated I did not use underwear. Before I started menstruating I used to bathe naked, and even when I was almost *kramom* I still bathed naked." The physical changes that a *kramom* undergoes also require a change in clothing and behavior. As Phea points out, when she still was a little girl she could walk in short skirts and bathe naked, but as a *kramom* she had to be more careful to cover her body, and especially the female parts of it. As girls' bodies develop into reproductive and sexual ones, concerns about sexuality increase for the women themselves as well as their family.

Descriptions of such concerns regarding the sexuality of young unmarried women are also common in the literature relating to gender in Cambodia. Ebihara (1968: 465) writes how, at the time she conducted her research, young women were "rather strictly chaperoned in that they are never permitted to go out alone at night, or even out to deserted rice fields in the daytime by themselves." These strict rules are related to "fears of possible rape or abduction by men" (Ebihara 1968: 465). Rape, according to Ledgerwood (1990: 186), is the "worst possible offense," as it is "directly related to Khmer concern with virginity and control of female sexuality."[11] There are no similar concerns regarding the loss of male virginity. Whereas unmarried girls are carefully kept under surveillance and chaperoned, and are well aware that loss of virginity before marriage causes "great shame" and "bad-smelling talk," sexual adventures on the part of young men are taken "fairly lightly" (Ebihara 1974: 314).[12]

This concern with female sexuality, especially virginity, and "double sexual standards" can be found in many societies around the world (see Stone 1998). Efforts to explain such concerns point to the notion of the honor of a family or kin group, which depends on the sexual purity of its women and is again interrelated with maintaining and transmitting status and wealth (Stone 1998: 233; Goody and Tambiah 1973). Most of the analyses of virginity have, according to Ortner (1981: 400), centered on its relationship with marriage implications, such as "keeping up the girl's 'value,' thus assuring her of a good marriage and/or assuring her family of good marital connections."

In the Cambodian context, meanings of virginity are predominantly expressed in terms of religious values, family honor, and marriage transactions. Ebihara (1968; 1974: 314) stresses, above all, the spiritual values relating to female virginity. She connects the value of female virginity to the third Buddhist precept: refraining from sexual misconduct, which forbids premarital and extramarital sex.[13] Further-more, she notes, "ancestral spirits frown upon and punish fornication." These ancestral spirits *(meebaa)* watch over the living members of a family and are capable of causing illness when someone in the family is guilty of sinful deeds or quarrels (Ebihara 1968: 430–431; Porée-Mas-pero 1985). The *meebaa* are especially concerned with the proper con-duct of young women before they are married, most notably preventing them from losing their virginity, but also with the prevention of adultery by married women and other discords within the family (Pou and Ang 1992: 106). Their anger evoked by broken moral codes may be directed at any, even an innocent, member of the family.[14] This indicates how virginity is connected to family values and family honor. When virginity is lost in premarital sexual relationships, it means that the "value of the woman, that which cannot be replaced, has been stolen—her reputation and that of her family. Reputation, honor, is everything, and the basis for a woman's honor lies in the control of her sexuality" (Ledgerwood 1990: 187).

In a similar sense, Oun, quoted above, speaks of the relationship between virginity and family honor. She, as well as other women, explained that a virgin has honor *(ketteyuh)* that extends to her whole family, which means that a girl who has premarital sex damages the reputation of her whole family. This is also expressed in the saying "To have a daughter is like having a jar of *prahok*, if it breaks the whole house smells." A daughter should carefully guard her virginity and thereby, as a sex worker stated, maintain the face of her parents or, in the words of a street trader, be careful not to break the family line *(kouc pouch)*.

While women know very well how to formulate such ideals, at the same time they criticize them. Phea thought that "Khmer are too tra-ditional. A Khmer woman has to keep her virginity for her husband. Only her husband can touch her body. A woman has to *sang kun* by saluting her parents at the wedding [*samphea kaa*]. They say that if we don't bow our head to the mat,[15] we don't *sang kun*." Phea contended that "although I am not a virgin daughter, I did send money to support [my parents]. I have a different idea. Even though I am not a virgin, I can still *sang kun*." While few women were as straightforward in their criticism of "Khmer tradition," many did criticize the values of female virginity in comparison to the relatively unconstrained behavior permit-ted to young men. Several women questioned the "double standard" and thought it not right that "men can have many women, so why can we not [have many men]?" Thea, for example, criticized the contradiction that, whereas a daughter cannot afford to behave immorally, a son can do whatever he wants. She referred to the saying that when a man falls down he is still red (as gold), but a woman who falls stinks and will never have a good smell anymore. This is a variation of the oft-quoted saying "Men are gold, women are cloth" *(proh douc mi'eh, srey douc somley):* in other words, when gold falls in the mud it can be cleaned and will be shiny again, whereas a piece of cloth will remain stained forever. Also, other women criticized the validity of such sayings: "They allow men to do bad, whereas women only have to do good, otherwise they look down on us." This fear of being looked down on *(meul niey)*, of shaming themselves and their family, and of being ashamed before them *(khmah kee)* is nevertheless still central in young women's considerations about sexuality and virginity (see also Ledgerwood 1990: 175).

Important in this respect are the connections between virginity and marriage. Men, so I was told, need "pure" women, not women who are "already broken" *(kouc haey)*. Map, a sex worker, explained that marriage with a nonvirgin could be compared with stealing a bracelet. Once someone has stolen something, her hand cannot stay quiet and can steal again. Thus, a woman who has had sexual relationships with other men before, could do so again once she is married. Therefore, Phea noted, "When we have lost our virginity, they do not take us."

The connection between marriage and virginity is often made using the image of white sheets turning red—even though white sheets are hardly used in the countryside. This image appears in songs as well as in soaps, and may have contributed much to teaching "ignorant" young women about this aspect of female sexuality. A factory worker described how she learned about this when she watched a Khmer soap opera. It contained a scene in which a man rapes a young woman by pulling her down on a bed. The next scene shows blood on the sheets, indicating that the man has raped a girl who was pure *(borisot)*. The next scene shows the girl, who is full of shame and washes herself in the rain in order to get rid of the badness.

A woman cannot undo her loss of virginity or redeem her "value" with regard to marriage. Sophiep, a factory worker, thought that when the woman appears not to be "pure," the marriage will be annulled and the family of the bride will have to pay back double the amount of the bridewealth. Sophiep's view is illustrative not so much of actual bridewealth arrangements, but more of how issues of honor and shame are related to marriage. Young women are told that if they keep their virginity before marriage they will have a future, meaning that they will be able to capture a suitor with "promising enough futures" (Ebihara 1974: 315). Ideally, the choice of such a suitor with promising enough futures lies with the parents, because they are "older and wiser and know what is best for their children, and since marriages link family with family, it is best that factors such as family reputation and financial resources be pragmatically researched and contemplated by the older generation" (Ledgerwood 1990: 178).

Yet parental supervision and authority, ideally functioning to keep control over young women's behavior, reputation, and choice of partner, have come under increasing attack as young women leave the

FIG. 10. Factory workers playing a game at Wat Phnom

village to live and work in the city. Whereas in former times pagoda festivals were the major "hunting grounds for potential spouses" (Ebihara 1968: 464), these "hunting grounds" are now extended to the factory floor, to Phnom Penh's public parks, and to urban housing compounds. Increased mobility and "modern" orientations have given young women new opportunities to meet potential marriage partners and, as parents fear, even to engage in (sexual) relations without their knowledge. I found that, although most migrant women speak about the importance of arrangement by, or at least the agreement of, parents concerning marriage, not all the marriages of the women I met were arranged or approved by parents. And although I was repeatedly told that marriage is the only legitimate form of cohabitation, not all couples living together were married.

This demonstrates that, while young women are very much aware of the ideals of female sexual behavior and the related concerns regarding marriage arrangements, they do not necessarily conform to them. Such contrast between the ideal and the reality is, of course, part of the everyday challenges in women's (and men's) lives, and as such part of the human condition, in which the real and the ideal seem impossible to bridge. Ledgerwood argues that "in considering the contrast ideal/ real—ideally girls are secluded and do not engage in or have the opportunity to engage in premarital sex, and in reality some girls do—we must bear in mind that the consequences are 'real' both in social and in religious terms" (1990: 176).

SEXUALITY AND URBAN EMPLOYMENT

In a city context, values regarding proper behavior and sexuality are challenged, if not in reality than in the imagination. For many *neak srae,* the city, besides being the "epitome of modernity," is a site of immorality, exemplified by the different valuations of the proper behavior of women. Villagers in Ebihara's research were convinced that "premarital sex is common in Phnom Penh where there are looser morals and prostitutes" (1968: 465). Such ideas, based on prewar observations, still hold relevance for Oun, who connected this attitude toward female sexuality to differences in moral and material values. She notes that "[i]n the village, if they know that a woman doesn't have good characteristics, they won't ask her to marry. But in Phnom Penh they don't think like that, they only think about the money." On the other hand, as Ledgerwood (1990:140) points out, city women claim to be morally superior to rural women because the latter are "uneducated" and "backward," and have "opportunities to sneak off 'to the forest' with men."

Thus young rural women who move to the city are seen both as "uneducated and backward" and as inhabiting a place with "looser morals" without the customary supervision of their family. For these women, living and working in the city means that they can visit new places, meet unrelated people and have a certain independence, which is part of the attraction but also the moral ambiguity of city life. Street traders fear that, because of their need and freedom to walk a lot and come in contact with various people, including men, others may accuse them of not being "good" women. Women like Peou, who work at a fruit shake stall at night, feel that certain male customers display such attitudes, joking that "*tik-kralok* sellers are easy to take, just drink their fruit shake, pay money and then take them to [a guesthouse]."

Not solely for fruit shake sellers, but for migrant women more generally is suspicion about their sexual propriety easily raised, as they are young women living outside the direct surveillance of their family. Kunthy remarked, "People say that a daughter who lives outside the family environment is no longer a virgin. They say that such women are selling their virginity." Factory workers therefore complained that some villagers, as well as city folks, associate them with *srey kouc,* or "deflowered women," because they live among peers away from the supervision of parents. Also young migrant women themselves clearly have doubts about the moral behavior of other young women who live among their peers. Peou, for example, remarked: "You know, these girls rent a room to stay in a place with ten to twenty rooms. There are always some guys around and they love each other. Some are honest and get married, some are not. That is possible for factory workers who have no parents around to take care of them."

The image of immoral behavior on the part of factory women runs counter to the picture that many of them have of themselves as dutiful daughters working hard to earn money for themselves and their families. Rha, therefore, when faced with accusations from some of her villagers regarding her being "broken," snapped back in reply that she was "broken by a machine" *(kouc ciemuey masin),* in order to make it clear that she had been working diligently and thus had neither the time nor the mindset to engage in relationships with men. Given the importance of the reputation that is at stake, reactions against such accusations are strong, as in the case of the garment factory workers who were on strike and called "broken women" by police who were trying to prevent the workers from blocking the road (see Chapter 4). The factory workers took this as a strong insult and wrote a letter of complaint, which they took all the way to the National Assembly.

This dilemma is, of course, even stronger for those working in the sex business. Sex workers are fully aware of the negative stigma their work entails. They feel that people look down on those who "earn money by selling their body." Sex work, I was often told, is not according to Khmer custom *(koh tomliep tomloap)*, counter to tradition *(koh propeinii)*, and illegal *(koh chbap)*. Melea noted: "Sex work is illegal. [. . .] The law doesn't permit women to earn money by working as sex workers, but it lets women work in factories or in farming." Although the actual legal status of prostitution is not as clearly defined as Melea assumed—according to the law it is the exploitation of prostitution, not prostitution as such that is prohibited—her remark does show the marginal position of and moral distinction that is commonly made in relation to sex work. When sex work is contrasted with the other kinds of work that women do, like small-scale trading or factory work, it is commonly considered as not *trem-trew,* or "correct." *Trem-trew,* in this context, is related to sexual morality and thus includes work in which women do not "sell their bodies" to earn an income.

Society's moral stance toward sex work is also challenged by sex workers' organizations that try to raise awareness about the legal and social position of sex workers in society. A sex worker involved in organizing sex workers stated that "society hates us" even though sex workers are people like anyone else. "We have rights too, because we earn money legitimately; we are not robbers. I earned my money by my own capacity." Similarly, Sokha found that: "To work as a prostitute, we can find money, but we have no *ketteyuh* [honor]. [. . .] Yet if there were no such opinions from others, I would think it is normal. I wouldn't think of anything else, just to earn money everyday. Yet, when many people talk bad about this job, I think a lot. [. . .] I think that I am human being. I do not deserve for people to evaluate me like that. I have arms and legs, I have fingers, why can't I do another job? Why do I work like this and let other people evaluate me like that?"

Sex workers see themselves as trying to earn money in the difficult situation of poverty and, in that sense, as not so different from young rural women performing other kinds of work. Yet they also know that since they are "broken already," and thus not "pure," they have lost something important. Since they *are* broken already, some sex workers argued, they might just as well pursue their aspirations for a better life for themselves and their families in the form of earnings as well as participation in urban consumption and social practice. It was commonly agreed that sex work is "the easiest business in which to earn a lot of money." Whereas for factory work one needs to pay a commission, and for trading one needs some start-up capital, sex work needs no such prior investment; on the contrary, it offers the chance to borrow money whenever it is urgently needed. In that sense, sex work allows women to comply with the ideal of supporting their families financially, while at the same time defying other ideals regarding their sexuality.

It must, however, be said that although sex workers are commonly referred to as *srey kouc,* not all sex workers identify themselves with other broken women and that not all broken women are sex workers. This is related to the fact that sex work itself is not easily defined and is practiced in a range of settings and by a range of people—brothel-based sex workers, but also orange sellers in parks, beer promotion girls in restaurants, singers in karaoke clubs and dancers in night clubs, who do not necessarily define themselves as sex workers. Melea, who worked in a brothel, was clear about the correctness of their work: "Women who work like me are bad women. These include beer promotion girls and also the fruit shake sellers on the sidewalk of the independence monument. When the price is set between the customer and the seller, they will go."

Fruit juice vendors, as well as female students and factory workers, are nowadays thought to be increasingly involved in "free sex" as well as sex in exchange for money or other material gains. It is interesting how some sex workers morally criticize other young women who have sexual relationships with their boyfriends. Unlike sex workers, these women do not receive any financial rewards; and thus, neither they themselves nor their families will profit from such relationships, which instead will only mark a loss in terms of honor. The increase in such relationships could, some sex workers fear, even mean that men will visit sex workers less often. This is not to say that, apart from certain street traders, most notably those selling fruit juices, now also factory workers have become competitors to sex workers. It does show, however, that young rural women working in Phnom Penh face similar prejudices regarding the connection between urban employment and sexuality.

SEX, MODERNITY AND BEAUTY

Recent studies indicate that young men as well as women, especially in urban areas, are increasingly negotiating their own sexuality
and sexual relationships (Tarr 1996; Population Services International
2002). Cambodians tend to criticize such changes as imitations of culture from abroad, whereby the consequences of Western-style modernity, promoted through television, commercials and music, are seen as
threatening local social and moral values, especially those regarding
female sexuality (see also Stivens 2002: 188). A health worker thought
that some women still want to keep their virginity, but because of their
relationships with others may not be able to do so. He related this to
changes occurring in society since the early 1990s when videos from
other cultures became available and "young people started to do like
in the video."

The allure of "modern" consumption and behavior is an important force for those eager to join those adolescents cruising on their
motorbikes in the early evening, who, as seen in romantic movies or
video clips, may carry on the backseat a girl openly showing affection for her male driver, with "her arms wrapped around his waist and
her head resting on his back" (Calvert and Nov 2001). Thea observed
how young girls like her, come from the countryside and selling along
the river boulevard, were attracted by boyfriends wearing nice clothes
and gold and eagerly followed them, only to end up "broken" *(kouc)*.
Sophiep also thought that urban experiences have changed women's
minds. In her view this process started after the arrival of the factories,
when women came from the rice fields to Phnom Penh. When they see
the city and lights, they become overjoyed. They are lacking their parents' supervision and have boyfriends in Phnom Penh, who take them
to one of Phnom Penh's many guesthouses where one can rent a room
for an hour.

The issue of young women being attracted by "money, cars and villas" is even taken up in a song, "Advice for Khmer Women," written
by Hem Sivorn:

> Sing this advice for Khmer women along with the music; correct
> the heart of the wrong man. Very coquettish girls behave without
> fear; accept without seeing the wealth belonging to others. The war
> of sensual desire causes severe anguish: money, car, villa for buy-
> ing virginity. To make her agree, she will have anything: stolen to

support one girl, and other one; stolen to support a girl, betraying children, wife.

Some have high rank, have a lot of wealth and forget about tradition. They have dollars to buy the girl's morale, build a new villa to make her look. They dare to exchange honor for passion. In addition [they] put a curse on child and wife, and cheat without being ashamed of sin: taking harm as thankfulness for child and wife; taking harm as thankfulness for child and wife.

Khmer girl be advised, please remember not to feel happy, aroused over another's sorrow, while destroying the happy life of women like you. There are no words for your heart, another's heart; they are women like you. Don't violate what you know already, to violate it will mean misfortune. Fear that sin will be returned to you when you have a daughter yourself; fear that sin will be returned to you when you have a daughter yourself.

Khmer women's advice advises husbands as well: don't cheat your wife, remember the *kun* of your mother; being honest will make you happy. Taking a young woman means shaming your child, [and] leads to misery. [Your] wife is gold, for what would you take bronze? Pity on our culture and tradition, which are almost lost, shamed before neighboring countries, [. . .] almost lost, shamed before neighboring countries.

Happiness, girl, you have to understand: be aware that by selling your body for money, car, villa, you lift your hand to embrace fire. Old words say that the hot wealth is poor already. To sell the honor of your mother is dangerous, it is like a mosquito without fear of fire. We will receive the fruit of sin we build up ourselves. Happiness only increases when wife and husband get on well with each other.

Young women are thus advised not to sell their virginity in return for some short-term gains and happiness, as they will bear the consequences of it in the future. The song associates these kinds of sexual relationships (especially with married men) not only with loss of honor, shame, sadness and *kam* (bad *karma*), but also with loss of Khmer tradition more generally.

Many factory workers and street traders told me about the negative consequences of having a *sangsaa* in Phnom Penh, and that they are wary of peers whom they consider "too modern." Those engaging in sexual relationships before marriage are depicted as "used food," "cheap," and, contrary to the sweet words used to talk them into sexual relations, left behind by their "sweetheart," who in the end will marry a "nice girl" selected by his parents. Thus women like Meng stress that they are careful to "take care of their body" in Phnom Penh, for men in the city will take a woman, steal her virginity, and then "throw her away" *(boh cau)*. Sex workers, on the contrary, evaluate their relationships with boyfriends in rather different terms. Besides love and affection, the more intimate relationship with a *sangsaa* provides a welcome break from the distinct and also more boring relationships with customers, as Phea commented: "Customers come to have sex, give money, and leave. But with my *sangsaa* I sleep until the next morning. We hug and play games with each other. We have fun together. When my *sangsaa* leaves me to see other girls, I am sad only for a short time. Then I just get a new *sangsaa* and forget about the former one."

In everyday speech, a woman displaying the kind of "promiscuous" behavior described by Phea is called Kaa Key, after the story about a beautiful young woman of this name who is married to a king but gets involved in sexual relationships with other men who seduce and kidnap her.[16] *Kaa Key* has come to mean the embodiment of a "bad woman, a woman who sleeps with many different men, and presumably enjoys it" (Ledgerwood 1990: 113). Once a woman gains such a reputation, her prospects for marriage are damaged, if only because the groom's family may oppose such a union. This shows that, while the sexual practices of young people are undergoing change, discourses about premarital sex, especially of women, remain more or less the same.

It is therefore not surprising that migrant women all emphasize the importance of virginity, even though some of them—not only sex workers—engage in premarital sexual relationships. I do not believe that young migrant women easily and commonly engage in sexual relationships, as is sometimes assumed. However, I have to admit that it was often difficult to assess the relationship between the ideal and the real regarding the sexual relationships of the women I met. There was much speculation, but very little spoken about openly, as Tarr succinctly expresses in her study entitled "People in Cambodia Don't Talk about Sex, They Simply Do It" (1996). Sophea, for example, talked about the importance of keeping her virginity in order to assure good marriage prospects. Her roommate, Sophoarn, thought, however, that Sophea in reality does not care about sexual propriety. One afternoon, after Sophea had gone to work, Sophoarn told me that when Sophea was still working in a factory, she once did not return home during the whole night. Sophoarn asked her the next day where she had been, and Sophea told her that she had spent the night in a guesthouse with her boyfriend. Sophoarn thought that Sophea is now already spoiled beyond all limits, because she continues to have sex with men who invite her to come to a karaoke shop after work. Sophea, she concluded, wants to have fun, go out, and wear sexy clothes, all of which is expressed in her work as a beer promotion girl.

What is interesting about this example of Sophea, in my opinion, is not whether or not Sophea did what Sophoarn accuses her of, but how Sophea defined her work, clothes, speech and behavior as components of a repertoire that, although challenging concepts of proper behavior, is necessary and thus proper for work and life in the city. For Sophea, there is speech and behavior that is proper for work but not outside of work, and she takes care to switch accordingly. Indeed, Sophea knew that "others might say that I am not a good woman." Yet she asserted, "I think of myself as a good woman." My neighbors, who had seen me together with Sophea, depicted her as a *srey kouc*. However, their evaluation of Sophea being a broken woman did not refer so much to her broken hymen, but more to her behavior and appearance.

Such evaluations suggest that social meanings of virginity do not necessarily correspond to definitions of virginity in the "modern language" of Western medicine.[17] Virginity is considered not only in relation to actual sexual intercourse, but also in relation to demeanor and visible bodily marks. For example, a factory worker claimed that Cambodians can read the signs of a woman's appearance, especially by looking at her body, face and skin. Her aunt, she said, only has to look at the face: when it is still round, the woman is full *kramom;* but when women who have worked in a garment factory come back to the village with sunken faces, it is a clear indication that they have lost their virginity in the city. Not only aunts warning nieces not to become sexually involved in the city but also others, including medical persons, are convinced that one can tell whether a young woman has lost her virginity from observing her appearance. Besides the face, other often mentioned indications are breasts and bottoms; virgins have small, tight breasts and buttocks, whereas the breasts and buttocks of a woman who has lost her virginity are "falling down" *(tleak doh; tleak kuut)*.

While women's bodies lose their beauty after they have lost their virginity, men's bodies are thought to become more beautiful after deflowering a virgin. To deflower a virgin *(khui kramom),* sex workers explained, not only gives men a pleasant feeling because of her narrow vagina, it also gives them strength and a nice skin. Some men are therefore prepared to pay a lot of money to deflower a virgin or, as sex workers explained, to suck the vaginal fluid of a virgin *(beut borisot).* Although a girl can only be deflowered once, some sex workers explained how they earn extra money as *kramom pomme* (lit. "apple virgin"). They, in collaboration with their brothel manager, take blood from a vein in their upper arms and put it on a cotton ball, which is then placed in the vagina. Then they use a traditional medicine *(tnam boraan)* "to make the mouth of the vagina smaller." When the client penetrates, his penis touches the bloody cotton, which leaves traces on his penis and will convince him that he has deflowered a virgin.

The strengthening and beautifying effects of deflowering a virgin are believed to be relevant not only for men but also for women who deflower a virgin boy. Sex workers noted that "eating [deflowering] a virgin boy contributes to a beautiful skin" *(sii komloh sac s'aat).* Yet, they lamented, virgin boys are not easy to find, and most of their customers are experienced men with whom having sex actually drains strength and beauty. Thou, who had been working as a sex worker for at least five years, said that with the years she lost her "body form and freshness." Interestingly, she connected this loss more to her many sexual relationships than to the fact that she had given birth to a child and that AIDS was destroying her body.

Sex thus may lead to strength and beauty when a virgin is "consumed," but drains strength and beauty once a woman has lost her virginity. Further, such loss is easily extended to others. In Khmer this is expressed by the saying that, if there is only one rotten fish in the basket, all will smell. For women moving to the city it means that they should not only take care to protect their own bodies but also be sure not to associate with others who might damage their reputation.

CODE SWITCHING

Migrant women find themselves in an ambiguous position as dutiful daughters earning money to support their families yet outside parental supervision, ignorant regarding their own sexuality yet warned to protect it, and although important contributors to the country's drive toward modernization and development, condemned for mimicking the "too modern" behavior so actively promoted by television, commercials and music. The ambiguity of such multiple and contradictory meanings attached to notions of the ideal woman (Ledgerwood 1996a: 139), or the ideal daughter, in Khmer society figures prominently in the various accounts of the migrant women. They are very well aware that this ambiguity gives rise to social concerns regarding the loss of traditional values, whereby they are easily depicted as "loose women" or "broken women."

The question of whether financial contributions can "make up" for women being considered "broken," and so earn acceptance from their families and in their villages is perhaps not as relevant as is often believed. The local saying "Don't try to bend the *sralew* tree,[18] don't try to advise [change] a broken woman" assumes that once a woman is "broken" she will not be able to change. Such perceptions are simultaneously used and resisted by the women themselves. Piseth thought that by becoming a sex worker she had "lost all characteristics of a proper woman," but only a little later claimed, "I can become a good woman as long as I speak gently and go somewhere properly." Another sex worker explained: "I behave like both, as expected of a 'normal' woman, and of a *srey kouc*. When I go home, I behave like a *srey kramom;* I am *sloot* (gentle, shy). But when I sleep with customers I can be *kaac* (nasty) because the customers are nasty."

Such remarks demonstrate how important it is for women to know and be able to navigate among the various languages, behavioral patterns, or "codes" that make up their lives in the village, the city, at work, and among friends. Women's mobility involves the possibility or necessity of switching codes for each situation. Yet, far from being "split personalities," as Kurt Weil's portrayal of Anna I and Anna II may suggest, women like Piseth intelligently and creatively, and at times forcefully, move among various positions. In the process, women may actively use codes of proper behavior, especially those regarding parental debts and sexuality, not only to comply with a given social order, but also to make sense of their own subjected positions.

Conclusion: Moving Women, Moving Selves

9

Having traced young Khmer women's experiences with migration, employment and urban life, the remaining question is how these can be placed in the context of the theoretical principles discussed in the Introduction. For example, what does the story of Sophea tell us about the way Khmer women deal with structures of inequity, experience "modernity," or play what Ortner called "serious games"? Sophea is one of the many young Khmer women who have left their villages in their desire to earn money for themselves in the more eventful city. Her urban career unequivocally shows the kinds of jobs in which young, poorly educated, rural women tend to end up in the city, from domestic service to trading to factory labor and finally to beer promotion work in restaurants. With time in the city, Sophea found new jobs, new friends, new accommodations, and changed her styles of dressing, talking and behaving. For this she was criticized by her family, her neighbors and her roommate, who thought her job as a beer promotion girl, and especially the associated intimate behavior toward men, her preference for tight clothes and high heels, as well as her regular going out or singing karaoke, not proper behavior for a Khmer woman. Yet Sophea was aware of the meanings of proper behavior and modified her speech, clothes and behavior according to the various contexts of work, leisure and the village in which she found herself, in the attempt to keep up an image of acceptable modernity. Sophea found work and life in Phnom Penh exciting and preferable to life in the village. She was therefore determined to enjoy her urban autonomy and "have some more fun."

Sophea's story did, of course, not end there. When I returned to her house a year later, I only found her roommate. Sophea, I learned, had left Phnom Penh several months earlier with her siblings, and had come back to Phnom Penh only once for a short visit. She was now staying with relatives, helping them out in a shop selling agricultural products, and was going to marry a man from her district after the Khmer New Year. The course of Sophea's story puzzled me at the time. Did Sophea select her prospective husband herself, as she once stated she wanted, or did her older brother arrange the marriage, as he had once tried to do unsuccessfully due to Sophea's resistance and determination to stay in Phnom Penh? Was Sophea's wedding grander than the weddings of her older brothers and sisters, as she once claimed she wanted it to be in order to impress the villagers and outdo her siblings? And did Sophea's urban adventure and independent behavior, which she always empha-sized and which set her apart from many other women of her age, end in accommodation to marriage and return to the village?

I have not had the opportunity to ask Sophea any of these questions. And, to be honest, I doubt whether answers are as relevant as I initially thought they might be. Although Sophea was criticized for not behav-ing properly, even for being a *srey kouc,* she never openly rejected, and even emphasized, the importance of ideals of female behavior for herself and the other women she worked and lived with. In her own way, she used, changed and accommodated gendered ideals in seeking to come to terms with her aspirations and the opportunities open to her. Her story thus vividly illustrates the ambiguities in the lives of rural young women who move to the city, and that require understanding in terms of the constraints and contradictions with which young women must contend, as well as in terms of the mobility and creativity women exude as they make sense of their lives. In this sense, I think Sophea's story is part of the complex interplay between young women's experiences and actions, constructions of gender, social and economic structures, and the histori-cal context in which these are set.

Individual life trajectories like those of Sophea need to be contex-tualized. When analyzing female migration and urban experiences, we find many forces operating together and influencing one another. Women's migration to and employment in the city is closely linked to the recent industrialization and expansion of services that occurred in Cambodia after 1993. New opportunities for employment are concen-trated in Phnom Penh, where garment factories appeared following the country's adoption of attractive investment regulations, where the sex business grew to serve both local and foreign visitors, and where the markets and street trading contribute to the city's colorful street scene. While the employment opportunities in these sectors are influenced by national policies and forces of globalization, they are at the same time shaped by the women working in them and by their social relationships. Their aspirations to work in the city are strengthened by their "modern" expectations and mediated through the family, the village and, especially, peer networks *(ksae)* that play a central role in migration motivations and their realization, as well as in the gendered organization of labor.

Other studies have highlighted the importance of social networks, the role of individual desires and modern aspirations, and the gender selectivity of migrant streams. In that sense, this study shows important parallels to the processes and practices of female migration and urban employment described in other parts of Southeast Asia (see, e.g., Ong 1987; Murray 1991; Wolf 1992; Mills 1999; Law 2000). Yet, as this study also shows, the meanings and outcomes of female migration and urban employment for, and among, Cambodian women and society more generally differ due to their situation within the specific Cambodian context and local idioms. The described phenomena came to play a role much later in Cambodia, and the processes of change that accompany them have been more abrupt. As a country emerging from years of warfare and communist experiments, Cambodia has been left behind the trends in countries like Thailand, Indonesia and Malaysia. The massive engagement of Cambodian women in industry and services, producing garments for the global market, selling sexual services to foreign visitors, and roaming the streets to sell foodstuffs was indeed unimaginable ten years before I conducted fieldwork on this topic. By now, female labor has come to play an essential role in the country's move toward economic development and modernization.

Within the process, existing values are reinterpreted to fit new circumstances. Women's motivations for seeking work in the city are commonly formulated in terms of family expectations and personal desires. Families hope that their daughters' work in the city will help increase family welfare through new commodities, agricultural inputs, or the education of younger siblings. Such family expectations are often formulated in terms of *sang kun,* "repaying debts of merit," which women working in the city seek to do by means of financial contributions. Urban work also offers new possibilities of "entering the shade" *(coul mlup)* by working indoors and thus out of the sun, which is valued due to its association with enhanced beauty. As we have seen, global factories in particular have been able to draw upon this image. Women not only physically but also symbolically "enter the shade," as their time in the city can be seen as a prolonged transition period between childhood and the responsibilities related to marriage and motherhood. Women often see that time as one in which they, unlike their mothers, can enjoy a certain degree of autonomy and pursue their own desire to be "modern," as promoted in advertising and the mass media and in stories of peers living and working in the city. For young women, this especially means engaging in consumption and explorations of the city, hoping for some fun, beauty, and new experiences.

As such, there seems to be nothing particularly Khmer about these "modern" aspirations or the way they are expressed. Yet the relevance of the idea of "modernity" for young women and their families in present-day Cambodia makes sense only when considered in relation to other times and places. The determination to leave behind the past of war and destruction and the influences of "modern" images from other countries has made the idea of "modernity" a strong force, not only in the aspirations of young rural women and their families, but also in the pursuit of national development and, ultimately, the search for global economic profit. While in order to experience modernity, women and their families depend on urban earnings. Being modern thereby ambiguously relates to the necessary commitment to and, at the same time, the constraints on women's urban positions within low-skilled and low-paid forms of employment.

This ambiguity also involves moral aspects of working in the city. Migrant women, whatever the work they end up doing, are often seen as "loose" or "broken," having left the watchful eyes of their family and the protection of the village boundary. Migration to the city means that women both fulfill and forsake financial and moral obligations. Being aware of this ambivalent position, migrant women emphasize the ways in which their work in, and earnings in, the city provide new opportunities to fulfill gendered ideals, particularly those relating to hard work, family support, and female beauty. They know that the reputation of a woman remains a cause for apprehension among concerned parents and gossiping villagers, but their urban earnings have allowed it to become expressed in visible, material terms. In a way, this suits perceptions of women as "primarily donors" (Ledgerwood 1990), more "worldly attached" (Kirsch 1985), and responsible for economic matters, which in the Southeast Asian context may not bring the highest prestige (Errington 1990) but has great influence on the status and position of their families in the village and society more generally.

This also makes it difficult to make distinctions between dutiful daughters and broken women on the basis of remittance patterns and sexual integrity, as the two of them do not necessarily correspond. Such easy distinctions conceal the various ways in which women are involved in, perceive and transform understandings of themselves through their interactions with the village and the city. The contradictory moralities and ideals regarding financial obligations, gendered ideals and individual desires lead to a balancing act between what is acceptable or desirable modern behavior and what should be cherished as so-called village values—that is, a balancing act between filial obligations and personal aspirations regarding urban earnings, female sexuality and parental authority. Migrant women variously comply with, struggle with, and challenge such cultural and social debts, values and ideals of obedient daughters, and proper women and do so in culturally appropriate ways.

The question is now how this interplay among personal desires, social obligations and structural constraints works out for women working in different sectors. While other studies have looked at the diversity and actual experiences of women in migration and urban employment, few studies have systematically examined how these relate to different types of employment. I have tried to do so by focusing on factory workers, sex workers and street traders. The data presented in this book indicate that it does not make sense to study the migration of these women separately, but rather that the processes and conditions are similar for all the women. As we have seen, the embeddedness in rural-based networks, reinforcing self-identifications as "rice people in the city," as well as modern aspirations, cut across all categories of work. More important, the borders between the different categories of work are not as clear-cut as the separate chapters in this book suggest. In reality, they are crossed according to perceived advantages and the following of new contacts and experiences in the city that induce women to move between factories, brothels, or markets, and sometimes also between forms of employment.

These forms of employment all belong to the kind of low-paid, low-status, and highly gendered occupations that offer little possibility for upward mobility. Notwithstanding such similarities, factory work, sex work and street trade differ in the kinds of skills required, the reputation of the work, and the role of peer groups in the organization of work and life in the city. While a young woman like Srey hopes that factory work will allow her to buy "modern" clothes and experience the city, she, and if not her village-based social environment, will ensure that she will not be considered "too modern" by those back in the village. But what Srey and her friends may call "too modern" is just part of the work and also the fun of urban life for a sex worker like Melea. At the same time Melea is well aware that her way of dressing and behaving is acceptable, and necessary, only within the confines of sex work, and that it requires adaptation as soon as she goes back to her village. Dha's work and life in the city is, in this sense, probably the most closely set within the village context. As a noodle seller with a child back in the village and with experience as a factory worker in the city, she is well aware of the limitations of her position, which is far from the easy life and modern images that were presented to her before she first left for Phnom Penh.

The conditions and perceptions of work in these sectors, however, relate not only to types of employment, but also to hierarchies and distinctions within each of them. Perceptions of sexual propriety differ between women working in upmarket night clubs and brothel-based sex workers; and women selling fruit shakes on the sidewalks at night represent a "modern" urban image that has more in common with some sex workers and factory workers than with traders selling vegetables from a basket. This again reflects the interconnections between the different forms of employment.

By taking into account women's own experiences and practices, this study challenges the one-dimensional and generalized views of rural women in factories, sex work, or trade. Factory workers do not primarily consider themselves as exploited workers providing cheap products for a global market; sex workers do not necessarily view themselves as victims of trafficking or of patriarchal structures of dominance; and street traders do not see their work as serving an exploitative capitalist economy while providing cheap products and services to low-paid urban workers. Cambodian women assess their migration and urban employment in the context of personal experiences and economic benefits. Their embeddedness in extending networks of fellow villagers, friends and colleagues allows them to react to difficulties and possibilities in relation to urban work, which may also mean shifting between employers and employment categories. This does, of course, not mean that women's involvement in these types of urban employment should be considered as simple acts of free choice. Rather, there is, to quote Law (2000: 121) again, a "negotiated tension" between free will and the constraints that make these particular types of employment an opportunity for them.

This negotiated tension between choice and constraint suggests that women have agency. Despite the dominant views of young rural women as pawns in the global economy and the pursuit of national development, or as poor and ignorant persons trapped in restrictive customs and the tragedy of Cambodia's history, Khmer women do have room to maneuver. Young migrant women's involvement in and ability to utilize networks of increasing size and complexity allows them to move into and between geographical and social spaces that extend far beyond the village context.

I saw this reflected in mobility as an important characteristic of young rural women's lives and work in the city. Their mobility is expressed in geographical movement from the countryside to the city as well as in their ever-changing work and living situations, and in the flexible patterns of behavior they display as they try to make sense of the ambiguities and contradictions in their pursuit of fulfilling personal desires, family obligations and cultural ideals while faced with the difficulties and possibilities they encounter in the city. Mobility is thus not just an expression of the ways in which labor regimes operate, but also of young women's creativity in dealing with the tensions among cultural constructions, objective determinants, "modern" imaginations and lived experiences. Moreover, mobility and creativity make these women important agents in bridging, or blurring, imagined separate worlds and perceptions of the rural and the urban, and of the traditional and the modern, regarding morality, material benefits, and identifications.

This book has shown that even those migrant women accused of forgetting their rural background, of making the "cake bigger than the scale" by courting or marrying according to their own wishes, or of being "broken" while enjoying the city too much or working in the sex business retain ties with their rural background and maintain images of themselves as proper women. Women can do so because they are increasingly experienced in interpreting, and acting in, the various worlds they bridge. They, as well as others, acknowledge that, just as children can never fully return *kun*, the kindness or merit of parents, also women will never fully attain the "ideals" of a properly virtuous Khmer woman. In this context, Moore's (1994: 66) "fantasies of identity," or "ideas about the kind of person one would like to be and the sort of person one would like to be seen to be by others" are useful. These involve the tensions between urban aspirations and rural identifications, between the lure of the city and the dreariness of everyday work in the factory, brothel, or street, as well as the multiple and ambiguous gender constructs and ideals that inform women's lives in constraining ways but can also be creatively used by women as they shift between various positions in their interactions with their rural home, urban work, and peers as well as the opposite sex. Ambiguities and contradictions are therefore important in understanding agency and the ways in which women juggle their positions as they move to the city.

And this is where Ortner's notion of "serious games" comes in. The notion of "serious games," as set out in the Introduction, tries to grasp the embeddedness of women's experiences and activities in material needs, cultural scripts, and webs of social relationships that are pervaded with inequality (see Ortner 1996; 1999). While offering a framework for understanding the dimensions related to the choices of and constraints on women, the idea of women playing games leaves open important questions. Is it just about playing, or does the seriousness of the games mean that there are winners and losers? If the latter, what does winning entail for the young women I studied: promotion at work, financial gains, being seen as a proper woman, or being able to choose one's own husband? Did Sophea win by getting married despite her "broken" past, or did she lose, by having to accommodate social pressure and give up her independence? What is at stake in losing? Sadly, for some women the stakes have been extremely high—particularly those who face the loss of their lives because of AIDS. So what are the gains? As we have seen, they are usually small in financial terms, although they may contribute to a slight upgrading of their rural houses, to the education of a younger sibling, to the medical treatment of a sick family member, or to the woman's own wardrobe. Gains are probably more significant in terms of personal experiences, since these will influence the ways they live their lives—whether or not they chose their partners, whether or not they return to their village, whether or not they will be economically successful—and thereby continue to actively and creatively shift positions and develop webs of relationships within the family, at work, in the city and wider society.

This suggests that it does not make sense to draw final conclusions about winning or losing. Women simultaneously take part in many "games" involving networks and hierarchies that affect cooperation and competition, solidarity and exploitation. Maintaining and creating networks requires knowledge of the different rules relating to gendered behavior, Buddhist values, selecting a spouse, and work, as well as creativity and skills to shift between different positions. In other words, women are agents who, with skill, knowledge, intelligence and wit, define their goals, interpret the rules and "switch codes" according to the relevant conditions. The game metaphor, therefore, pertains not so much to the lives of these young women—life is not a game—as to their actions and interactions in different contexts.

This is why I introduced the concept of code switching as a way of referring to the creative use of different elements of language, behavior, or self-presentation within interactions in different contexts. When women move to the city, they not only move between the rice field and the urban world but also between ideals of the proper woman and the modern woman, between stereotypes of the docile and industrious and the obstinate, lazy worker, between being dutiful and being broken, and between fantasies of the ignorant, shy and obedient farmer's daughter and of the streetwise, sexy woman engaging in relationships with potential husbands. Women forcefully and creatively switch between the various positions and discourses in accordance with social circumstances. And thus, as women move, they also move selves.

The diversity in the outcomes and meanings of female migration and urban employment shows that women interpret ideals, formulate goals, or engage in webs of social relationships in many various ways. According to the situation, they actively use codes of proper behavior and local concepts, not only in a sense of complying with a given social order, but also to their advantage, while pursuing their needs and desires or making sense of their own subject positions. It is such "play" with traditional concepts of gender that, as Ledgerwood (1994: 128) formulates, smoothes the transition to new types of order in a rapidly changing society like that of Cambodia. And as women continue to shape their own stories creatively in the face of the difficulties and constraints that permeate their lives, those stories will eventually influence the (his)story of Cambodia.

APPENDIX

BIOGRAPHIES

These short biographies are meant to help the reader recognize and become acquainted with the names of those women who appear most regularly throughout the book. However, they include neither all informants nor all the women named in this study. I have used fictional personal names out of respect for the women's privacy. The reported ages are those given by the women themselves. But it should be noted that Cambodians tend to calculate their ages in a different way than do Europeans, starting with year one from birth and counting on the basis of a particular (Khmer) calendar year, not the day of their birth.

Dha
Dha is a twenty-one-year-old noodle seller from Kampot. She first came to Phnom Penh when she was sixteen to work, together with some friends, in a garment factory. She quit after four months and returned to her village. Her grandmother, with whom she had lived since her parents separated when she was seven years old, arranged for her to marry a man in her village. Dha and her husband divorced when their only child was four years old. Dha, leaving her child in the care of her grandmother, returned to Phnom Penh with the support of a relative who introduced her to the trade of noodle selling *(num-bancok)*.

Lim
Lim is a twenty-two-year-old vegetable seller from Kampong Chnang. She has been in Phnom Penh for two years. She first stayed with relatives and tried to earn some money as an itinerant trader, then was introduced to vegetable trading on the street outside Psar Tuol Sangkeo. Her younger sister and brother joined her to look for work in a garment factory in Phnom Penh. They shared a small room in a housing compound in Tuol Sangkeo.

Manny
Manny is a twenty-three-year-old factory worker from Battambang. Manny worked in Phnom Penh for almost three years. She lived in a house along with about twenty women from her *srok* (including Srey).

Manny returned to live in her village after her mother arranged her marriage and it turned out to be difficult for her and her husband to live and work together in Phnom Penh.

Melea

Melea is a twenty-four-year-old sex worker from Kampong Cham. She did not feel at home with either of her parents, who were divorced and had both remarried, so she stayed with an uncle and aunt. Melea came to Phnom Penh for the first time after she ran into problems with her uncle. She was eighteen years old and followed a friend who had found work as a domestic servant in Phnom Penh. However, her father fetched her back to her village and arranged a marriage. A few months after the wedding, Melea and her husband divorced. Melea returned to Phnom Penh, where she found a job in a drink shop and started working as a sex worker. She has since changed establishments several times. She ran away, with her boyfriend *(sangsaa),* from the brothel owner in Boulding where I met her, leaving debts and no clue as to where she went.

Mom

Mom is a twenty-one-year-old sex worker from Kampong Speu. She came to Phnom Penh after her husband was arrested and sent to prison for being involved in a robbery. She first worked as a babysitter and domestic servant, and changed to sex work in order to earn more money. She has worked for over four years in several brothels in Tuol Kork, albeit not continuously. Mom was in the brothel of Rho when I met her, and later moved to a nearby brothel when the son of the brothel owner promised to marry her.

Nary

Nary is a seventeen-year-old factory worker from Battambang. She came to Phnom Penh along with Srey and other friends to look for a job. She was unsuccessful and went back home to her village, but returned to Phnom Penh whenever she heard that factories were selecting new workers again. She eventually found a job and stayed in the house with Srey and other women from her *srok.*

Peou

Peou is a twenty-one-year-old fruit shake seller from Prey Veng. She has been in Phnom Penh for three years, helping her sister on the nighttime fruit shake stall along one of the main boulevards. Her older sister, Heang, bought the stall with the financial help of a relative and has managed to expand her business to include a telephone booth and fried noodle cart. Their mother is widowed and lives by herself in the village now that the youngest sister has also come to join Peou and Heang in Phnom Penh.

Phea

Phea is a twenty-year-old sex worker from Prey Veng. She was brought into the sex business by a *meekcol,* who had promised to get her a job as a babysitter. Ever since, Phea has worked in brothels in various parts of the country. She contracted AIDS and was hired as a peer educator by an NGO.

Piseth

Piseth is a thirty-two-year-old sex worker from Kampot. Her parents died during the Pol Pot regime, and she and her four younger siblings grew up with their grandparents. When she was young, Piseth took various odd jobs in order to earn money for her young siblings. When she was twenty-two years old, she followed a friend to work as a beer promotion girl in Phnom Penh. She has worked as a sex worker in various establishments ever since. She later rented a room from a brothel owner in Tuol Kork, where she lived with her "husband," but continued to work as a sex worker, and occasionally tried to earn some money by trading.

Rha

Rha is a twenty-eight-year-old sex worker from Kampong Cham. She worked in various nightclubs as a *srey roam,* dancing girl, and then found work in a karaoke bar. Rha married when she was about twenty years old and has a child. She separated from her husband, who drank and beat her. She then left her child with her mother and followed a friend to find work in Phnom Penh in order to support the child.

Sophanna

Sophanna is a nineteen-year-old factory worker from Battambang. She is the oldest of seven children and comes from the same district as Srey. She came to Phnom Penh when she was sixteen years old to work in a factory in Phnom Penh. She had to interrupt her work and return to her village for several months when she fell ill, which also led to the cancellation of her marriage to a man she met in Phnom Penh. She returned to work in another factory and rented a room with her sister Sophiep.

Sophea
Sophea is a twenty-four-year-old beer promotion girl from Kampong Cham. She is the youngest of eight children; her parents died when she was very young. She came to Phnom Penh when she was sixteen years old and found work as a domestic servant, a market trader, a factory worker and a beer promotion girl. She shared a room with Sophoarn, whom she befriended in the factory, and another friend from her village. She later left Phnom Penh to stay with relatives and marry a man from her *srok*.

Sophiep
Sophiep is an eighteen-year-old factory worker from Battambang. She is Sophanna's sister. Sophiep has had a boyfriend who visited her parents to ask their permission to marry her. The negotiations, however, were cancelled after a fortuneteller warned that Sophiep was still too young and neither side could not come to an agreement regarding the bridewealth.

Sophoarn
Sophoarn is a twenty-four-year-old factory worker from Siem Reap. She is the youngest of three children. Sophoarn left for Phnom Penh to stay first with an aunt. She later found work in a garment factory where she befriended Sophea. She then shared a room with Sophea and another friend. After Sophea left to live with her relatives, she continued to live in that room together with a self-chosen husband.

Srey
Srey is an eighteen-year-old factory worker from Battambang. She came to Phnom Penh after her father died in the hope of earning money to help her mother repay her debts and to buy clothes and explore Phnom Penh, as other women in her village had done before her. She stayed in a house with about twenty other women from her *srok;* however, she could not find a job and returned home. After about half a year, when friends told her about upcoming selections in garment factories, Srey came back to Phnom Penh and did find one.

Thea

Thea is a seventeen-year-old street trader from Kampong Chnang who came to Phnom Penh with her family. She sells mixed pickles at Wat Phnom and later changed to selling apples from a basket in a nearby market.

Vanna

Vanna is a twenty-three-year-old sex worker from Prey Veng. She is the oldest of three children; her younger sister also came to work as a sex worker in Tuol Kork. Vanna used to work in Boulding. After the area was destroyed and her brothel owner left the business, Vanna rented a room with three other women and started working from the public parks.

Vy

Vy is a thirty-year-old factory worker from Prey Veng. She is divorced; her husband takes care of the younger child while she kept the older, who was nine years old. She left the child in the care of her older sister when she came to Phnom Penh. Vy paid a broker to find work for her in a garment factory. She later switched to another factory where she did not have to work the night shift. Her younger brother came to join her in Phnom Penh to look for a job. Vy used to go home regularly to visit her child; and her child occasionally came to visit her in Phnom Penh with her older sister.

NOTES

CHAPTER 1. INTRODUCTION

1. See Winter (2003) about Angkor as a contested landscape, dominated by discourses of architectural conversation and archeology on the one hand, and models of tourist development on the other.

2. See, for example, Ortner and Whitehead (1981: 1). This constructivism was further developed by authors such as Butler (1999), who argue that sex, long seen as the biological essence of the socially constructed gender, is as culturally constructed as gender. The focus is thus on sex, as well as on gender, as something people do in their daily practices and performance, not by means of free choice, but through discursive means in which factors such as race and class distinctions also play a role (Visweswaran 1997).

3. This is related to the fact that traveling and conducting research was for several decades impossible in the country. The most prominent work on gender within the Khmer context, conducted by Judy Ledgerwood, is therefore based on her research among Khmer in the United States.

4. See also Mills (1999: 5) about women as symbols of modernity in Thailand.

5. Scholars now tend to consider modernity not merely as an objective reality or as a pursuit of development, but as a phenomenon working upon experience (e.g., Berman 1988; Brenner 1998; Mills 1999). Marshall Berman (1988: 15) pointedly writes that "to be modern is to find ourselves in an environment that promises us adventure, power, joy, growth, transformation of ourselves and the world—and, at the same time, that threatens to destroy everything we have, everything we know, everything we are." This experience of modernity is something that is shared, or, as Appadurai (1996) formulates, "at large," and yet it is nowhere the same and unequally distributed in the present world.

6. Marston develops this in the actions and thoughts of the Democratic Kampuchea cadre, who created their "own type of modernity" or "own type of non-modernity" (2002: 58).

7. Habitus, according to Bourdieu (1977), is the principle of generation and structuration of practices and representations that individuals develop in the course of their life. The habitus engenders all the thoughts, all the perceptions, and all the actions consistent with the historical and socially situated conditions by which it is constituted. Habitus is thus the internalization of objective structures, which are again reproduced through the externalization of internality.

8. Ortner draws here especially on the work of Giddens and Sahlins.

CHAPTER 2. RICE PEOPLE IN THE CITY

1. According to legend, an elderly lady called Péñ found a tree floating in the Mekong which had four bronze Buddha statues and one stone statue of Vishnu caught in its branches. She asked her neighbors to help her construct a small hill (*phnom* in Khmer) with a sanctuary on top in which she placed the Buddhas. The city that developed at this place was named after this hill and the lady: Phnom Penh (Coedès 1913).

2. After the foundation of Phnom Penh as the capital city in mid-fifteenth century, the royal and ceremonial capital of Cambodia was shifted several times to Longveak and Udong (Mabbett and Chandler 1995).

3. French control in Cambodia was interrupted due to the Japanese presence during WWII.

4. Sihanouk had been crowned king in 1941, under French rule, but abdicated from the throne in 1955 in order to become leader of the political movement Sangkum Reastr Niyum (People's Socialist Community) (Osborne 1994; Chandler 1996a).

5. Architectural style that developed among progressive architects (e.g., Le Corbusier) and gained momentum after WWII. The "Modern Movement" is characterized by functionality and clarity of design, the employment of new technology and materials (concrete, glass, iron), clean lines, and a renunciation of ornaments. Paris-educated Khmer architects, most notably Vann Molyvann, adapted this style to the Khmer context and used it in the construction of ministries, the university, the Chaktamuk theater and the Olympic Stadium (Lemarchand 1997; Vann Molyvann 2003).

6. The reasons the Khmer Rouge gave for the evacuation of the city were fear of American bombings, food shortages, epidemics, and the implementation of a necessary security measure against resistance; it may, however, also have been related to their lack of experience with city management (Chandler 1991: 247; McIntyre 1996).

7. After the evacuation of Phnom Penh, the CPK set in motion other migration streams, most notably from the populated southeast to the fertile northwest, thereby completely uprooting families and existing social structures (Vickery 1984; Chandler 1996a; Kiernan 1996).

8. Enemy *(khmang)* was a broad term including those with middle-class backgrounds, intellectuals, Vietnamese and other minorities, and those with connections to the West or with foreign-language skills. Later it came to also include high-ranking members of the party, military commanders, and officials accused of plotting against Pol Pot and his associates or of allying themselves with the Vietnamese and Americans (Chandler 1996a; 1996b).

9. See the home page of the municipality (www.phnompenh.gov.kh).

10. While *neak srae* is often translated as "rice people," a more accurate translation would be "people from the rice field."

11. This disinclination to increase agricultural production is, as critics point

out, related to increased colonial taxation on the harvest. In order to pay these taxes, peasants became more dependent on the sale of their produce and on moneylenders or usurers, increasing their indebtedness and therewith their poverty (Becker 1998: 39).

12. In the case of rural incomes, there may have been some underreporting regarding income from agricultural activities.

13. The relatively high proportion of agricultural workers in urban areas reflects the fact that cities also contain areas that are agricultural in nature. The nature of the census of 1998 may also have influenced this relatively high number. People were asked for their usual, or main, economic activity over the previous twelve months. Seasonal laborers, for example, may thus have been recorded as agricultural workers, whereas their occupation in the city may well have been different (National Institute of Statistics 2000a: 27).

14. Some of them returned later, in the 1990s, when they saw opportunities in the liberalized political and economic situation for their own position or their country's development.

15. The columns in Table 2 distinguish between migrants, or those who at some point had moved to the place of enumeration from last previous place of residence, and recent migrants who moved within the five years prior to the census/survey.

16. For both male and female migrants in urban areas, migration rates were highest for those between twenty and twenty-four years old. Yet, whereas male rates were comparatively higher in the age groups above twenty-four, female migration rates exceeded male rates in the age group between fifteen and nineteen years (National Institute for Statistics 2004: 36). This suggests a situation in which, on the one hand, young, unmarried women are in great demand as migrant laborers and, on the other hand, married women with children face more restrictions in their mobility.

17. *Ksae* literally means "string," "rope," or "line" (Headley 1977: 111), but is used more commonly to refer to patronage networks (Chandler 1999: 89).

18. *Meekcol* can be seen as a category of individuals who are considered to have certain leadership skills or a potential that can be used to organize community activities (Collins 1998: 26–27) but also, as here, to recruit people for work elsewhere. They are not necessarily individuals with high status, but they do have certain capacities or contacts that allow them to operate as mediators in specific situations.

CHAPTER 3. WOMEN, IDEALS, AND MIGRATION

1. For a similar discussion on Javanese gender, see Wolf (1992, esp. chap. 3).

2. See also Rosaldo (1980) and Ortner and Whitehead (1981).

3. While often considered to be a mark of the "high status" of women, Southeast Asian women's control over, and preoccupation with, economic mat-

ters can be the opposite of the kind of power or potency that brings the greatest "prestige," as has been discussed in the case of Javanese notions of spiritual potency and Thai Buddhist notions of attachment (Errington 1990; Brenner 1995; Kirsch 1985).

4. Ledgerwood (1990: 22–23) argues that the Khmer terms for political power, physical strength, religious efficacy and military might are all thought of as male. But women do have a different type of power, through which they exert positive or negative influence on the status of their husbands, fathers and sons.

5. "Karma" literally means action and relates to the Buddhist belief that acts bring about their retribution, usually in a subsequent existence (Buswell 2004: 415).

6. "Dharma" refers to a uniform norm, universal and moral order, natural law, including one's social and proper conduct, as well as to the truth taught by the Buddha (Buswell 2004: 217–219).

7. Such other positions include *achar*, a lay Buddhist specialist. Women do, however, enter the pagoda as *doun chii* or *yeey chii*, who are usually women who want to retreat from the secular world such as the elderly or those who, for various reasons, want to renounce daily social life.

8. The word *chbap* refers to this particular genre of didactic texts of social and moral laws and also to the judicial laws of the country. More generally, Pou (1988: 4) defines *chbap* as "an ensemble of rules to follow, imposed on all individuals within the society with a view to maintain order." In that sense, the *chbap*, prescribing "harmony, balance, regularity, and conformity" (Ayres 2000: 14), is important to overcome the disorder that is associated with ignorance and the wild, *prey* (Chandler 1996b: 49).

9. The most benevolent female spirit is the *mnieng pteah*, who has also been called a *srey krup leakkhana* (Porée-Maspero 1961; Ebihara 1968; Ledgerwood 1990). The *mnieng pteah* are house spirits who guard the domestic order; they do not get angry when members of the house break rules but instead flee the house (Ang 1992). Other kinds of female spirits have more negative characteristics. The *mdaay toam*, or original mother, is a woman who has died but has not been reborn. Instead, she exists as a spirit who seeks to find and retrieve her child from her previous lifetime. She has a chance of recapturing it while the child is very young by causing it to become ill and die (Ledgerwood 1990: 50). For an extended overview of the array of spirits in Khmer folk beliefs, see Ang (1986).

10. These characteristics are not unlike the "widow ghosts" in northeast Thailand described by Mills (1995).

11. Menstrual blood and the blood of delivery are considered dangerous, as they can cause illness in both women and men, and have the potential of weakening the power of traditional and religious healers (Ledgerwood 1990; Ang 1986).

12. This concerns some verses regarding women's role in containing the fires

within and outside the house, as well as some verses advising women to walk silently and elegantly (so as not to make the skirt rustle) and to be orderly.

13. See also the M.A. thesis of Aing Sok Roeun (2004), which shows that while most of the women she interviewed could not remember or recite the text, the meaning of it was passed on from grandmother to mother to daughter.

14. The title of Ebihara's article "Khmer Village Women in Cambodia: A Happy Balance" was not chosen by herself but by the editors of the volume (Ledgerwood, personal communication; 1990: 170n).

15. Ebihara (1968) writes (in the 1960s) that in her village the ritual had not been observed for forty years. None of the young women I encountered had, indeed, "entered the shade." However, the custom, in reduced form, is still observed in certain areas. Soun Cendep observed for his B.A. thesis (2003) the *coul mlup* ceremony in eight families in Srey Ambel, Koh Kong province.

16. It is not necessarily evident what is meant by sexual violation. Tarr (1996: 160) notes that hugging and kissing can be considered sexual activities, or at least preludes to sexual activity, and are thus seen as highly sexual in nature. This also raises the question of local understandings of sexual violation.

17. This may be true not only for premarital sexual relations but also for extramarital affairs. In 1996, I was involved in a research project on "conflict resolution," during which I heard several stories of women involved in relationships with married men. While I did not get into the subtle differences between seduction and coercion that may have existed in such relationships, it was clear that naming, or renaming, such extramarital affairs as rape would acquit the woman of most of the blame and require that, depending on the situation, she would either receive a financial payment from or marry the man who had "caught" her.

18. The importance of parents' involvement in marriage arrangements is reflected in the saying "before planting the rice look at the grass, before marrying off a child look at the lineage."

19. This freedom to choose or reject a marriage partner was limited during the Khmer Rouge time, when marriages were arranged by the *angkar* and carried out en masse between couples brought together without looking at the status or wealth of the respective families, and without checking with the spirits about whether the couple would fit together.

20. Distinctions between the kinds of *srey meemay* are made in the full terminology: a widow is a *srey meemay pdey slap,* that is, a woman whose husband has died, while a divorced woman is called a *srey meemay leeng pdey* or a *srey meemay pdey leeng*, depending on whether the wife or the husband initiated the divorce. A woman who has been abandoned by her husband is also called a *srey meemay pdey rut choul.*

21. A favorite joke among my neighbor kids was to chant *kramom-meemay* along to the rhythm of the gecko in my house. The final cry of the gecko

would end their chanting with either *kramom* or *meemay,* thus predicting the marital state of their future bride.

22. See, for a similar observation about women without men in a completely different context, in this case Algeria, Jansen 1987.

23. In 1996 the State Secretariat of Women's Affairs was upgraded to the Ministry of Women's Affairs. After the formation of a new government in 1998, the name and responsibilities of the Ministry of Women's Affairs was extended to include Veteran's Affairs. Within the latest government formation (July 2004) the ministry was again renamed the Ministry of Women's Affairs. I use the term Ministry of Women's Affairs for all periods for convenience.

24. Quoted in Derks (1997: 21).

25. Sixty-four percent of females aged fifteen and above are literate (compared to 85 percent of males); 64 percent of Cambodian women above twenty-five have not completed primary-level education (as opposed to 46 percent of men). Furthermore, while Cambodian boys and girls have similar high enrollment rates (almost 90 percent) until the age of fourteen, the percentage attending school after this age decreases sharply, with girls being more likely to drop out of school at a later age (National Institute of Statistics 2004).

26. Male mobility has been much less associated with such moral considerations regarding sexual propriety. This can be explained by the fact that male mobility has a precedent in off-farm labor during the slack season, as in the cases of monks, traveling merchants, or men who move for administrative purposes. Moreover, the double standard regarding sexual morality, which allows men to have sexual experiences from which women should be protected, also makes male mobility in that sense less problematic.

CHAPTER 4. FACTORY WORK

1. *Damlung* is a unit of weight for gold that is equal to about 37.5 grams. One *damlung* is ten *cii,* which was worth about 340 US dollars at the time of research.

2. In 2004, 91 percent of the poor lived in rural areas (World Bank 2006).

3. *Hun* is a unit of weight for gold that is equal to about 3.75 grams. Ten *hun* is one *cii,* which was worth about thirty-four US dollars at the time of research.

4. Fermented fish paste.

5. At the time of the research, one US dollar equaled about 3,800 riel.

6. Although this is a generally held view, it was not confirmed in an USAID study on competitiveness and labor productivity in Cambodia's garment industry. The study concluded that, although comparatively weak in training, work methods and production specification, Cambodia's overall factory performance ranked behind more advanced countries like Turkey and

Mexico, on a par with the Brazilian industry, and actually ahead of industries in China and Egypt (Sok Hach 2005).

7. Interestingly, these women referred to the *khmauc* of a living person, whereas the term *khmauc* is normally used to refer to a ghost or spirit of a dead person (Ang 1986).

8. Now an independent ministry (Ministry of Labor and Vocational Training), formerly the Department of Labor and Manpower under the Ministry of Social Affairs, Labor, Vocational Training and Youth.

9. See for more information the Web site of Better Factories (www .betterfactories.org).

10. According to the ILO Minimum Age Convention No. 138, the minimum age for admission to work is fifteen years or, as an exception, fourteen years in countries covered by article 2.4 of the ILO Convention.

11. In order to monitor adherence to the code of conduct, monitors travel between the factories producing for their companies in order to explain and demand adherence to their code of conduct. This monitoring, as is often emphasized, is a work in progress. In the case of H&M in Asia, for example, monitoring starts with checking on the presence and state of fire extinguishers, since this is seen as a necessary first step in achieving better working conditions in other facets of the working process. Implementation of a full code of conduct is, however, limited in most factories in Cambodia.

12. This became very clear when in 2000 the BBC documentary "GAP Nike— No Sweat?" on working conditions in the Cambodian garment industry shed light on the use of child labor and abusive practices within Cambodia's garment industry. It focused on one factory producing for, among others Nike and the Gap, and accused these companies of breaking their codes of conduct. The documentary showed a twelve-year-old factory worker, who later claimed to have lied about her age for ten dollars, as well as other underaged workers who complained about forced overtime and abusive working conditions. Already before broadcasting, the documentary drove the accused clothing companies to react by canceling job orders for this particular factory, leading again to job losses for workers.

13. The president of the FTUWKC, Chea Vichea, was killed in January 2004. The investigation into his murder led to arrests, but the case was dismissed due to lack of evidence.

14. See, for more information, the Web site of the Arbitration Council (www .arbitrationcouncil.org).

CHAPTER 5. SEX WORK

1. Boulding, which is how Khmer pronounce "building," is a modern-style apartment complex built in the Bassac area in the early 1960s and turned into a squatter area in the 1990s.

2. A healing practice in which coins are used to systematically scratch over the body (especially the back, chest, and shoulders) in order to alleviate certain symptoms of illness (headache, cold, etc.).

3. See, for an overview of the different estimates of the total number of sex workers according to various reports, Derks et al. 2006.

4. In the two brothel areas in Phnom Penh where I conducted the research, Toul Kork and Boulding, medical organizations operating in the areas counted 453 and 99 sex workers in brothels in the respective areas between late 2001 and early 2002.

5. See Ten Brummelhuis 1999 for a description of the various and changing meanings of *kathoey* in a Thai context.

6. See also Jansen 1987.

7. I use the terms "sex work" and "prostitution" interchangeably, depending on the context and translations within the text. Yet, since the focus of my study is on three kinds of economic activities in which rural women engage when they come to Phnom Penh, the term "sex work" expresses a more equal understanding of these alternative categories.

8. The region in question is still known among Cambodians as Kampuchea Krom, or "Lower Cambodia."

9. The 1997 survey by the National Assembly Commission on Human Rights and the Reception of Complaints estimated that 18 percent of the brothel-based sex workers nationwide were Vietnamese; the 1998 PSI census found 38 percent Vietnamese among the sex workers in the various sex establishments in Phnom Penh; and Steinfatt et al. (2002) calculated that Vietnamese sex workers formed 47 percent of the total number of sex workers in Phnom Penh.

10. A brothel area eleven kilometers north of Phnom Penh. It was closed down in 2004.

11. Code name used by the Khmer Rouge regime—literally, "organization."

12. The Khmer word used for deflowering is derived from the Vietnamese word *khui*. Literally, *khui* means "to open a bottle," "to uncork," or "to make a hole." The term *khui* is also used figuratively to describe having sex with a girl or woman who is still a virgin. Deflowering a young girl is by some (especially Chinese) men also believed to have a rejuvenating effect. After having been deflowered, these girls or women are so-called *khui haey* or *kouc haey* ("deflowered already") and therefore reduced in their special symbolic as well as financial "value." Those who have been recruited as virgin prostitutes often continue, like Phea, to work as prostitutes.

13. Sex workers often calculated their income in *cii*, or the gold measure worth about thirty-four dollars.

14. Social and health workers who target sex workers often complain about the unprofessional attitude of Cambodian sex workers, who (unlike their Vietnamese counterparts) have sweethearts with whom they have unpro-

tected sex and whom they support. A health worker thought that Khmer sex workers have a poor understanding of relationships with men. They develop intimate relationships with customers who regularly visit them. At the beginning, these still pay money, but after a while they stop paying for sex and may even receive money from the sex worker: these men *deik sii* (sleep and eat) off her. And, in the worst cases, they also infect her. A brothel owner may not notice at first, only with time, when she notices that the two stay in the room for a long period. Yet, he concluded, the brothel owner cannot force too much upon the woman, because she is afraid the woman will run away.

15. The practice of child prostitution is believed to have increased over recent years, since young, fresh and healthy—that is, not skinny—girls are seen as being free from HIV. Although it is difficult to obtain reliable numbers regarding child prostitution in Cambodia, studies indicate that it involves Vietnamese children in particular.

16. See also Crochet 1998 and Eisenbruch 1997.

17. Lately much more attention is being given to this phenomenon of gang rape *(bauk)* following NGO and media reporting (see Gender and Development for Cambodia 2003).

18. These initiatives have been greatly reduced due to the guidelines of the US aid policy asking NGOs to denounce prostitution and refrain from activities that would change laws regarding prostitution or enhance sex workers' rights as a condition for receiving funds.

CHAPTER 6. STREET TRADE

1. Although trade still forms the second-largest employment category for urban women, the rise of the garment industry has led to an increasing proportion of women working in manufacturing, apparently at the expense of their involvement in trade (Godfrey et al. 2001).

2. Alexander developed the concept of "*pasar* system" within the Javanese context. It can, however, just as well be used to describe the ways in which Cambodian markets function.

3. A similar distinction was made by Alexander (1994; 1998) among Javanese traders: wholesale, the domain of Chinese merchants; and the independent, small-scale traders, mostly women, dealing in a range of agricultural and manufactured commodities.

4. This argument resembles the one that men's absence from trade in Java can be explained by the belief that such activity will undermine "spiritual potency" and "status" (Brenner 1995).

5. The landlady buys the rice noodles for four hundred riel per kilo and sells them to the vendors for seven hundred riel per kilo.

6. This refers not only to such items as clothes and sunglasses, but also to

street-food items. For example, foods like apples and doughnuts, which used to be rare or unknown, have during the past years become increasingly popular.

7. See also the rotating saving association *(arisan)* in Indonesia (e.g., Wolf 1992; Brenner 1998).

8. This means that those who take up the first loans pay more money (always as much as the first contribution) than those who take up the later loans (the contributions decrease with each participant taking a loan).

9. *Sraoc tik* ceremonies can be performed in different ways. Most generally, water in a container or bucket is endowed with magical power through the chanting of Buddhist mantras, incense smoke, and candles, after which the monks spray it over the person for whom the ceremony is organized. Cambodians may organize a *sraoc tik* ceremony for various reasons—to avert danger, to ensure safety before a long trip, to recover from illness, to boost prosperity in business, to increase happiness in the family. *Sraoc tik* ceremonies are also held during the Khmer New Year, or before marriage or other transitional events in life. The more general terms for the different versions, which may be part of one ceremony, are *romdoh kru'eh,* to free or save from danger; *creah cungrei,* to avert misfortune or bad luck; and *leuk riesei,* to return to prosperous times (Derks 1998b: 25).

10. Geertz (1978) explored this tendency to establish continuing relationships between buyers and sellers in a town in Morocco. Similar client relationships can be found in Indonesia, called *langganan* (see also Alexander 1994).

11. Although Bijlmer (1989) based this categorization on his study of street workers in Surabaya, it can be easily adapted to Cambodia.

CHAPTER 7. CITY LIFE AND MODERN EXPERIENCE

1. The expression is borrowed from an article by Chandara Lor and Brian Calvert, "Capital Ambitions. For Pur Sat Villagers, Phnom Penh Is a Place of Wonder—and Danger," *Cambodia Daily,* January 13–14, 2001.

2. See Appadurai 1996: 66–85 for a more detailed description of the relationship between time and consumption.

3. Distinctions made by Khmer regarding complexion usually go unnoticed among foreigners, indicating the social construction of these distinctions. See also Rozario 2002: 47 for a description of the social construction of complexion in Bangladesh.

4. Such views on the differences between the village and the city have been repeated in different times and about different parts of the world (see, e.g., Wirth 1975; Hannerz 1980; Ferguson 1992; Rapport and Overing 2000).

5. This also refers to the easy ways of earning an income.

6. Food stalls outside factory compounds offer the opportunity to eat three meals a day for a fixed amount per month (around eighteen dollars) or, for

those who do not eat at a fixed stall, to write down what they eat and pay once a week or month.

7. Mills (1997; 1999) uses the phrase *than samay* for "modern" in Thai, which she also translates as "up-to-date."

8. A night of anti-Thai riots took place in Phnom Penh in 2003 after rumors circulated that a Thai actress had suggested that Angkor Wat belonged to Thailand. The riots brought considerable damage to Thai-owned businesses, hotels, and the Thai Embassy.

9. In 2004, according to a World Bank report (2006).

10. Martel (1975: 253–254), for example, describes two tendencies in Lovéa, the village in which she conducted her research: those who represent the religious and modern world, and a "modern" group linked with administration and oriented toward a consumer society.

11. This is also the premise of several publications on the "modern woman" in Asia that pay special attention to the local forms of being modern (see, e.g., Mills 1997; Sen and Stivens 1998; Schein 1999; Munshi 2001).

12. It was hard to obtain consistent information on spending for personal consumption. This is partly related to the fact that most women do not keep accounts of their earnings and spending, but also because of the actual monthly variations in women's earnings as well as in monthly personal spending, such as those related to festivals, trips home, or other occasions. Women may, however, also be wary of actually keeping accounts of their personal spending (in relation to remittances). Mills (1999: 130) similarly noted that the young women to whom she spoke were often reluctant to reveal exactly how much of their wages they spent in the city, especially on nonessential items.

13. See Chapter 3 for a description of the *coul mlup* custom.

14. The manuscript is a small booklet consisting of wooden pages, each of which contains a small story. This booklet is held above the head and one "selects" one story by sticking, without looking, a pin or incense stick between the pages. The *achar* then reads the selected text and explains its meaning.

15. Going to the movies was a popular activity during the 1960s, when many new movie theaters opened in Phnom Penh and the provinces (Ly and Muan 2001). Phnom Penh had more than thirty movie theaters in the 1960s that, due to the ongoing war, were closed or abandoned and, after a short revival in the early 1980s, later used as gas stations, restaurants, or other businesses. A few cinemas have recently opened up again.

16. A series of restaurants-cum-guesthouses along the Mekong, southeast of Phnom Penh.

17. The Water Festival, with boat races between teams from all the provinces, takes place in November and marks the reversal of the current of the Tonle Sap river at the beginning of the dry season (when water from Lake Tonle Sap flows back into the Mekong).

CHAPTER 8. DUTIFUL DAUGHTERS, BROKEN WOMEN

1. These are sloth, pride, anger, gluttony, lust, covetousness and envy.

2. Roseman (2002: 24) "extends the concept of 'code switching' to the broad array of cultural expressions of class and linguistic identity from its original use in sociolinguistic analysis to describe individuals regularly switching in patterned ways between different languages or between language varieties." See also Heller 1988 about micro-level and macro-level sociolinguistic approaches to code switching.

3. Ebihara (1968: 207) describes how villagers among themselves, as well as with close relatives, may avoid open confrontation in expressing their disapproval and criticism regarding deviant behavior. More typically, such criticism is voiced behind an offender's back.

4. Various studies about female labor migration in Southeast Asia refer to the conflict between the pursuit of "modern" experiences and family obligations. From these studies we learn that the ways in which migrants deal with this dilemma are dependent on their gender, life-cycle factors, social and economic backgrounds, and their kind of employment, as well as "those factors which condition and colour female agency in the community, and the capacity of young women to be architects of their own lives" (Elmhirst 2002: 152; see also Wolf 1992; Mills 1999).

5. Other studies on the remittances of factory workers come up with similar amounts (World Bank 2006: 67).

6. The importance of filial obligations has been observed widely in female migration studies and is commonly thought to be stronger for daughters than for sons (Strauch 1984; Curran 1996; Mills 1999). In Thailand, for example, studies have indicated that, although men and women are equally likely to migrate, women remit wages and gifts to their parents' home at a significantly higher rate, and are expected to do so (Curran and Saguy 1997).

7. See Mills (1999: 76) about "debt of merit," or *bun khun*, in a Thai context. Also, Cambodian women sometimes explained *sang kun* as a form of earning merit *(tweu bon)*. Similar conceptions of (moral) indebtedness can be found in Indonesia *(hutang budi)* and the Philippines *(utang-na-loob)* (Pye 1985).

8. A Cambodian researcher on Buddhism told me the story to explain the concept of *sang kun*. The story is also described in Keyes 1984 with the name "Blessing of Ordination."

9. The story continues with the intention of the son to save his father. This, however, is not easy and requires the son to be ordained as a monk, i.e., to follow a much longer and stricter route in the footsteps of the Buddha (Keyes 1984: 228).

10. Chant and McIlwaine (1995: 273), in their study about female labor in the Philippines, point to the differences between migrant women in vari-

ous kinds of employment and their ties with their homes. They argue that, unlike women working in factories or tourism, sex workers, due to the shame attached to their work, tend to sever contacts with their families, allowing them more personal and behavioral freedom and liberating them from a sense of duty and obligation. This view, however, seems inconsistent with the general assumption that it is principally the pressure daughters face regarding their responsibility for family survival, and the high earnings they can achieve in comparison to those from other kinds of work available to them, that pushes women into prostitution (e.g., Muecke 1992; Lim 1998: 12). I found both patterns among the sex workers I met. The intensity of ties with home varied considerably between, for example, women like Khim (Chapter 4) whose mother and siblings stayed close to the brothel in which she worked, and women like Piseth who had hardly any contact with her family back home.

11. See Surtees 2003 for a description of Cambodian understandings and forms of rape.

12. Premarital sex on the part of men, although not considered unproblematic, is seen as a common phenomenon, as is also evident from Meng's estimation that "out of ten men only one thinks of remaining *borisot* [before marriage]."

13. There is, however, no agreement as to what "sexual misconduct" means. Some Cambodians I talked to maintained that virginity is not a Buddhist value but rather a remnant of Indian-Hindu influence or a result of colonial (Christian) influence, which considered sex before marriage as sinful.

14. Porée-Maspero (1985: 68) describes illnesses or other punishments affecting the family members of young women and men who have engaged in premarital relationships, as well as the ceremony to heal the affected person. Also Ledgerwood (1990: 176f.) gives examples of how, among Khmer living in the United States, ancestral spirits caused illnesses or accidents because of the immoral conduct of some other family members.

15. To "bow the head to the mat" *(kbaal dol kanteel)* is an expression referring to the wedding ceremony, at which the married couple bow their heads, both palms together in front of the chest with the fingers pointing upwards, in front of their parents as a sign of respect and as an homage to ancestral spirits.

16. A representative of a woman's organization, who had read the story at school, described the story as follows. The first wife of a king feels neglected because he is preoccupied with gambling and his other wives. She falls in love with a man who used to come to play chess with her husband. The man kidnaps her and takes her to his place, where they live happily together. When he abandons her one day to *kan sel* (respect the precepts), she meets another man who tells her he loves her. She believes him and follows him. The man, however, is a messenger of the king. He brings her back to the king, who punishes her for her promiscuous behavior by putting her on a

raft and letting it float away on the sea. This is how she dies. For a somewhat different version of the story, see Ledgerwood (1990).

17. For example, Leclerc-Madlala (2001: 539–540) states that markers of female virginity are, in the case of KwaZulu-Natal province in South Africa, not so much related to hymens as to particular folk constructs of the body and ethnomedical beliefs about health and illness, whereby the importance of the eyes (innocent or knowing), breasts and abdomen (firm and taut or flabby and loose), and muscles behind the knees (tight and straight or not), are the important markers in assessing a young woman's virginity. Within the practice of "virginity testing," examinations of the genitalia are performed in regard to color, size, wetness and visibility of "white dot."

18. A tall hardwood tree.

GLOSSARY

achar	lay Buddhist teacher, wise man
angkar	organization; in Pol Pot's time used for regime
'at leakkhana	improper, lacking quality
baap	badness, sin, immoral action
barang	French; foreigner
bong	elder sibling
bong-p'oun	brothers and sisters, relatives
bong srey	older sister
Bon No'ael	Christmas
Bon Pcum Ben	Buddhist ceremony to commemorate one's ancestors
Bon Sangsaa	Valentine's Day (February 14)
Bon Set Neary	Women's Day (March 8)
boraan	old, ancient, from former times
borisot	pure, good, perfect
chamkar	garden farmland
chbap	law, didactic code, code of conduct
Chbap Srey	Code of Women's Behavior
cih coan	to oppress
cii	unit of weight of gold equal to about 3.75 grams (ten *hun*), worth about 34 US dollars at the time of research
coul mlup	"entrance into the shade"; the ceremony to mark a girl's reaching puberty, when she is kept in the house and out of the sun
cumnueñ	business, commerce, (wholesale) trade
dae leeng	to go out (for fun, for a walk)
damlung	unit of weight for gold that is equal to about 37.5 grams (ten *cii*), worth about 340 US dollars at the time of research
dondeng	to ask for a woman's hand in marriage
kaa	to marry (v.); marriage (n.)
kaac	nasty, bad, wicked
kaliip	probably from French *calibre*; high-class; sexy
kam	karma, fate (usually bad)
kañcraeng	basket
karma	action; concept related to the Buddhist belief that acts bring about their retribution, usually in a subsequent existence
kcil	lazy, unmotivated

ketteyuh	honor
khmah kee	to be ashamed, embarrassed, lose face
khmauc	ghost
khui	to deflower
koh	wrong, incorrect, different
komlah	unmarried young man, bachelor
kouc	broken, damaged, ruined, bad
kouc haey	broken (deflowered) already
kouc kluen	to be spoiled, lose virginity
koun	child, kid
koun 'akateñu	ungrateful child
kramom	virgin, young unmarried girl
krom	group
krup kaa	marriageable; sexually mature
kruu	teacher; traditional healer
ksae	string, rope; (patronage) networks
kun	kindness, goodness, merit
luek-dou	lit. "to sell-change"; to trade
mcah pteah	house owner
mdaay (mae)	mother
mee	leader
meebaa	ancestral spirits
meebon	brothel owner/keeper/manager
meekcol	lit. "leader of the wind"; person with leadership and mediating skills, such as in relation to labor recruitment
meekrom	group leader (in factories, supervisor)
meemay	divorced or widowed woman
meul niey	to look down on, scorn, have contempt for someone
mlup	shade
mooy	regular customer
motodup	motorbike-taxi
neak chamkar	people from the garden farmlands
neak krong	city people
neak srae	"rice people," people from the rice fields
neak taa	guardian spirit
niyiey daem	to talk bad behind one's back, slander
num-bancok	rice noodles with a curry-like sauce and fresh vegetables
numpan	bread
opsuk	boring
p'oun srey	younger sister
pñiew	guest, customer

prahok	fermented fish paste
(prak-)daem	initial investment for a business
prak-khae	monthly salary
prey	forest; wild, savage, undomesticated
proh	man, male
propeinii	tradition
prothien	leader; supervisor
prummecaarey-phiep	virginity
psar	market
riel	Cambodian currency; at the time of research 1 US dollar equaled about 3,800 riel
rook sii	lit. "to find food"; to do business, earn an income
rook sii luek kluen	to earn money by selling one's body (sex work)
s'aat	beautiful
samay thmey	new time, modern
sang kun	to return kindness, merit
sangsaa	sweetheart, boyfriend/girlfriend
sapbaay	happy, fun, enjoyable
sii	to eat (esp. applies to animals)
sii khae	to be paid per month
sloot	gentle, sweet, shy, compliant
srae	rice field
srey	woman
srey kouc	broken woman, prostitute
srey kramom (prummecaarey)	virgin woman
srey krup leakkhana	perfectly virtuous, proper woman, woman with full qualities
srey rook sii plew peet	sex worker
srey samay	modern woman
srok	district
srok srae	countryside, farm village
taipan	pimp
thawkae	boss, manager, owner of a shop (Ch.)
tik-kralok	fruit-shake
toan samay	modern, up-to-date
toan samay cruel	beyond modern
toan samay peek	too modern
tontine	saving association
yeey	grandmother, elderly woman

BIBLIOGRAPHY

Abu-Lughod, Lila. 1990. "The Romance of Resistance: Tracing Transformations of Power through Bedouin Women." *American Ethnologist* 17, no.
1, 41–55.

ADHOC. 1999. "Report on Special Activities of Human Rights and Research
on Causes of the Prostitution in Cambodia." Phnom Penh: ADHOC.

Ahearn, Laura A. 2001. "Language and Agency." *Annual Review of Anthropology* 30: 109–137.

Aing Sok Roeun. 2004. "A Comparative Analysis of Traditional and Contemporary Roles of Khmer Women in the Household. A Case Study in Leap
Tong Village." M.A. thesis, Royal University of Phnom Penh.

Alexander, Jennifer. 1994. "Markets, Gender and the State." Working paper,
University of Bielefeld.

———. 1998. "Women Traders in Javanese Marketplaces: Ethnicity, Gender,
and the Entrepreneurial Spirit." In *Market Cultures: Society and Morality in
the New Asian Capitalisms,* edited by Robert W. Hefner, 203–223. Boulder,
CO: Westview Press.

Andaya, Barbara Watson. 2002. "Localising the Universal: Women, Motherhood and the Appeal of Early Therevada Buddhism." *Journal of Southeast
Asian Studies* 33, no. 1: 1–30.

Ang, Choulean. 1986. *Les êtres surnaturel khmer dans la religion populaire
khmère.* Paris: Cedoreck.

———. 1992. "Le sacré au féminin." *Seksa Khmer* 1987–1990, nos. 10–13:
3–30.

Appadurai, Arjun. 1996. *Modernity at Large: Cultural Dimensions of Globalization.* Minneapolis: University of Minnesota Press.

Arbitration Council. www.arbitrationcouncil.org (accessed August 30, 2006).

Asian Development Bank. 1996. "The National Policy for Women: Cambodia." Manila: ADB.

Atkinson, Jane Monning, and Shelly Errington, eds. 1990. *Power and Difference: Gender in Island Southeast Asia.* Stanford, CA: Stanford University
Press.

Ayres, David M. 2000. *Anatomy of a Crisis: Education, Development, and the
State in Cambodia, 1953–1998.* Honolulu: University of Hawai'i Press.

Banwell, Suzanna Stout. 2001. "Vendor's Voices: The Story of Women Micro-
Vendors in Phnom Penh Markets and an Innovative Program Designed to
Enhance Their Lives and Livelihoods." Phnom Penh: The Asia Foundation.

Barry, Kathleen. 1995. *The Prostitution of Sexuality.* New York: New York
University Press.

Barth, Fredrik. 1994. "A Personal View of Present Tasks and Priorities in Cultural and Social Anthropology." In *Assessing Cultural Anthropology,* edited by Robert Borofsky, 349–361. New York: McGraw-Hill.

———. 2002. "An Anthropology of Knowledge." *Current Anthropology* 43, no. 1: 1–18.

Becker, Elizabeth. 1998. *When the War Was Over: Cambodia and the Khmer Rouge Revolution.* New York: Public Affairs.

Bennett, Linda Rae. 2002. "Modernity, Desire and Courtship: The Evolution of Premarital Relationships in Mataram, Eastern Indonesia." In *Coming of Age in South and Southeast Asia: Youth, Courtship and Sexuality,* edited by Lenore Manderson and Pranee Liamputtong, 96–112. Richmond, UK: Curzon.

Berman, Marshall. 1988. *All That Is Solid Melts into Air: The Experience of Modernity.* New York: Penguin Books.

Better Factories. www.betterfactories.org (accessed August 30, 2006).

Better Factories Cambodia. 2006. "Cambodia Garment Industry: One Year Later. Fact Sheet." ILO, www.betterfactories.org/content/documents/One%20year%20later%20–%20May%2006%20(en).pdf.

Beyrer, Chris. 1998. *War in the Blood: Sex, Politics and AIDS in Southeast Asia.* London: Zed Books.

Bijlmer, Joep. 1989. "The Informal Sector as 'Lucky Dip': Concepts and Research Strategies. Some Critical Notes Based on Research among Ambulatory Street-Workers in Surabaja, Indonesia." In *About Fringes, Margins and Lucky Dips. The Informal Sector in Third World Countries: Recent Developments in Research and Policy,* edited by Paul van Gelder and Joep Bijlmer, 141–159. Amsterdam: Free University Press.

Bit, Seanglim. 1991. *The Warrior Heritage: A Psychological Perspective of Cambodian Trauma.* El Cerrito, CA: Seanglim Bit.

Blancot, Christiane. 1997. "La reconstruction." In *Phnom Penh: Développement urbain et patrimoine,* edited by Christiane Blancot and Dominique Petermüller, 61–70. Paris: Atelier parisien d'urbanisme.

Blancot, Christiane, and Aline Hetreau-Pottier. 1997. "1863–1953, Une ville neuve dans un site d'occupation ancienne." In *Phnom Penh: Développement urbain et patrimoine,* edited by Christiane Blancot and Dominique Petermüller, 29–39. Paris: Atelier parisien d'urbanisme.

Blancot, Christiane, and Dominique Petermüller, eds. 1997. *Phnom Penh: Développement urbain et patrimoine.* Paris: Atelier parisien d'urbanisme.

Bolwell, Dain. 2004. "Cambodia Trade Union Survey 2004." Phnom Penh: ILO Worker's Education Project.

Boserup, Ester. 1970. *Women's Role in Economic Development.* New York: St. Martin's Press.

Bourdieu, Pierre. 1977. *Outline of a Theory of Practice.* Translated by Richard Nice. Cambridge: Cambridge University Press (1972).

———. 1984. *Distinctions: A Social Critique of the Judgement of Taste.* Translated by Richard Nice. Cambridge, MA: Harvard University Press (1979).

Bowen, John R. 1995. "The Forms Culture Take: A State-of-the-Field Essay on the Anthropology of Southeast Asia." *Journal of Asian Studies* 54, no. 4: 1047–1078.

Brenner, Suzanne A. 1995. "Why Women Rule the Roots: Rethinking Javanese Ideologies of Gender and Self-Control." In *Bewitching Women, Pious Men: Gender and Body Politics in Southeast Asia,* edited by Aihwa Ong and Michael Peletz, 19–50. Berkeley: University of California Press.

———. 1998. *The Domestication of Desire: Women, Wealth and Modernity in Java.* Princeton, NJ: Princeton University Press.

Brooks, Ann. 2003. "The Politics of Location in Southeast Asia: Intersecting Tensions around Gender, Ethnicity, Class and Religion." *Asian Journal of Social Science* 31, no. 1: 86–106.

Brown, David L. 2002. "Migration and Community: Social Networks in a Multilevel World." *Rural Sociology* 67, no. 1: 1–23.

Brydon, Anne, and Sandra Niessen, eds. 1998. *Consuming Fashion: Adorning the Transnational Body.* Oxford: Berg.

Brydon, Lynne, and Sylvia Chant. 1989. *Women in the Third World: Gender Issues in Rural and Urban Areas.* Aldershot, UK: Edward Elgar Publishing.

Burgler, R. A. 1990. *The Eyes of the Pineapple: Revolutionary Intellectuals and Terror in Democratic Kampuchea.* Saarbrücken: Verlag Breitenbach Publishers.

Buswell, Robert E., ed. 2004. *Encyclopedia of Buddhism.* Vol. 1. New York: MacMillan Reference USA.

Butler, Judith. 1999. *Gender Trouble.* New York: Routledge.

Cabinet du Résident-Maire de la ville de Phnom Penh. 1906. "Arrête sur la proposition du commissaire central de police." Phnom Penh.

Calvert, Brian, and Ana Nov. 2001. "Adolescent Sex—and Its Risks—on the Rise." *Cambodia Daily,* February 12.

Cambodia Development Resource Institute. 2006. "Economy Watch—Indicators." *Cambodia Development Review* 10, no. 1: 18–19.

Cassell, Philip, ed. 1993. *The Giddens Reader.* Stanford, CA: Stanford University Press.

CEDAW (Convention on the Elimination of all Forms of Discrimination against Women). 2006. "Cambodia: Responses to the List of Issues and Questions for Consideration of the Combined Initial, Second and Third Periodic Report." United Nations. <cambodia.ohchr.org/download.aspx?ep_id =274> (accessed on 29.08.2006).

Chambers, Iain. 1994. *Migrancy, Culture, Identity.* London: Routledge.

Chan Dina. 1999. "Trafficking and Prostitution." In *Looking Back, Moving Forward: Proceedings of the First National Conference on Gender and Development in Cambodia.* Phnom Penh: GAD/C.

Chan Sophal, and Kim Sedara. 2003. "Enhancing Rural Livelihoods." *Cambodia Development Review* 7, no. 1: 1–4.

Chandler, David. 1991. *The Tragedy of Cambodian History: Politics, War and Revolution since 1945.* New Haven, CT: Yale University Press.

———. 1996a. *A History of Cambodia.* 2nd ed., updated. Boulder, CO: Westview Press.

———. 1996b. *Facing the Cambodian Past.* Chiang Mai: Silkworm Books.

———. 1999. *Voices from S-21: Terror and History in Pol Pot's Secret Prison.* Berkeley: University of California Press.

Chant, Sylvia. 1992. *Gender and Migration in Developing Countries.* London: Bellhaven Press.

Chant, Sylvia, and Cathy McIlwaine. 1995. *Women of a Lesser Cost: Female Labour, Foreign Exchange and Philippine Development.* London: Pluto Press.

Chant, Sylvia, and Sarah A. Radcliffe. 1992. "Migration and Development: The Importance of Gender." In *Gender and Migration in Developing Countries,* edited by Sylvia Chant, 1–29. London: Bellhaven Press.

Chapkis, Wendy. 1997. *Life Sex Acts: Women Performing Erotic Labor.* New York: Routledge.

Chhoy Kim Sar, Touch Varine, Kham Phalin, and Prak Sophea. 1997. "Rural Women and the Socio-Economic Transition in the Kingdom of Cambodia." Phnom Penh: Ministry of Women's Affairs.

Choldin, Harvey M. 1973. "Kinship Networks in the Migration Process." *International Migration Review* 7, no. 2: 163–175.

Chommie, Michael. 1998. "Census of Commercial Sex Establishments." Phnom Penh: PSI.

Chou Kim. 1993. "The Problem of Prostitution in Cambodia: Is It Normal for the Khmer Society?" *Khmer Conscience* 7, no. 2: 17–19.

Coèdes, George. 1913. "La fondation de Phnom Pén au xve siècle d'après la chronique cambodgienne." *Bulletin d'École française d'Extrême-Orient* 6: 6–11.

Cohen, Monique. 1984. "The Urban Street Food Trade in Developing Countries." Washington, DC: Equity Policy Center.

Collins, William A. 1997. "Dynamics of Dispute Resolution and Administration of Justice for Cambodian Villagers." Phnom Penh: USAID.

———. 1998. "Grassroots Civil Society in Cambodia." Phnom Penh: Center for Advanced Study.

Commission on Human Rights and Reception of Complaints. 1997. "Report on the Problem of Sexual Exploitation and Trafficking in Cambodia." Phnom Penh: National Assembly.

Council for the Development of Cambodia (CDC). "A Guide to Investment in Cambodia." Phnom Penh: Cambodian Investment Board, CDC, n.d.

Council of the State of Cambodia. 1989. "Cambodian Law of Marriage and Family (Unofficial Translation)." National Assembly, Phnom Penh.

Crochet, Soizick. 1998. "Activités et idéologies des agences internationales en charge de programmes de Sida au Cambodge." *Eglises d'Asie* 98, no. 4: 1–33.

Cross, John C. 2000. "Street Vendors, Modernity and Postmodernity: Conflict and Compromise in the Global Economy." *International Journal of Sociology and Social Policy* 20, no. 1/2: 30–52.

Curran, Sara. 1996. "Intra-Household Exchange Relations: Explanations for Gender Differentials in Education and Migration Outcomes in Thailand." Seattle Population Research Center Working Paper, University of Washington.

Curran, Sara R., and Abigail C. Saguy. 1997. "Migration and Cultural Change: A Role for Gender and Social Networks?" Working Paper Series, Center for Migration and Development, Princeton University.

Curtis, Grant. 1998. *Cambodia Reborn? The Transition to Democracy and Development*. Geneva: UNRISD.

CWDA (Cambodian Women's Development Agency). 1995. "The Prostitution and Traffic of Women: A Dialogue on the Cambodian Situation." Paper presented at the Workshop-Conference, Phnom Penh, 4–5 May.

De Jonge, Huub. 2000. "Trade and Ethnicity: Street and Beach Sellers from Raas on Bali." *Pacific Tourism Review* 4: 75–86.

Delvert, Jean. 1961. *Le paysan cambodgien*. Paris: Mouton & Co.

Derks, Annuska. 1997. "Trafficking of Cambodian Women and Children to Thailand." Phnom Penh: IOM/CAS.

———. 1998a. "Trafficking of Vietnamese Women and Children to Cambodia." Phnom Penh: IOM/CAS.

———. 1998b. "Reintegration of Victims of Trafficking in Cambodia." Phnom Penh: IOM/CAS.

———. 2004. "The Broken Women of Cambodia." In *Sexual Cultures in East Asia. The Social Construction of Sexuality and Sexual Risk in a Time of AIDS,* edited by Evelyne Micollier, 127–155. London: RoutledgeCurzon.

Derks, Annuska, Roger Henke, and Ly Vanna. 2006. "Review of a Decade of Research on Trafficking in Persons, Cambodia." Phnom Penh: TAF/CAS.

Doezema, Jo. 1998. "Forced to Choose: Beyond the Voluntary V: Forced Prostitution Dichotomy." In *Global Sex Workers. Rights, Resistance and Redefinition,* edited by Kamala Kempadoo, 34–50. New York: Routledge.

Ebihara, May. 1968. "Svay, a Khmer Village in Cambodia." Ph.D. diss., Columbia University.

———. 1974. "Khmer Village Women in Cambodia: A Happy Balance." In *Many Sisters: Women in Cross-Cultural Perspective,* edited by Carolyn J. Matthiasson, 305–347. New York: Free Press.

———. 1987. "Revolution and Reformulation in Kampuchean Village Culture." In *The Cambodian Agony,* edited by David A. Ablin and Marlowe Hood, 16–61. New York: M. E. Sharpe.

Ebihara, May, and Judy Ledgerwood. 2002. "Aftermaths of Genocide: Cambodian Villagers." In *Annihilating Difference: The Anthropology of Genocide,* edited by Alexander L. Hinton, 272–291. Berkeley: University of California Press.

Ebihara, May, Carol Mortland, and Judy Ledgerwood, eds. 1994. *Cambodian Culture since 1975: Homeland and Exile.* Ithaca, NY: Cornell University Press.

Edwards, Louise, and Mina Roces, eds. 2000. *Women in Asia: Tradition, Modernity and Globalization.* St Leonards: Allen & Unwin.

Edwards, Penny. 1996. "Ethnic Chinese in Cambodia." In *Interdisciplinary Research on Ethnic Groups in Cambodia, Final Draft Reports,* 109–175. Phnom Penh: Center for Advanced Study.

Eisenbruch, Maurice. 1997. "Doctor Hansen and the Crouching Mango: STD and HIV/AIDS (Unpublished Paper)." Phnom Penh: National AIDS Review.

Elmhirst, Rebecca. 2002. "Daughters of Displacement: Migration Dynamics in an Indonesian Transmigration Area." *Journal of Development Studies* 38, no. 5: 143–166.

Englund, Harri, and James Leach. 2000. "Ethnography and the Meta-Narratives of Modernity." *Current Anthropology* 41, no. 2: 225–248.

Enloe, Cynthia H. 1983. "Women Textile Workers in the Militarization of Southeast Asia." In *Women and Men in the International Division of Labor,* edited by June Nash and María Patricia Fernández-Kelly, 407–425. Albany: State University of New York Press.

Errington, Shelly. 1990. "Recasting Sex, Gender, and Power: A Theoretical and Regional Overview." In *Power and Difference: Gender in Island Southeast Asia,* edited by Jane Monnig Atkinson and Shelly Errington, 1–58. Stanford, CA: Stanford University Press.

Evers, Hans-Dieter. 1994. "Javanese Petty Trade." In *The Moral Economy. Ethnicity and Developing Markets,* edited by Hans-Dieter Evers and Heiko Schrader, 68–75. London: Routledge.

Fawcett, James T. 1989. "Networks, Linkages, and Migration Systems." *International Migration Review* 23, no. 3: 671–680.

Featherstone, Mike. 1995. *Global Modernities: Globalization, Postmodernism and Identity.* London: Sage Publications.

Ferguson, James. 1992. "The Country and the City on the Copperbelt." *Cultural Anthropology* 7, no. 1: 80–92.

Fernández-Kelly, María Patricia. 1983. "Mexican Border Industrialization, Female Labor Force Participation, and Migration." In *Women, Men and the International Division of Labor,* edited by June Nash and María Patricia Fernández-Kelly, 205–223. Albany: State University of New York Press.

Fischer, Michael M. J. 1999. "Emergent Forms of Life: Anthropologies of Late or Postmodernities." *Annual Review of Anthropology* 28: 455–478.

FitzGerald, E. V. K. 1994. "The Economic Dimension of Social Development and the Peace Process in Cambodia." In *Between Hope and Insecurity:*

The Social Consequences of the Cambodian Peace Process, edited by Peter Utting, 71–94. Geneva: UNRISD.

Forest, Alain. 1992. *Le culte des génies protecteurs au Cambodge. Analyse et traduction d'un corpus de textes sur les Neak Ta.* Paris: Éditions L'Harmattan.

Fornäs, Johan. 1995. *Cultural Theory and Late Modernity.* London: Sage Publications.

Freeman, Carla. 1998. "Femininity and Flexible Labor: Fashioning Class through Gender on the Global Assembly Line." *Critique of Anthropology* 18, no. 3: 247–262.

Friedman, Jonathan. 1994. *Cultural Identity and Global Process.* London: Sage Publications.

Frieson, Kate. 2001. "In the Shadows: Women, Power and Politics in Cambodia." Working Paper No. 26, University of Victoria.

Geertz, Clifford. 1993. *The Interpretation of Cultures.* London: Fontana Press (1973).

———. 1978. "The Bazaar Economy: Information and Search in Peasant Marketing." *The American Economic Review* 68, no. 2: 28–32.

Gender and Development for Cambodia. 2003. "Paupers and Princelings: Youth Attitudes towards Gangs, Violence, Rape, Drugs, and Theft." Phnom Penh: Gender and Development for Cambodia.

Giddens, Anthony. 1991. *Modernity and Self-Identity: Self and Society in the Late Modern Age.* Cambridge: Polity Press.

Godfrey, Martin, et al. 2001. "A Study of the Cambodian Labour Market: Reference to Poverty Reduction, Growth and Adjustment to Crisis." Phnom Penh: Cambodia Development Resource Institute.

Goody, Jack, and S. J. Tambiah. 1973. *Bridewealth and Dowry.* Cambridge: Cambridge University Press.

Gorman, Siobhan. 1997. "Implications of Socio-Economic Change for Women's Employment in Cambodia: A Case Study of Garment Factory Workers." M.Ed. thesis, University of Manchester.

———. 1999. "Gender and Development in Cambodia: An Overview." Working Paper No. 10, CDRI.

Gottesman, Evan. 2003. *Cambodia after the Khmer Rouge: Inside the Politics of Nation Building.* New Haven, CT: Yale University Press.

Goulain, Christian. 1967. "Phnom Penh: Notes de géographie urbaine." *Cahiers d'Outre-Mer* 22, no. 77: 5–36.

Green, Caroline. 2002. "Gender Equality and Equity Are Minister's Aims (Interview with Mu Sochua, Minister for Women's and Veteran's Affairs)." *Phnom Penh Post,* June 7–20.

Groslier, Bernard Philippe. 1998. *Mélanges sur l'archéologie du Cambodge. Textes réunis et présentées par Jacques Dumarçay.* Réimpression ed. Paris: École Française d'Extrême-Orient.

Gupta, Akhil, and James Ferguson. 1992. "Beyond 'Culture': Space, Identity, and the Politics of Difference." *Cultural Anthropology* 7, no. 1: 6–23.

Guthrie, Elizabeth. 2004. "Khmer Buddhism, Female Asceticism, and Salvation." In *History, Buddhism, and New Religious Movements in Cambodia,* edited by J. Marston and E. Guthrie. Honolulu: University of Hawai'i Press.

Gyer, Judith von. 2005. *Situation Analysis of Peadophilia in Sihanoukville. Study of Perceived Demand for Child Sex in Sihanoukville.* Phnom Penh: Cosecam, Village Focus International.

Ham, Samnang. 2000. "First Movie House since '93 Set for Imminent Opening." *Cambodia Daily,* December 29.

Hanks, L. M. 1962. "Merit and Power in the Thai Social Order." *American Anthropologist* 64, no. 4: 1247–1261.

Hann, Chris, Caroline Humphry, and Katherine Verdery. 2002. "Introduction: Postsocialism as a Topic of Anthropological Investigation." In *Postsocialism. Ideals, Ideologies and Practices in Eurasia,* edited by Chris Hann, 1–28. London: Routledge.

Hannerz, Ulf. 1980. *Exploring the City: Inquiries toward an Urban Anthropology.* New York: Columbia University Press.

Headley, Robert K. 1977. *Cambodian-English Dictionary.* Vol. 1. Washington, DC: The Catholic University of America Press.

Heller, Monica, ed. 1988. *Codeswitching: Anthropological and Sociolinguistic Perspectives.* Berlin: Mouton de Gruyter.

Heyzer, Noeleen. 1986. *Working Women in Southeast Asia: Development, Subordination and Emancipation.* Milton Keynes, UK: Open University Press.

———, ed. 1988. *Daughters in Industry: Work, Skills and Consciousness of Women Workers in Asia.* Kuala Lumpur: Asian and Pacific Development Centre.

Hinton, Alexander L. 1998. "A Head for an Eye: Revenge in the Cambodian Genocide." *American Ethnologist* 25, no. 3: 352–377.

———. 2002. "Purity and Contamination in the Cambodian Genocide." In *Cambodia Emerges from the Past: Eight Essays,* edited by Judy Ledgerwood and Kheang Un, 60–90. DeKalb, IL: Southeast Asia Publications.

Hodgson, Dorothy L., ed. 2001. *Gendered Modernities: Ethnographic Perspectives.* New York: Palgrave.

Holter, Uta, ed. 1994. *Bezahlt, Geliebt, Verstossen: Prostitution und Andere Sonderformen Institutionalisierter Sexualität in Verschiedenen Kulturen.* Vol. 8, *Kölner Ethnologische Arbeitspapiere.* Bonn: Holos Verlag.

Hou Youn. 1982. "The Peasantry of Kampuchea: Colonialism and Modernization." In *Peasants and Politics in Kampuchea, 1942–1981,* edited by Ben Kiernan and Chanthou Boua, 34–68. London: Zed Press.

Hugo, Graeme J. 1993. "Migrant Women in Developing Countries." In *Internal Migration of Women in Developing Countries: Proceedings of the United*

Nations Expert Meeting on the Feminization of Internal Migration, Aguascalientes, Mexico, 22–25 October 1991. New York: United Nations Department for Economic and Social Information and Policy Analysis.

Hüsken, Frans, and Jeremy Kemp, eds. 1991. *Cognition and Social Organization in Southeast Asia.* Leiden: KITLV Press.

Igout, Michel. 1993. *Phnom Penh Then and Now.* Bangkok: White Lotus.

Institut Bouddhique. 1995. *Chbap Phseeng Phseeng (Chbab Divers).* Phnom Penh: Institut Bouddhique.

———. *Procum Reung Preeng Khmaei (Collection of Khmer Folktales).* Vol. 1. Phnom Penh: Institut Bouddhique, n.d.

International Labour Organization (ILO). 1973. "C138 Minimum Age Convention—Convention Concerning Minimum Age for Admission to Work." Geneva.

Jacobsen, Trudy. 2004. "Threads in a Sampot: A History of Women and Power in Cambodia." Ph.D. diss., University of Queensland.

Jansen, Willy. 1987. *Women without Men: Gender and Marginality in an Algerian Town.* Leiden: E. J. Brill.

Jellinek, Lea. 1976. "Life of a Jakarta Street Trader." Working Paper No. 9, Monash University.

Kahn, Joel. S. 2001. "Anthropology and Modernity." *Current Anthropology* 42, no. 5: 651–680.

Kalab, Milanda. 1968. "Study of a Cambodian Village." *Geographical Journal* 134, no. 4: 521–537.

Kampuchea Suriya. 1966. "*Roboh Proh Setrey* (Rules for Men and Women)." *Kampuchea Suriya* 38, no. 12: 1254–1257.

Karim, Wazir Jahan, ed. 1995. *'Male' and 'Female' in Developing Southeast Asia.* Oxford: Berg Publishers.

Kearney, Michael. 1986. "From the Invisible Hand to Visible Feet: Anthropological Studies of Migration and Development." *Annual Review of Anthropology* 15: 331–361.

———. 1995. "The Local and the Global: The Anthropology of Globalization and Transnationalism." *Annual Review of Anthropology* 24: 547–565.

Keyes, Charles F. 1984. "Mother or Mistress But Never a Monk: Buddhist Notions of Female Gender in Rural Thailand." *American Ethnologist* 11, no. 2: 223–241.

———. 1995. *The Golden Peninsula: Culture and Adaptation in Mainland Southeast Asia.* Honolulu: University of Hawai'i Press.

Kiernan, Ben. 1982. "Introduction." In *Peasants and Politics in Kampuchea 1942–1981,* edited by Ben Kiernan and Chanthou Boua, 1–28. London: Zed Press.

———. 1996. *The Pol Pot Regime: Race Power and Genocide in Cambodia under the Khmer Rouge, 1975–79.* New Haven, CT: Yale University Press.

Kiernan, Ben, and Chanthou Boua, eds. 1982. *Peasants and Politics in Kampuchea, 1942–1981.* London: Zed Press.

Kirsch, A. Thomas. 1985. "Text and Context: Buddhist Sex Roles/Cultures of Gender Revisited." *American Ethnologist* 12, no. 2: 302–320.

Krisnawati, Tati, and Artien Utrecht. 1992. "Women's Economic Mediation: The Case of Female Petty Traders in Northwest Lombok." In *Women and Mediation in Indonesia,* edited by Sita van Bemmelen, Madelon Djajadiningrat-Nieuwenhuis, Elsbeth Locher-Scholten, and Elly Touwen-Bouwsma, 47–64. Leiden: KITLV Press.

Kusakabe, Kyoko. 2003. "Market, Class and Gender Relations: A Case of Women Retail Traders in Phnom Penh." *International Feminist Journal of Politics* 5, no. 1: 28–46.

Law, Lisa. 2000. *Sex Work in Southeast Asia: The Place of Desire in a Time of AIDS.* London: Routledge.

Leclerc-Madlala, Suzanne. 2001. "Virginity Testing: Managing Sexuality in a Maturing HIV/AIDS Epidemic." *Medical Anthropology Quarterly* 15, no. 4: 533–552.

Leclère, Adhemard. 1974. *Histoire du Cambodge.* Phnom Penh: Noko Thom Editeur (1914).

Ledgerwood, Judy. 1990. "Changing Khmer Conceptions of Gender: Women, Stories, and the Social Order." Ph.D. diss., Cornell University.

———. 1992. "Analysis of the Situation of Women in Cambodia." Phnom Penh: UNICEF.

———. 1994. "Gender Symbolism and Cultural Change: Viewing the Virtuous Woman in the Khmer Story 'Mea Yoeung.'" In *Cambodian Culture since 1975: Homeland and Exile,* edited by May Ebihara, Carol A. Mortland, and Judy Ledgerwood, 119–128. Ithaca, NY: Cornell University Press.

———. 1995. "Khmer Kinship: The Matriliny/Matriarchy Myth." *Journal of Anthropological Research* 51, no. 3: 247–261.

———. 1996a. "Politics and Gender: Negotiating Conceptions of the Ideal Woman in Present Day Cambodia." *Asia Pacific Viewpoint* 37, no. 2: 139–152.

———. 1996b. "Women in Development: Cambodia." Manila: Asian Development Bank.

Ledgerwood, Judy, May Ebihara, and Carol Mortland. 1994. "Introduction." In *Cambodian Culture since 1975: Homeland and Exile,* edited by May Ebihara, Carol Mortland, and Judy Ledgerwood, 1–26. Ithaca, NY: Cornell University Press.

Ledgerwood, Judy, and Kheang Un. 2002. "Introduction." In *Cambodia Emerges from the Past: Eight Essays,* edited by Judy Ledgerwood, 1–15. DeKalb, IL: Southeast Asia Publications.

Lee, Sharon M. 1996. "Issues in Research on Women, International Migration and Labor." In *Asian Women in Migration,* edited by Graziano Battistella and Anthony Paganoni, 1–21. Quezon City: Scalabrini Migration Center.

Lemarchands, Guy. 1997. "Phnom Penh, capitale de l'état indépendant du Cambodge." In *Phnom Penh: Développement urbain et patrimoine,* edited by Christiane Blancot and Dominique Petermüller, 44–49. Paris: Atelier parisien d'urbanisme.

Leonard, Christine S. 1996. "Becoming Cambodian: Ethnic Identity and the Vietnamese in Kampuchea." In *Interdisciplinary Research on Ethnic Groups in Cambodia, Final Draft Reports.* Phnom Penh: Center for Advanced Study.

Li, Tana. 1996. "Peasants on the Move. Rural-Urban Migration in the Hanoi Region." Occasional Paper No. 91, Institute of Southeast Asian Studies, Singapore.

Lim, Lin Lean, ed. 1998. *The Sex Sector: The Economic and Social Bases of Prostitution in Southeast Asia.* Geneva: International Labour Office.

Long Chinta. 1997. "Labour Force and Migration in Cambodia, 1996." Phnom Penh: National Institute of Statistics, Ministry of Planning.

Lor, Chandara, and Brian Calvert. 2001. "Capital Ambitions. For Pur Sat Villagers, Phnom Penh Is a Place of Wonder—and Danger." *Cambodia Daily,* January 13–14.

Ly, Daravuth, and Ingrid Muan, eds. 2001. *Cultures of Independence: An Introduction to Cambodian Arts and Culture in the 1950s and 1960s.* Phnom Penh: Reyum.

Mabbett, Ian, and David Chandler. 1995. *The Khmers.* Oxford and Cambridge: Blackwell Publishers.

Malhotra, Anju, and Deborah S. DeGraff. 1997. "Entry versus Success in the Labor Force: Young Women's Employment in Sri Lanka." *World Development* 25, no. 3: 379–394.

Manderson, Lenore, and Pranee Liamputtong, eds. 2002. *Coming of Age in South and Southeast Asia: Youth, Courtship and Sexuality.* Richmond, UK: Curzon.

Marston, John. 2002. "Democratic Kampuchea and the Idea of Modernity." In *Cambodia Emerges from the Past: Eight Essays,* edited by Judy Ledgerwood, 38–59. DeKalb, IL: Southeast Asia Publications.

Martel, Gabrielle. 1975. *Lovea, village des environs d'Angkor. Aspects démographiques, économiques et sociologiques du monde rural cambodgien dans la province de Siem-Réap.* Paris: École Française d'Extrême-Orient.

Martin, Marie A. 1994. *Cambodia: A Shattered Society.* Translated by Mark W. McLeod. Berkeley: University of California Press (1989).

Massey, Douglas. 1990. "Social Structure, Household Strategies, and the Cumulative Causation of Migration." *Population Index* 56, no. 1: 3–26.

Matthei, Linda Miller. 1996. "Gender and International Labor Migration: A Networks Approach." *Social Justice* 23, no. 3: 38–53.

McIntyre, Kevin. 1996. "Geography as Destiny: Cities, Villages and Khmer Rouge Orientation." *Comparative Studies in Society and History* 38, no. 4: 730–758.

Mehra, Rekha, and Sarah Gammage. 1999. "Trends, Countertrends, and Gaps in Women's Employment." *World Development* 27, no. 3: 533–550.

Mies, Maria. 1986. *Patriarchy and Accumulation on a World Scale: Women in the International Division of Labour.* London: Zed Books.

Miller, Daniel. 1995. "Consumption and Commodities." *Annual Review of Anthropology* 24: 141–161.

Mills, Mary Beth. 1995. "Attack of the Widow Ghosts: Gender, Death, and Modernity in Northeast Thailand." In *Bewitching Women, Pious Men: Gender and Body Politics in Southeast Asia,* edited by Aihwa Ong and Michael G. Peletz, 244–273. Berkeley: University of California Press.

———. 1997. "Contesting the Margins of Modernity: Women, Migration, and Consumption in Thailand." *American Ethnologist* 24, no. 1: 37–61.

———. 1999. *Thai Women in the Global Labor Force: Consuming Desires, Contested Identities.* New Brunswick, NJ: Rutgers University Press.

———. 2001. "Auditing for the Chorus Line: Gender, Rural Youth, and the Consumption of Modernity in Thailand." In *Gendered Modernities: Ethnographic Perspectives,* edited by Dorothy L. Hodgson, 27–51. New York: Palgrave.

———. 2003. "Gender and Inequality in the Global Labor Force." *Annual Review of Anthropology* 32: 41–62.

Ministry of Commerce. 2000. "Business and Investment Handbook 2000." Phnom Penh: Ministry of Commerce.

Ministry of Planning. 1998. "Cambodia Human Development Report 1998: Women's Contribution to Development." Phnom Penh: Ministry of Planning.

———. 1999. "Cambodia Human Development Report 1999: Village Economy and Development." Phnom Penh: Ministry of Planning.

Ministry of Women's Affairs. www.mwva.gov.kh/about_mwva.html (accessed August 29, 2006).

Ministry of Women's and Veteran's Affairs. 1999. "*Neary Rattanak*—Women Are Precious Gems: Five-Year Strategic Plan." Phnom Penh: Ministry of Women's and Veteran's Affairs.

Mitchell, J. Clyde. 1974. "Social Networks." *Annual Review of Anthropology* 3: 279–299.

Mohanty, Chandra Talpade. 1997. "Women Workers and Capitalist Scripts: Ideologies of Domination, Common Interests, and the Politics of Solidarity." In *Feminist Genealogies, Colonial Legacies, Democratic Futures,* edited by M. Jacqui Alexander and Chandra Talpade Mohanty, 3–29. New York and London: Routledge.

Moore, Henrietta L. 1994. *A Passion for Difference: Essays in Anthropology and Gender.* Cambridge: Polity Press.

Mop Sarin. 1999. "Prostitution and Trafficking: Policies, Strategies and Constraints." In *Looking Back, Moving Forward. Proceedings of the First*

National Conference on Gender and Development in Cambodia. Phnom Penh: GAD/C.

Muecke, Marjorie. 1992. "Mother Sold Food, Daughter Sells Her Body: The Cultural Continuity of Prostitution." *Social Science and Medicine* 35, no. 7: 891–901.

Muller, Gregor. 2006. *Colonial Cambodia's 'Bad Frenchmen.' The Rise of French Rule and the Life of Thomas Caramann, 1840–87.* London: Routledge.

Municipality of Phnom Penh. www.phnompenh.gov.kh (accessed August 25, 2006).

Munshi, Shoma, ed. 2001. *Images of the 'Modern Woman' in Asia: Global Media, Local Meanings.* Richmond, UK: Curzon.

Murray, Alison J. 1991. *No Money, No Honey: A Study of Street Traders and Prostitutes in Jakarta.* Oxford: Oxford University Press.

———. 2001. *Pink Fits: Subcultures and Discourses in the Asia-Pacific.* Clayton, Victoria, Australia: Monash Asia Institute.

Mysliwiec, Eva. 1988. *Punishing the Poor: The International Isolation of Kampuchea.* Oxford: Oxfam.

National AIDS Authority of Cambodia. 2005. "Monitoring the Declaration of Commitment, January 2004–December 2005." United Nations General Assembly Special Session on HIV/AIDS.

National Institute of Statistics. 1995. "Report on the Socio-Economic Survey of Cambodia 1993/1994." Phnom Penh: Ministry of Planning.

———. 1996. "Demographic Survey of Cambodia 1996: General Report." Phnom Penh: Ministry of Planning.

———. 1999. "General Population Census of Cambodia 1998: Final Census Results." Phnom Penh: Ministry of Planning.

———. 2000a. "General Population Census of Cambodia 1998: Labour Force and Employment." Phnom Penh: Ministry of Planning.

———. 2000b. "General Population Census of Cambodia 1998: Spatial Distribution and Migratory Movements." Phnom Penh: Ministry of Planning.

———. 2004. "Cambodia Inter-Censal Population Survey 2004, General Report." Phnom Penh: Ministry of Planning.

———. 2005a. "Cambodia Inter-Censal Population Survey 2004, Spatial Distribution and Migratory Movements." Phnom Penh: Ministry of Planning.

———. 2005b. "Cambodia Inter-Censal Population Survey 2004, Labour Force and Employment." Phnom Penh: Ministry of Planning.

Népote, Jacques. 1992. *Parenté et organisation sociale dans le Cambodge moderne et contemporain. Quelques aspects et quelques applications du modèle les régissant.* Geneva: Olizane.

Nov, Ana. 2000. "Television Stations Heed Calls for Modesty." *Cambodia Daily,* October 9.

O'Connell, Stephen, and Vong Sokhen. 2000. "Axe Hovers Unfairly over Legal Child Workers." *Phnom Penh Post,* December 8–21.

O'Neill, Maggie. 2001. *Prostitution and Feminism: Towards a Politics of Feeling.* Cambridge: Polity Press.

Ong, Aihwa. 1987. *Spirits of Resistance and Capitalist Discipline: Factory Women in Malaysia.* Albany: State University of New York Press.

———. 1991. "The Gender and Labor Politics of Postmodernity." *Annual Review of Anthropology* 20: 279–309.

———. 1996. "Anthropology, China and Modernities: The Geopolitics of Cultural Knowledge." In *The Future of Anthropological Knowledge,* edited by Henrietta L. Moore, 60–92. London: Routledge.

Ong, Aihwa, and Michael G. Peletz, eds. 1995. *Bewitching Women, Pious Men: Gender and Body Politics in Southeast Asia.* Berkeley: University of California Press.

Ortiz, Sutti. 2002. "Laboring in the Factories and in the Fields." *Annual Review of Anthropology* 31: 395–417.

Ortner, Sherry B. 1981. "Gender and Sexuality in Hierarchical Societies: The Case of Polynesia and Some Comparative Implications." In *Sexual Meanings: The Cultural Construction of Gender and Sexuality,* edited by Sherry B. Ortner and Harriet Whitehead, 359–409. Cambridge: Cambridge University Press.

———. 1984. "Theory in Anthropology since the Sixties." *Comparative Studies in Society and History* 26, no. 1: 126–166.

———. 1995. "Resistance and the Problem of Ethnographic Refusal." *Comparative Studies in Society and History* 37, no. 1: 173–193.

———. 1996. *Making Gender: The Politics and Erotics of Culture.* Boston: Beacon Press.

———. 1999. *Life and Death on Mt. Everest: Sherpa and Himalayan Mountaineering.* Princeton and Oxford: Princeton University Press.

———. 2001. "Specifying Agency: The Comaroffs and Their Critics." *Interventions* 3, no. 1: 76–84.

Ortner, Sherry B., and Harriet Whitehead, eds. 1981. *Sexual Meanings: The Cultural Construction of Gender and Sexuality.* Cambridge: Cambridge University Press.

Osborne, Milton E. 1994. *Sihanouk: Prince of Light, Prince of Darkness.* Chiang Mai: Silkworm Books.

———. 1995. *Southeast Asia: An Introductory History.* St. Leonards, Australia: Allen & Unwin.

———. 1997. *The French Presence in Cochinchina and Cambodia.* Bangkok: White Lotus Press.

Ovesen, Jan, Ing-Britt Trankell, and Joakim Öjendal. 1996. *When Every Household Is an Island: Social Organization and Power Structures in Rural Cambodia, Uppsala Research Reports in Cultural Anthropology.* Uppsala: Uppsala University.

Parkin, Robert. 1990. "Descent in Old Cambodia: Deconstructing a Matrilineal Hypothesis." *Zeitschrift für Ethnologie* 115: 209–227.

Pheng Criev. 1963. *"Euwpuk Mdaay Mien Oupakaa Kun Leu Koun Mèèn Ru Men Mèèn* (Do Parents Possess Merit toward Their Children or Not)." *Kampuchea Suriya* 35, no. 6: 594–605.

Phnara Khy. 1974. "La communauté vietnamienne au Cambodge a l'époque du protectorat français 1863–1953." Doctoral thesis, Université de la Sorbonne Nouvelle, Paris III.

Pon Dorina, and Sarthi Acharya. 2001. "Earnings of Vulnerable Workers: Reflections on Poverty in Phnom Penh." *Cambodia Development Review* 5, no. 4: 9–11.

Population Services International (PSI). 2002. "Sweetheart Relationships in Cambodia: Love, Sex and Condoms in the Time of HIV." Phnom Penh: PSI.

Porée, Guy, and Eveline Maspero. 1938. *Moeurs et coutumes des khmèrs.* Paris: Payot.

Porée-Maspero, Evelyne. 1961. "Kron Pali et Rites de La Maison." *Anthropos* 56: 198.

———. 1985. *Cérémonies privées des cambodgiens.* Réimpression de l'édition de la Commission des Moeurs et Coutumes du Cambodge, Phnom Penh ed. Paris: Cedoreck.

Portes, Alejandro. 1995. "Economic Sociology and the Sociology of Immigration: A Conceptual Overview." In *The Economic Sociology of Immigration: Essays on Networks, Ethnicity, and Entrepreneurship,* edited by Alejandro Portes, 1–41. New York: Russell Sage Foundation.

Portes, Alejandro, and Julia Sensenbrenner. 1993. "Embeddedness and Immigration: Notes on the Social Determinants of Economic Action." *American Journal of Sociology* 98, no. 6: 1320–1350.

Pou, Saveros. 1988. *Guirlande de Cpap'.* Paris: Cedoreck.

Pou, Saveros, and Choulean Ang. 1992. "Le vocabulaire khmer relatif au surnaturel." *Seksa Khmer* 1987–1990, no. 10–13: 59–129.

Prasso, Sheri. 1995. "Violence, Ethnicity and Ethnic Cleansing: Cambodia and the Khmer Rouge." Department of Social Anthropology, University of Cambridge.

Pred, Allan, and Michael John Watts. 1992. *Reworking Modernity: Capitalisms and Symbolic Discontent.* New Brunswick, NJ: Rutgers University Press.

Pye, Lucian W. 1985. *Asian Power and Politics: The Cultural Dimension of Authority.* Cambridge, MA: Harvard University Press.

Rao, Rajalaskhmi R. 1996. "Women in the Urban Informal Sector." Phnom Penh: Urban Sector Group.

Rao, Rajalakshmi R., and Binie Zaan. 1997. "An Analysis of Female-Headed Households in Cambodia." Phnom Penh: National Institute of Statistics.

Rapport, Nigel, and Joanna Overing. 2000. *Social and Cultural Anthropology: The Key Concepts.* London: Routledge.

Reid, Anthony. 1988. *Southeast Asia in the Age of Commerce 1450–1680.* Vol-

ume One: The Lands Below the Winds. New Haven, CT: Yale University Press.

———. 1993. *Southeast Asia in the Age of Commerce 1450–1680. Volume Two: Expansion and Crisis.* New Haven, CT: Yale University Press.

Reynolds, Rocque. 1996. "Trafficking and Prostitution: The Law in Cambodia." Unpublished paper. University of New South Wales.

Rigg, Jonathan. 1997. *Southeast Asia: The Human Landscape of Modernization and Development.* London: Routledge.

———. 1998. "Rural-Urban Interactions, Agriculture and Wealth: A Southeast Asian Perspective." *Progress in Human Geography* 22, no. 4: 497–522.

Rofel, Lisa. 1992. "Rethinking Modernity: Space and Factory Discipline in China." *Cultural Anthropology* 7, no. 1: 93–114.

Rogers, Alisdair, and Steven Vertovec. 1995. "Introduction." In *The Urban Context. Ethnicity, Social Networks and Situational Analysis,* edited by Alisdair Rogers and Steven Vertovec, 1–33. Oxford: Berg Publishers.

Rosaldo, Michelle Z. 1980. "The Use and Abuse of Anthropology." *Signs* 5, no. 3: 389–417.

Roseman, Sharon R. 2002. " 'Strong Women' and 'Pretty Girls': Self-Provisioning, Gender, and Class Identity in Rural Galicia (Spain)." *American Anthropologist* 104, no. 1: 22–37.

Royal Kingdom of Cambodia. 1996. "Law on Suppression of the Kidnapping and Trafficking/Sales of Human Persons and Exploitation of Human Persons." Unofficial translation. National Assembly, Phnom Penh.

Rozario, Santi. 2002. "Poor and 'Dark': What Is My Future? Identity Construction and Adolescent Women in Bangladesh." In *Coming of Age in South and Southeast Asia,* edited by Lenore Manderson and Pranee Liamputtong, 42–57. Richmond, UK: Curzon.

Saptari, Ratna. 2000. "Production Processes and the Gendering of Industrial Work in Asia." *Asian Studies Review* 24, no. 2: 147–159.

Saptari, Ratna, and Rebecca Elmhirst. 2004. "Studying Labour in Southeast Asia: Reflections on Structures and Processes." In *Labour Processes in a Globalised World,* edited by Rebecca Elmhirst and Ratna Saptari, 15–46. London: RoutledgeCurzon.

Sassen, Saskia. 1998. "Notes on the Incorporation of Third World Women into Wage Labor through Immigration and Offshore Production." In *Globalization and Its Discontents,* 111–131. New York: The New Press (1984).

Schein, Louisa. 1999. "Performing Modernity." *Cultural Anthropology* 14, no. 3: 361–395.

Schlegel, Alice. 1991. "Status, Property, and the Value of Virginity." *American Ethnologist* 18, no. 4: 719–734.

Schulte-Nordholt, Henk, ed. 1997. *Outward Appearances: Dressing State and Society in Indonesia.* Leiden: KITLV Press.

Scott, James. 1985. *Weapons of the Weak: Everyday Forms of Peasant Resistance.* New Haven, CT: Yale University Press.

Seligmann, Linda J., ed. 2001. *Women Traders in Cross-Cultural Perspective: Mediating Identities, Marketing Wares.* Stanford, CA: Stanford University Press.

Sen, Krishna, and Maila Stivens, eds. 1998. *Gender and Power in Affluent Asia.* London: Routledge.

Shatkin, Gavin. 1998. "'Fourth World' Cities in the Global Economy: The Case of Phnom Penh, Cambodia." *International Journal of Urban and Regional Research* 22, no. 3: 378–393.

Shawcross, William. 1986. *Sideshow: Kissinger, Nixon and the Destruction of Cambodia.* London: Hogarth Press.

Smith, M. Estellie. 1989. "The Informal Economy." In *Economic Anthropology,* edited by Stuart Plattner, 292–317. Stanford, CA: Stanford University Press.

Sok Hach. 2005. "Measuring Competitiveness and Labor Productivity in Cambodia's Garment Industry." *Economic Review* 2, no. 2: 2–7.

Sok Hach, Chea Huot, and Sik Boreak. 2001. "Cambodia's Annual Economic Review 2001." Phnom Penh: CDRI.

Solé, Jacques. 1993. *L'âge d'or de la prostitution: De 1870 à nos jours.* Paris: Plon.

Sophal Ear. 1995. "Cambodia's Economic Development in Historical Perspective: A Contribution to the Study of Cambodia's Economy." Undergraduate thesis, University of California.

Soun Cendep. 2003. "*Pitie Coul Mlup* (Coul Mlup Ceremony)." B.A. thesis, Royal University of Fine Arts, Phnom Penh.

Standing, Guy. 1999. "Global Feminization through Flexible Labor: A Theme Revisited." *World Development* 27, no. 3: 583–602.

Steedly, Mary Margaret. 1999. "The State of Culture Theory in the Anthropology of Southeast Asia." *Annual Review of Anthropology* 28: 431–445.

Steinberg, David J. 1959. *Cambodia: Its People, Its Society, Its Culture, Survey of World Cultures.* New Haven, CT: HRAF Press.

Steinfatt, Thomas M., Simon Baker, and Allan Beesey. 2002. "Measuring the Number of Trafficked Women in Cambodia: 2002." Honolulu: Globalization Research Center, University of Hawai'i-Manoa.

Stivens, Maila. 1998. "Theorising Gender, Power and Modernity in Affluent Asia." In *Gender and Power in Affluent Asia,* edited by Krishna Sen and Maila Stivens, 1–34. London: Routledge.

———. 2002. "The Hope of the Nation: Moral Panics and the Construction of Teenagerhood in Contemporary Malaysia." In *Coming of Age in South and Southeast Asia,* edited by Lenore Manderson and Pranee Liamputtong, 188–206. Richmond, UK: Curzon.

Stoler, Ann. 1992. "Sexual Affronts and Racial Frontiers: European Identities and the Cultural Politics of Exclusion in Colonial Southeast Asia." *Comparative Studies in Society and History* 34, no. 3: 514–551.

Stone, Linda. 1998. *Kinship and Gender: An Introduction*. Boulder, CO: Westview Press.

Strauch, Judith. 1984. "Women in Rural-Urban Circulation Networks: Implications for Social Structural Change." In *Women in the Cities of Asia: Migration and Urban Development*, edited by James T. Fawcett, Siew-Ean Khoo, and Peter C. Smith, 60–77. Boulder, CO: Westview Press.

Surtees, Rebecca. 2003. "Rape and Sexual Transgression in Cambodian Society." In *Violence against Women in Asian Societies*, edited by Lenore Manderson and Lina Rae Bennett, 93–113. London: Routledge.

Tanabe, Shigeharu, and Charles F. Keyes, eds. 2002. *Cultural Crisis and Social Memory: Modernity and Identity in Thailand and Laos*. London: RoutledgeCurzon.

Tarr, Chou Meng. 1992. "The Vietnamese Minority in Cambodia." *Race & Class* 34, no. 2: 33–47.

———. 1996. "People in Cambodia Don't Talk about Sex, They Simply Do It! A Study of the Social and Contextual Factors Affecting Risk-Related Sexual Behavior among Young Cambodians." Phnom Penh: UNAIDS.

Tarr, Chou Meng, and Peter Aggleton. 1999. "Young People and HIV in Cambodia: Meanings, Contexts and Sexual Cultures." *AIDS Care* 11, no. 3: 375–384.

Ten Brummelhuis, Han. 1999. "Transformations of Transgender: The Case of the Thai Kathoey." In *Lady Boys, Tom Boys, Rent Boys: Male and Female Homosexualities in Contemporary Thailand*, edited by Peter A. Jackson and Gerard Sullivan, 121–140. Binghamton, NY: Haworth Press.

The Strait Times. 2000. "Cambodia Bans Chart-Topper." *Camnews*, February 25.

Thierry, Solange. 1985. *Le Cambodge des contes*. Paris: L'Harmattan.

Thion, Serge. 1993. *Watching Cambodia*. Bangkok: White Lotus.

Thomas, Fréderic, and Florence Plasnik. 2002. "Survey on the Behaviors and Attitudes of Tourists and Foreign Clients with Sex-abused Children and Young Women, Kingdom of Cambodia 2001–2002." Phnom Penh: AIDéTouS.

Thompson, Ashley. 2000. "Introductory Remarks between the Lines: Writing Histories of Middle Cambodia." In *Other Pasts: Women, Gender and History in Early Modern Southeast Asia*, edited by Barbara Watson Andaya, 47–68. Honolulu: Center for Southeast Asian Studies.

Timothy, Dallen J., and Geoffrey Wall. 1997. "Selling to Tourists: Indonesian Street Vendors." *Annals of Tourism Research* 24, no. 2: 332–340.

Tinker, Irene. 1997. *Street Foods: Urban Food and Employment in Developing Countries*. New York: Oxford University Press.

Tomlinson, John. 1999. *Globalization and Culture*. Chicago: University of Chicago Press.

Truong, Thanh-Dam. 1990. *Sex, Money and Morality: Prostitution and Tourism in South-East Asia*. London: Zed Books.

Ty Yao. 1997. "1979–1990, Le retour et la réorganisation de la vie urbain." In *Phnom Penh, développement urbain et patrimoine,* edited by Christine Blancot and Dominique Petermüller, 54–59. Paris: Atelier parisien d'urbanisme.

UNAIDS. 2000. "Cambodia. Epidemiological Fact Sheets on HIV/AIDS and Sexually Transmitted Diseases." Geneva: UNAIDS/WHO.

Van Esterik, Penny, ed. 1996. *Women of Southeast Asia.* DeKalb, IL: Center for Southeast Asian Studies, Northern Illinois University.

———. 2000. *Materializing Thailand.* Oxford: Berg.

Vann Molyvann. 2003. *Modern Khmer Cities.* Phnom Penh: Reyum.

Vickery, Michael. 1984. *Cambodia 1975–1982.* Boston: South End Press.

———. 1986. *Kampuchea: Politics, Economics and Society.* London: Pinter.

Visweswaran, Kamala. 1997. "Histories of Feminist Ethnography." *Annual Review of Anthropology* 26: 591–621.

Weil, Kurt. 1933. "Die Sieben Totsünden." In *Programm der Münchner Philharmoniker, Konzertsaison 1999/2000.*

Weitzer, Ronald. 2000. *Sex for Sale: Prostitution, Pornography, and the Sex Industry.* New York: Routledge.

Wikan, Unni. 1992. "Beyond the Words: The Power of Resonance." *American Ethnologist* 19, no. 3: 460–482.

———. 1995. "The Self in a World of Urgency and Necessity." *Ethos* 23, no. 3: 259–285.

Wilson, Tamar Diana. 1998. "Approaches to Understanding the Position of Women Workers in the Informal Sector." *Latin American Perspectives* 25, no. 2: 105–119.

Winter, Tim. 2003. "Tomb Raiding Angkor: A Clash of Cultures." *Indonesia and the Malay World* 31, no. 89: 58–68.

Wirth, Louis. 1975. "Urbanism as a Way of Life." In *City Ways: A Selective Reader in Urban Anthropology,* edited by John Friedl and Noel J. Chrisman, 26–45. New York: Crowell (1938).

Wolf, Diana L. 1992. *Factory Daughters: Gender, Household Dynamics, and Rural Industrialization in Java.* Berkeley: University of California Press.

Wolters, O. W. 1982. *History, Culture, and Religion in Southeast Asian Perspectives.* Singapore: Institute of Southeast Asian Studies.

World Bank. 1999. "Cambodia Poverty Assessment." East Asia and Pacific Region: Poverty Reduction and Economic Management Sector Unit and Human Development Sector Unit, World Bank.

———. 2006. "Cambodia: Halving Poverty by 2015? Poverty Assessment 2006." East Asia and Pacific Region: World Bank.

Yasmeen, Gisèle. 2001. "Stockbrokers Turned Sandwich Vendors: The Economic Crisis and Small-Scale Food Retailing in Southeast Asia." *Geoforum* 32: 91–102.

Yun Samean. 2002. "When Love Hits: Proposed Marriage Law Would Require More Consent." *The Cambodia Daily,* November 2–3.

Yuval-Davis, Nira. 1997. *Gender and Nation*. London: Sage Publications.

Zalduondo, Barbara O. 1999. "Prostitution Viewed Cross-Culturally: Toward Recontextualizing Sex Work in AIDS Prevention Research." In *Culture, Society and Sexuality*, edited by Richard Parker and Peter Aggleton, 307–324. London: UCL Press.

Zhou Taguan. 1993. *The Customs of Cambodia*. Translated by Gilman d'Arcy Paul. Bangkok: The Siam Society.

Zimmerman, Cathy. 1994. *Plates in a Basket Will Rattle: Domestic Violence in Cambodia*. Phnom Penh: The Asia Foundation.

Zimmerman, Gerd R. 1997. "Phnom Penh as the 'Primate City' of Cambodia and Its Revival since 1979." *Asien*, no. 63: 56–70.

INDEX

ABOUT THE AUTHOR

Annuska Derks received her Ph.D. in cultural and social anthropology from Radboud University Nijmegen in the Netherlands. She is presently a coordinator and researcher with a comparative research project on contemporary forms of bonded labor in Southeast Asia at the universities of Berne and Geneva.